To This
Northern
Shore

For Alexandre, Thomas and Luke

To This Northern Shore

Pieces of a life
from
South to North

A MEMOIR

Jean-Luc Barbanneau

Published 2023 by Voices
an imprint of
Lexus Ltd
47 Broad Street, Glasgow G40 2QW, Scotland
© Jean-Luc Barbanneau, 2023

Cover photograph by Jean-Luc Barbanneau
Cover design by Elfreda Crehan

All rights reserved. No part of this publication may be reproduced or stored in any form without permission from the publisher, except for the use of short sections in reviews.

British Library Cataloguing in Publication Data.
A catalogue record for this book is available from the British Library.
ISBN: 9781904737636

Printed and bound in Europe by Pulsio SARL

www.lexusforlanguages.co.uk

VOICES brings you lives of remarkable people. What lies at the heart is not the glitz of celebrity but the vastness of human experience. Made into words.

Contents

On a northern shore 11
Auld Lang Syne 14
"Where do you come from in France?" 17
Beachcombing 20
Life can be a beach, briefly... 25
From one river to another 29
What's in a name? 36
The multifarious triggers of memory 42
On the shoulders of short men 48
What can never be shed 53
The madness of crowds 56
The strange case of the absence of regrets 61
Childish pursuits 64
Scorched earth 71
One up, one down 74
Jack the lad – part one 79
Suitcase or coffin 82
Different welcomes 86
Double dose of adolescent spleen 93
Mother, martyr and matriarch 100
Jack the lad – part two 109
Awakened by the Master 117
The old ways of a French provincial town 123
Another world across the road 127
Lesson drawn, with help... 133

In limbo – flux and uncertainty 141
On the road 145
At last... 151
The 'Duke of Zellidja Award' 157
In Graham Greene's footsteps 163
In the time of fear – part one 173
Fitting in 178
'Sois jeune et tais-toi' 183
Spiral 189
'Imagination has seized power' 193
In the Gray zone 201
In praise of pubs 204
A sense of community 210
A Brighton honeymoon 215
The power of parsley 220
A view of the 70s from my seventies 225
In the time of fear – part two 231
Lost in the labyrinth of language 235
From school to books 243
Throwaway thoughts 256
Discovering the New World 263
The romance of wine 273
Listening to the secrets of strangers 286
Myths and legends 293
My first vote 304
The random pursuit of happiness 311
The lure of imagination 316
A glimpse into the hinterland 321
My generation 325
Time for a last good-bye 331
A thread of beads 341

On a northern shore

Today I find myself on a northern shore, looking out to a grey, angry sea under louring, fast-moving clouds, the cold wind stinging my face, and yet it brings to mind another long-lost and very different seashore: a southern Mediterranean beach in the heart of Algiers, the beach of my childhood.

It may be the presence of a scattering of rocks on the edge of both places that makes images of today's reality and memories of an estranged past collide. I see small groups of early-morning swimmers, most of them with no other protection than an ordinary swimsuit, laughingly making their way in what must be icy cold water. On other days, under blue skies and bright sunshine, I have been tempted... It all seems so piercingly revivifying, as they come out, thrilled and joyful. Then I think of my already narrowed arteries, and the shock of the cold bringing about extreme stenosis (a word I have had to learn in recent years). When my cousin and I ran down the narrow Rue Cadix to that other seafront in Bab-el-Oued, our only worry as we rushed into the clear water was not to tread on sea urchins. His mother, Nadia Guardascione (of southern Italian stock), had other, greater concerns, shouting at us from her third-floor balcony in her peculiar mix of anger and hilarity, "Jean-Claude, be careful! If you drown, I'll kill you!" We laughed and ran down towards the rocks.

And here today, looking at different rocks, I ponder the strange and unexpected arc of my life, from south to north, from warm to cold, from the Mediterranean to the Scottish North Sea, over just a bit more than seven decades. I have retrospective visions of what at the time, in the mid-1950s, I imagined my life would be – no arc, just roots: a life lived in one place, within the comforting reach of an extended family, a local scattering of aunts and uncles and cousins, around the twin focal points of my parents' and my grandparents' flats, almost all of them in just one area of Algiers, in Bab-el-Oued. (It was, after all, the life of most of the people I knew.) Maybe this is the vision of all children, this phantasy of stability, before late adolescence replaces it with a desire to break away. But in my case, events were to prevent this from happening.

By the time my cousin and I were seven or eight, our after-school swims were already under the flight path of army helicopters bringing wounded soldiers to the nearby military hospital – the Algerian war of independence had started. Not that it was known as such at the time, a rebellion at most, but a long, bloody war it proved to be. And by June 1962, it would be exile for Jean-Claude and me, the whole family, the whole tribe, nearly one million people departing in a period of a few weeks.

There is of course no shortage of stories of exile in the second half of the twentieth century, and even less so in the early decades of the twenty-first. But most of them have in common the moral legitimacy of their displacement: people who have fled their homeland because of persecution, war, destitution – victims. I belong to a tribe that has no claim to righteousness, a tribe cursed with being on the wrong side of historical change – both culprits and victims.

There would be two other exiles in my life, voluntary ones, but this first one, bringing about a dramatic end to the chimera and illusions of childhood, has remained an open wound.

Neither the thrills of student days in Paris culminating in a near revolution in 1968, nor the romance of falling in love with England, nor lately the search for political comfort after England chose Brexit and finding a seaside refuge in Scotland, none of these has softened that original wrench – there is still a pain like the phantom ache of an amputated limb.

Auld Lang Syne

In one of my memory boxes, I have a photograph torn from an old *Paris Match* magazine. It shows a small crowd of people on the deck of a passenger ship, their backs to the camera, above them, on top of a small mast, a French flag fluttering in the wind. In the distance, tiered along the hills of the bay, the white buildings of the centre of Algiers. The men, women and children gathered closely are catching a last sight of their city, and, as the caption says, singing "*Ce n'est qu'un au revoir...*" – 'it's only goodbye', or perhaps 'we'll meet again'. But for almost all of them, it was *adieu*. There would be no return to their native land.

In my fifties, I trained as a psychotherapist. On one occasion we were asked to show an emotionally charged object during a group session and speak about its significance. I chose this image. I started confidently, explaining the background and what the photo meant to me, only to be shocked to find myself suddenly unable to carry on speaking as I ran out of breath and voice, and my eyes brimmed with tears. And yet this was in fact a kind of appropriated memory – I did not leave on one of those crowded boats. In those last few chaotic weeks before Algerian independence, my father felt we could not wait days to queue up for a passage and he managed to exchange his newish car for plane tickets. So, we flew to Bordeaux and did not have that searing vision of a receding Algiers across the sea. But that image of departure remains just as potent.

Auld Lang Syne

People close to me, the Guardasciones, did queue up for a ship. I went down to the port to say goodbye to Jean-Claude, who was standing in line on the quayside by the warehouses and cranes, along with hundreds of others. The whole family was there – mother and father, Jean-Claude and his two older brothers, the grandparents – their few possessions gathered on the ground around them, a sort of makeshift, sparse encampment. Each person was allowed only two suitcases. Every case you could see was full to bursting. Some people had tried to supplement this limitation by wearing several layers, coats over jackets, an incongruous sight in the early summer heat. There seemed to be a strong matriarch in charge of each family group, keeping control of bored children, telling off angry young men and trying to ignore despondent husbands. Old men sat on suitcases, silent and uncomprehending. For many, like my own grandfather, it would be the first time they had set foot in France since fighting as young men in the trenches of the First World War. For these people were not the rich, land-owning colonialists or the administrative and political elite – all of whom had long since transferred their wealth to France or Switzerland and left by plane. The thousands queuing up were the *petit peuple*, the 'poor white' of the so-called French of Algeria. So-called because most of their family backgrounds were not French, but Italian, Spanish, Maltese or Sephardic Jewish from various countries – and if their background was French, their surnames were often Schmitt, Meyer or Weber, showing they had come as refugees from the troubled history of Alsace-Lorraine.

My grandfather's name was Adamo, his first name Giovanni which he changed to Jean when he was called up for his French military service. His father had emigrated from Sicily. My grandmother was a Sanchis – I never found out whether that was a mistaken rendering of Sanchez from when her family arrived in Algeria from Spain, or the original Valencian name.

For many of them, never rich enough to cross the Mediterranean for a holiday in France, this would be the first and last time they would see their native city from the sea in all its white splendour. And so, in packed, overloaded ships, there they were crowding the decks, clinging to each other and singing *"Ce n'est qu'un au revoir..."*

It was only years later, in my student days at a New Year's Eve party in Brighton, that I discovered that song was in fact a French version of Auld Lang Syne, the words adapted rather than translated from the original but retaining their nostalgic power, and the tune with its lamenting melody acutely conveying the pathos of those days of exodus. Every New Year's Eve, after all these years, I still can't hear that tune without that image from *Paris Match* being conjured up and having to contain tears amidst others' celebrations.

"Where do you come from in France?"

It inevitably comes up in the small talk that follows an introduction. "Jean-Luc... are you French?" To which I reply, "Well, yes, sort of...", or "Yes but a lapsed kind of Frenchman", or "Yes, but I've given it up..." This is usually followed by, "Where do you come from in France?" Then I have to say nowhere in France, I was born in Algeria. Ah you're Algerian then? No, I can't claim to be that... So, are you French Algerian? – er, no, that's usually French citizens born in France of Algerian immigrants. At this point, and at the risk of pomposity, a few more words need to be expended: I'm of European descent, born in Algeria when Algeria was still a French colony. (I don't go into the euphemisms used by successive French governments.) Ah, so your parents were from France originally – well, yes, my father was but my mother was born in Algeria. Occasionally I get, does that make you partly Arab then? I have to explain about the one million 'Algerians' of various European backgrounds, many established for several generations in the country, almost all of whom went into exile when Algeria became independent following a long and complex war. Often this rings a bell and sometimes it brings up: "Oh, I remember that film...", meaning Pontecorvo's *The Battle of Algiers*, which graphically depicts the French army's fierce campaign in the mid-fifties to quell the growing rebellion in the Arab quarters of Algiers with unfettered use of force and torture. "Did you live through that?" Yes, but on the other side, as it were – and as a child among the people on the receiving end of the bombs planted by the nationalists. At this point the more Francophile or generally the more informed may come up with the historically correct label: "So, you're a *pied-noir*?" Yes, I am, I have to say. But this is where it gets even more complicated, because I then feel that if they know enough to be familiar with the term, then they must have an idea of what's associated with it, right-wing extremism, racism and generally voting for Le Pen. I usually just have time to venture an individual denial of what's implied before it's time for my listener to change the subject or to move on to find someone else to talk to. I can't blame them – I too wish I had a more straightforward answer to the original question.

The next thing that often comes up with those who are interested enough to take the conversation further, admittedly for well-meant reasons, is a playing down of the experience of war on a child: "You were so young when you left, you can't have been that affected by it all." Yes, I was young but how to explain that children in times of conflict rapidly grow older than their years. I did not feel like a thirteen-year-old. I did not follow a football team or who was winning the Tour de France. Instead, my childhood passions were for the symbols and heroes of our doomed *Algérie Française* cause, for the flag, the songs, the slogans, the generals who rebelled to take our side. In the last two turbulent years of my life in Algiers, I followed every daily development in the conflict, particularly on my side of it. My day-to-day life was filled with the bloody twists and turns of the descent into a three-way civil war, much of it happening on the streets. And by then, as is common with this type of conflict, children spent much of their time in the streets, in the midst of it. Just picture images from the Troubles in Northern Ireland or from the streets of

"Where do you come from in France?"

Gaza. Like all my peers, I was very quickly a grown-up child. Only, in the wider context of history unseen at the time, on the wrong side. It is a childhood of intense emotions, but one now that I am really grown up, and grown old, I can't easily own without awkwardness and embarrassment. I certainly can't freely revel in the memories of it.

Yet, I cannot claim what I am not, a Frenchman from somewhere in France, nor fully what I have tried to be for the last 50-odd years, a signed-up and assimilated citizen of Britain. I cannot wholly escape the original locus of my tribe. Algeria has stuck to me even though I cannot belong to it.

Nor can I claim that I wholeheartedly belong to my cursed *pied-noir* tribe. There could be too many political meanings attached to that. I have known other displaced people who have the relative comfort of righteousness – they had to flee war or persecution – but this is not granted to people who were blind to their historical circumstances and ended up fighting a rearguard colonial battle. Having lost everything, most of them have still clung to their delusions.

Even though I have long lost my childhood attachment to their original cause, I have recently become acutely aware that the *pieds-noirs* are about to disappear. Those disparate Europeans of Algeria, who in 1962 stumbled, bloody and destitute, out of what they felt was their homeland and found an often-unwelcoming refuge in France and other countries, are about to die off. And part of what I want to write about here in these fragments will be to leave a trace of them, to bear witness to some aspects of their lives through an evocation of the ones I knew best, my family. Not a eulogy by any means, more of a lament, even if one largely undeserved.

Beachcombing

Coming to this windy shore of the Forth of Firth has felt like a liberation after 25 years of living in the Thames valley, in a city that had become too crowded and somehow, strangely, too oppressively hot. Maybe because I became tired of pounding the hard pavements on my spells of daily walking. Here, five minutes' walk from our front door, are long sandy beaches, a varied seascape dotted with rocky islands, the imposing Bass Rock shining out among them and, most importantly, an open horizon. Several times a day I am drawn to one or the other of the town's beaches for long walks, usually keeping as close to the shoreline as possible, not only because it is easier to tread on the wet sand but also because I find the endless repetition of the breaking waves comforting: an affirmation of the continuously renewed vitality of the natural world distracting me from familiar thoughts, all too frequent these days, of my own impermanence.

These walks have become an ingrained daily routine, needed almost as much as food and drink. When I mentioned this to an old French friend in answer to, "What do you do in this new place?", his response was "a beach is always the same, isn't it boring?" He lives near the comparatively unchanging Mediterranean beaches of the Languedoc so I could understand his reaction, but how it made me want to transport him instantly to this place of constant mutation. This place of clear and distant horizons giving way to the rolling in of the haar, of dark clouds being whisked off by strong winds to reveal limpid blue skies, of roaring high tides all but crashing into the walls of beachside houses and then retreating to reveal vast areas of sand and rocks, and a mirror-like calm sea. Each tide leaves behind a different configuration of beach, varying areas of wet and dry sands, changing marbled patterns of sand colours, shifting strands of washed-up seaweeds ranging from the lightest pale cream to the darkest black via all shades of green, red and pink too.

If you lift your gaze and look out to the open sea as it meets the sky, you have a whole other ever-shifting palette of blues, greens and greys, constantly rearranged by the vagaries of the weather. The horizon itself can be a merging combination of clouds and the hills on the opposite shore of the firth or, by contrast, a distinct line of the small white houses in the fishing villages of the East Neuk of Fife shining in the sun, so well-defined you feel it would be a short hop to step into their streets. The Isle of May similarly can appear near enough for the vertical dark stony stripes of its sheer cliffs to be clearly visible or as an indistinct grey shape, half lost in the mist, that could just as easily be a slow-moving ship.

And as a study in constant alteration of appearance you cannot get better than that preposterous rocky promontory just off the coast, the majestic Bass Rock. Its sheer sides and inclined top change colour with every passing cloud, every small variation in sunlight, as well as, when looked at from different angles, an endless play of all shades between bright white and almost black. It makes this inert volcanic plug look like it could be some strange, slow-moving live monster. It's the home of the northern gannet – a species whose spectacular feeding method I have only recently discovered on my beach walks. At certain times of day, you can see them circling above the waves not far from the shore, spotting their catch, and then diving down vertically, kamikaze-like, and disappearing completely (they are big birds!) below the surface for quite a few seconds. There is a great array of birds around at all times – low-flying crows or jackdaws pecking at the seaweed, firmly standing their ground as you walk past; tiny wagtails, almost as tame as robins, sometimes hop alongside me.

Occasionally at the edge of the surf there are small groups of oystercatchers – or, more technically, small 'parcels' of oystercatchers – moving rather elegantly on their thin legs, red beaks standing out against their black and white 'dinner jackets'. More frequently seen are groups of eider ducks close to the shore, their presence often signalled by their unlikely sounding cooing, and naturally, ever-present, is an aerial circus of squawking seagulls of all kinds. On early low tide mornings, I can also spot a lone heron who regularly comes to stand still or haughtily step around in the same cluster of exposed rocks at the far end of West Beach. So often that it has the feel of an encounter with a friend. There is no exchange of greetings but it lets me approach quite close, keeping a sideways wary eye on my slow movement and reciprocating in an equally ponderous manner – except with a high lifting of knee which I could not possibly match.

When you stop taking in the whole beach landscape, forego the open sea and wide skies, and get your eye into where you are putting your feet down, you discover an inextinguishable treasure trove of multicoloured small stones, shells and other washed-up small shards of mainly natural debris. Miraculously, there is very little plastic pollution on this shore – this is a highly civic-minded area and I sometimes see local volunteers picking up any stray pieces of rubbish along the beach. Paradoxically, it is a particular category of broken objects from the human world that I have become fascinated by: small broken bits of glass and china that have been so worn by sun, sand, sea, wind and time that they are transformed into enticing fragments of what one could imagine being a naturally formed puzzle. Not that they fit together, but in a way it is their very imperfection that makes them attractive. They have become misshapen, their sharp angles rounded off, their asperities made smooth, their colours opaque, often in a variegated way, their feel soft as if sandpapered. Once I started noticing them it became difficult to stop, and so it is now a habit. To the hypnotic accompaniment of rolling waves, I walk along this windy edge of the North Sea and look out for these tiny pieces as if they were rare and precious finds. I usually keep one in my hand that I play with like a worry bead; it has become part of the ritual. Now that I have accumulated a large number, I have become more discriminating, which makes me give in to the irresistible human tendency to anthropomorphise: and so, I pick up and hesitate to discard as if they were small sentient beings that I am already fond of, creating a story in my head of successive selections, adoptions and rejections – a repeated narrative of short-lived joy and pain.

I have taken to collating the many I have kept into a growing display on a white laminated surface in a bright bathroom – and every time I see this, particularly when there is sunlight shining on it, I am struck by the overall look of this little amateur art installation, by the beauty emanating from these bits of everyday glass and porcelain that are surely now far more interesting than ever they were in their original state. Not much by any accepted aesthetic standards perhaps but it still gives me a thrill. (As I slide into old age, I am more than ready to delight in every pleasurable moment, however small.) I am conscious that they can be seen as illustration of what a long life does to us. Some broken pieces, inescapably, but transformed, rounded off, made smoother, more opaque but more interesting too. It is the sight of them and the thoughts they gave rise to that also triggered the writing of this. It suddenly felt like the time had come to collect my own personal fragments, these short pieces which could perhaps form an interesting enough whole, a fragmented picture of a fragmented life. An old-fashioned collage that encompasses three exiles across four countries, life in two languages, from an urban civil war in childhood to the noxious culture war of Brexit in old age. No shortage of broken pieces...

Life can be a beach, briefly...

I have very few memories of my father, or at least of my father acting like a father. There is, however, a photograph of him standing on a beach-side path showing me a locust he'd caught. I am looking up at it and he is smiling down at my look of awe. I must have been five or six years old, and we are probably in a town that used to be called La Madrague – understandably, most of the places of my Algerian childhood were given Arabic names after independence. It was a small beach resort a short distance from Algiers, and a sought-after weekend spot for the better-off *pieds-noirs* of the capital. Not that we were better-off ourselves, living as we did in a one-bedroom flat in the poorest part of town (at least for Europeans), but my father had the knack of getting himself (and his family) 'adopted' by people above his station. He would be adept at this all his life, using charm and a kind of streetwise resourcefulness, as well as, to be fully honest, a readiness to be helpful at all times. Jacky, as he was known (my father's name was Jack, not the more common French version, Jacques), could always be counted on to go out of his way to do you a favour, with a winning smile and a witty retort. I think he had a way of doing this that came just short of being cringingly ingratiating – there was, too, a confidence and cockiness about it. Occasionally, I saw people take advantage of it but by and large he got away with it with his dignity intact. I suppose you could say he knew how to display the right level of chutzpah.

As a result, we mixed with people who owned what were referred to as *cabanons* in La Madrague and similar small towns along the coast. These were a far cry from what the name implies, not a type of *cabane* (shed or cabin), but usually large, well-appointed beach-side villas. Their owners liked to entertain large parties of guests at the weekend, showing off the views from their terraces, taking people out on their speedboats for water-skiing or fishing. We often stayed in a villa which belonged to my father's boss, the oddly named (for that place, at that time) Monsieur Prescott, who, in a fashion that was to be often repeated, had become fond of my father in a rather patrician sort of way. His son, the same age as my father, made a show of being very friendly with him, but I suspect there was a degree of jealousy lurking there as he could be patronising. It was noticeable that Jacky always ended up being given the dirty or awkward jobs to do with the speedboat. It was also obvious, even to a child, that both vied for the attention of the women in the group. My mother put on a brave smile through this when in company but simmering resentment could give way to bad-tempered exchanges on our drive back into town on Sunday night.

However, these were happy times for me. Times when I was discovering the pleasures of being among a large group of friends, the joys of conviviality: laughter and good humour all around. Times also when we were doing things as a family, which would soon become rarer as my father started to work on road-building in the Sahara and was away from home for long periods. As one of the few children there, I was fussed over and indulged by the women in the group, and teased by the men, whom I looked up to, wishing to be older, to be like them. I could not have known that buried in that desire was a portent of disappointment, of events taking a turn so that a longed-for, imagined life would never be lived – something that would become a recurring feature of my Algerian childhood.

Memories of these weekends were summoned up from deep recesses of my mind in an unexpected and rather incongruous way. I rarely used to eat crisps but not long ago I tried a packet of one of those 'superior', 'artisan' types of crisps – and indeed, not only was it a gustatory delight but their consistency and taste brought back instantly, and insistently, the flavour and smell of what were then called in French '*chips*'. We used to eat those as a treat at the terrace of a small-town café on our Sunday evening returns to Algiers. Friends drove back in a convoy of cars and although it was not a long journey, everyone was keen to squeeze a last pleasure out of the weekend, so they always stopped at this particular café, where the owner, now a sort of friend, would pull several tables together and greet them with a loud "The usual then?" It was *apéritif* time. The grown-ups drank the local *anisette*, a *pastis*-like drink, with a stronger smell of aniseed – in fact more like *ouzo* – which at the time was not common in France but would become an emblematic *pied-noir* drink. The children were given *menthe à l'eau* or *grenadine*. The tables were soon covered in small dishes, a kind of meze known as *kemia*, again typically *pied-noir*. The olives and small pieces of pickled vegetables were not to the children's taste. Instead, we waited with glee for *les chips* to arrive in large bowls. Crisps were a new thing in Algeria at that point – you certainly could not get them in a packet and here it was this café's latest specialty. (I think the owner must have learnt how to cook them from American servicemen stationed nearby towards the end of the Second World War.) Being home-prepared, they were slightly thicker than the normal modern ones, usually more cooked, with small darker, almost burnt areas – but so much tastier. And it is that taste, or at least a close approximation of it, that I rediscovered in a small packet of crisps bought in Oxford sixty years later and which rushed back memories of these fleeting moments of happiness. These weekends soon came to an end. Not only because of my father's absence but also because of the growing rebellion, as it was then called.

Whilst the *pieds-noirs* played, some of their Arab compatriots, having given up hope of progress in any other way, had been organising for a war of independence. The *pieds-noirs*' insouciance and joie de vivre was matched by an almost total blindness to the reality of their historical circumstances.

From one river to another

For about twelve years prior to this third and latest exile, I spent time by two rivers, the Thames in Oxford (which of course they have to call something different there, the Isis, enabling the locals to have immediate recognition of outsiders…), and the Charente, just outside a small village in the French *département* of the same name (which could certainly be described as typical of *la France profonde*). Several times a year I travelled between an Edwardian terraced house near riverside meadows in north Oxford and an ancient farmhouse perched above the meandering Charente – from a centre of culture to a region where agriculture reigned supreme. The purchase of the farmhouse had been made possible by my share of the proceeds from the sale of my mother's property after her death, and my choice had surprised people around me. My very urban brothers, one in La Rochelle, the other in Geneva, both asked, "Do you really want to bury yourself deep in the country, where nothing happens?" I did explain that having a chance to escape from what felt like an exiguous city home to the larger spaces of an old rambling house in its own large wooded grounds would bring about a sense of invigorating release – and it did, every time I went there. But there was a lot more to it.

My father was not a real *pied-noir*: unlike my mother, he was not born in Algeria. He came from a small village, oddly named Frontenay-Rohan-Rohan, near Niort, not very far from the house we bought. He came to Algiers to do his

French military service just after the war and, having met my mother, he stayed, and, like many converts, he espoused the *pied-noir* way of life and later, the *pied-noir* cause with enthusiasm. His own father had died during the war, not on the battlefield but from pneumonia. Whilst I obviously did not get to know this grandfather, I was certainly embraced by the extended family on summer holiday visits. As the first grandchild I was fussed over not only by my grandmother, Mamie, but also by three stout aunts of about the same vintage, Henriette, Germaine and Madeleine (names wonderfully evocative of the period), all very much stereotypical French aunties, demonstratively affectionate, chatty and extrovert. They were, in fact, great-aunts, sisters of the dead grandfather. There was also a real aunt, Monique, my father's younger sister, and her husband, Jacques. For these summer stays with the French family, I was often sent on my own, flying from Algiers to Bordeaux, a small boy with a large suitcase and a sizeable official sign tied with ribbons around my neck. In those days, on getting off the plane, you walked across the tarmac to the terminal building, and I remember crossing that space holding the hand of a solicitous air hostess and scanning the people waving on a balcony for the known faces of the aunt and uncle that had come to collect me. It was usually *Tante* Henriette and *Tonton* André because they lived not far from Frontenay and had a car.

On my earliest trips André drove a classic black Citroën Traction Avant but he soon acquired, the moment it was launched, the spectacularly smooth and ultra-modern Citroën DS, which was treated with great pride and reverence. (He lived a long life, had many cars but never bought anything other than a Citroën.) I was told in no uncertain terms that I had to ask for an early stop if ever I felt in the least bit carsick and I did my childish very best to avoid it. This was not helped by the unusually soft and gentle wave-like suspension, or when occasionally *Tante* Henriette would sit in the back with me and insist on pulling me close to her, enveloping me in a cloud of her pungent perfume. I can still, after all these years, recognise that scent on other people, and strangely it releases not nausea, but instead a rather pleasant, hazy nostalgic feeling.

There was also an air of mystery to these journeys which only became clear later. My uncle seemed quite nervous whenever policemen were spotted by the road or overtook us on motorbikes, and cryptic words were exchanged with my aunt. The tension hung in the air until we drove through the gates of their courtyard. Then, usually under cover of falling darkness, there was a somewhat ceremonious emptying of the boot, a careful unloading of several cases which, obvious from the clinking noises, contained bottles of wine. I realised later on that my uncle took advantage of these trips to Bordeaux airport to call on local wine producers on the way there and buy supplies without having to pay duties. I would have had no idea at the time but they must have been very fine and expensive clarets. There was something incongruous about my stern and very respectable uncle acting in this surreptitious way, taking risks for the sake of good wine. I realise as I write this that this must have been the first time I became aware of the significance of wine in French culture, my first small step on a life-long fascination with all things to do with wine, with what I would come to think of, in my adult life, as the romance of wine. Uncle André was a civil engineer and was in charge of the local branch of *Ponts et Chaussées*, the government service that looked after road-building and maintenance. They lived in a large 1930s villa, in a village called Brioux-sur-Boutonne, also not far from Niort, and I usually stayed with them for a few days before being taken to my grandmother's house in Frontenay.

I loved the peace and comfort of those days – though alone, with no one my age that is, I always seemed to find enjoyable ways of occupying my time. There was a large attic full of boxes of oddments I was allowed to open and play with. Downstairs, there was a kind of conservatory room with cane furniture and piles of *Paris Match* and other glossy magazines which I spent hours happily leafing through. And there was an extensive garden, where I first discovered the intense taste of freshly picked, fully ripe raspberries – a taste I've pursued my whole life but rarely recaptured as sharply. I was also sent out to pick green beans, lettuces or parsley in time for each meal, collecting a whole batch of new smells and sensations that I had never come across in my city life in Algiers. At the back of the garden, there were kennels for two or three dogs, retrievers for *la chasse*, hunting, a much talked about ritual activity which André took part in assiduously. My uncle would come back from hunting outings, rifle over his shoulder, and wordlessly put down a brace of pheasants or partridges on the kitchen table. These were greeted with howls of congratulatory delight from Henriette. Theirs was a very traditional set-up, typical of the time and place. Henriette saw her role as looking after the home and supporting her husband – and it would be more accurate to say venerating her husband. I do not recall her ever being anything but complimentary about André. And he did seem to be devoted to her too, but in a more aloof, non-demonstrative manner. (Thereby laying down, deep in a child's mind, images of a model of relationships that would be totally unsuited to the later experiences of my generation.) Henriette always painted him as a severe man who would not tolerate any misbehaviour from a child, but I did not have occasion to experience that. They both saw me as a very well-behaved little boy but what I was really was a very *serious* little boy, preoccupied by what he was living through in Algiers, at home, at school and more dramatically in the streets, and grateful for days of peace and calm.

Over a meal, looking for a topic of conversation, my uncle asked me if I was enjoying Cub Scouts sessions, which I had recently started going to. These took place at the weekend in a school playground in the centre of Algiers. I had to walk there from Bab-el-Oued in the west of the city and the route included a boulevard which ran along the bottom of the Casbah. This was at the height of the campaign of bombings and killings launched by the FLN (the *Front de Libération Nationale*), and I was all too aware that the 'rebels' were based in the labyrinth of lanes to the right of me as I hurried along, keeping to the arcaded galleried pavement on the left, trying not to look up the narrow alleys. Once, I had to walk past a still bleeding corpse lying in the middle of the pavement – he was an Arab, perhaps shot as a suspected informer. People walked around without stopping as if death on the streets was not unusual, which in those days it had begun not to be. I liked being part of the Cubs but on my way there and back I could never shake off a feeling of being under threat, of being in imminent danger. I answered André by telling him about activities and going to camp but did not speak of my walks of fear.

After some time with them, I would usually be taken to stay with my grandmother in Frontenay. She lived in a very small house on the main road through this typical, sleepy

French village, with most of the shutters permanently closed. Mamie was the secretary in the local *mairie*, a part-time job but one of great influence in the *commune*. I could sense that whenever I dropped in at her office and saw the reverence with which people would treat her. The mayor took on all the formal aspects of the role but she was the real power. With me though, her first grandchild, she was nothing but indulgent and spoiling, like the aunties. At first, it could be quite boring being there, with not much to do in the house or the small garden, but then a local cousin, slightly older than me, Jean, turned up, and with him came another chance to have more normal childhood experiences than what I had in Algiers. The first day he appeared on his bike he impressed me by showing me that if you waved enthusiastically when convoys of American army vehicles trundled past (there was a base not far away), the soldiers would often throw out packets of chewing-gum.

More lastingly, he made me discover the countryside on long rides on unmade-up lanes during what seemed like endless summer days. We would cycle along small roads of compacted sandy gravel, ribbons of yellow cutting through fields lined with green hedges which took us to a nearby area known as the Marais Poitevin, a network of waterways in long-ago recovered marshland, by now a lush mosaic of small fields and canals where local people still used flat barges to travel between fields and move their animals around. We dumped our bikes right by the water's edge and set small net traps to catch crayfish. Whilst waiting we ate baguette sandwiches filled with chocolate bars and drank Orangina. Jean knew someone from whom we could borrow a barge and he showed me how to use the paddle, called a *pigouille*. We navigated our way for hours through the labyrinth of narrow canals under a canopy of greenery, in what felt like a universe of our own.

When in my late fifties I started searching for an old French farmhouse I first thought of looking around Frontenay. Although the main high street was much the same, the outskirts had been transformed, invaded by ever-expanding estates of new-build houses for people commuting to the thriving insurance companies in Niort. Worse than that was the fate of the surrounding countryside. Gone were the yellow unmade-up lanes, now turned grey or black with macadam. Gone too were all the hedges and trees that marked the small fields. Agribusiness had destroyed it all to leave in its stead a vast expanse of open fields, which, to me, in spite of the crops growing there, felt like a desert. In contrast, but no less affecting, the sleepy villages of the Marais Poitevin had become tourist hotspots and there were queues to hire the black barges for trips on the now crowded canals. It felt a bit like a second loss, less dramatic admittedly than the first, of the settings of my childhood. It turned memories of these peaceful summer interludes into something hazy and unreal. Eventually I found my longed-for rural domain in a quiet corner of the Charente Limousine, an area of hedge-lined fields and small hills, what the French call *bocage*, which was reminiscent enough of the vanished backdrop of my childhood summer wanderings with my cousin Jean.

What's in a name?

I don't like being called Jean. This is something that happens a lot in Britain, where the concept of a hyphenated first name does not seem to be widely understood. I often have to make it explicit that Jean-Luc is one name, not a first and middle name. In online forms, it is frequently impossible to enter a hyphenated first name, which means that in all sorts of situations, from banks and insurance companies to supermarkets and shops, I can only be registered as Jean. This, not always amusingly, has given me a gender-fluid online identity. I am regularly addressed as Ms Jean Barbanneau and receive appropriately tailored messaging: there was a phase when I got an abundance of advice about how to "cope better with my menopause", and I am never short of special offers on face creams and perfumes.

In the same vein, and maybe the apex of absurdity, there was an occasion some years ago when after a meeting with Japanese publishers (which I had attended in my, at the time, bearded male self) I received a thank you note addressed to Ms Jean McBarbanneau. Not just a gender change but also the creation of a new Franco-Scottish clan. Maybe I should use this now that I live in these parts... And with those who do get the single hyphenated first name concept, the interesting thing is that in many cases after I have been introduced, Jean-Luc does not seem to stick. Instead, I am often called Jean-Paul (could it be because of Sartre?), occasionally Jean-Pierre (mysteriously). I had hoped that

Jean-Luc Godard's fame would help but it clearly did not have the reach of Sartre. For a short time in the 1990s there was a Belgian prime minister called Jean-Luc Dehaene who was occasionally mentioned in the news, but like most Belgian prime ministers he did not last long enough for the name to make an impression. Then, a few years ago, things improved a bit – there was a revival of *Star Trek* and with it came much more exposure for the Jean-Luc Picard character, which had a much broader reach than any other Jean-Luc. Even though I remained totally impervious to the appeal of all science-fiction, I was grateful.

Once the obstacles of Jean-Luc are surmounted, I still have to face the multifarious pronunciation and spelling challenges of Barbanneau. Phone conversations can go something like this:

- What is your name?
- Barbanneau, I'll spell that, B... A... R...
- B... A... R...
- B... A...
- Yes, I've got that already...
- No, it's B... A... again...
- Ah...
- Double N...
- Double M...
- No, not M, N... like November...
- Ah, yes double N...
- E... A... U...
- E... W...
- No, E... A... U...
- Say that again?

Then the letter or email arrives, addressed to Dear Ms Jean Barabannew. Not surprisingly, when making reservations or leaving things at dry cleaners, I am plain John Luke.

My *pied-noir* maternal grandfather was called Jean but that too was the result of a name change. He was born Giovanni Adamo. His parents emigrated from Sicily to Algeria, where his father set up a photographer's shop in Oran. I was never entirely sure about this, but I was aware as a child of allusions to the fact that at least some members of the original Sicilian family were Jewish. However, by the time I knew my grandfather, he had shed not only that aspect of his origin but had also fully embraced his French identity and had long since become Jean, rather than Giovanni, Adamo. His conversation though was still sprinkled with Italian words and he sometimes called me Gianluca. On the rare occasions he needed to admonish me for making too much noise, it was often with a firm sounding *basta!* His time serving in the French army during the First World War was at the centre of his existence. He had been in the trenches of Verdun and came back with his eyesight badly damaged by the effects of gas. All the years I knew him he was active in war veterans' activities, putting on his medals for the frequent commemorations and always wearing on the lapel of his jacket the tiny red ribbon of the *Légion d'honneur*, of which he was inordinately proud. He sat in an armchair by an old wireless to listen to the news and consult his many *dossiers*, multicolour files containing paperwork from the various *ancien combattant* associations he was involved in, holding them very close to his narrowed rheumy eyes. It can't have been an easy task and his silent determination left a lasting impression on me. Like most of his peers he did not recount stories of his time in the trenches but he did tell me once that it had been four years of hell. Because of his bad eyesight, he walked slowly and cautiously, but he always stood very upright, with his head held up high. I remember watching him from the balcony in Rue Cadix in Bab-el-Oued, walking to a veterans' parade with a companion, looking so dapper and dignified. His deeply patriotic allegiance to the French Republic had become a reason for living and as the complex disintegration of French Algeria unravelled, what was happening around him became increasingly beyond his comprehension. By March 1962, when the *pieds-noirs* of Bab-el-Oued were in open rebellion against the French government and he had had to cower on the floor between his bed and his wardrobe to avoid strafing by war planes of the French air force, he was a broken man. By June, he stood, still just about upright, still wearing his *Légion d'honneur* ribbon, along with my grandmother, each holding their allowed two suitcases, in a long queue on the quayside of the port of Algiers, waiting for a ship to take them to Marseille. On arrival, no one saluted him. He never went to another veterans' reunion and less than a year later he died – younger than I am now.

My *pied-noir* grandmother also had a change of name. She was born Francisca Sanchis in a small Spanish town south of Valencia, and when her parents emigrated to Algeria when she was a child, she became Françoise. She too considered herself French but as she went about her daily chores, I often heard her come out with Spanish expressions – or perhaps more accurately words from the Valencian dialect she still used with her sisters. Towards the end of her life, I asked her why her parents had uprooted their large family and the answer had a surprising aspect. Predictably enough, they had only been scratching a living on a small farm but the main reason was that a son was being called up to fight in the Spanish–American war of 1898 in Cuba – an historical event totally unknown to me until then – and they had already lost another son in that conflict. There were plenty of jobs in the still relatively new and expanding French colony of Algeria and her mother convinced her father to make the move to avoid the risk of losing another son. I wish I had asked a lot more but, as with my grandfather and his wartime experiences, *Mémé*, as she was known, did not seem to enjoy talking about the past. I now feel I should have encouraged her and my grandfather more to fill the gaps – and this applies to my mother and father, and the uncles and aunts as well.

It is a cause of great regret in my eighth decade that, as a child, I was too preoccupied by events around me, as a young adult too distracted by the desires of that age, and as an adult too far away, exiled in another country, and busy with my own family life, to be curious enough about the lives of my elders. It is not unusual, I know, but a great loss all the same. Francisca, by then Françoise, Sanchis must have met Giovanni, by then Jean, Adamo in Oran where they both lived. Probably involving a typical *pied-noir* courting scenario, which I got to observe as a boy in Bab-el-Oued: young men would hang around in small groups on the streets or squares where young women, arm in arm, in twos or threes, took their evening *passegiata*. Looks were exchanged, jokes attempted, laughter shared and eventually, often after many weeks of this ritual, questions were answered, and couples were tentatively formed...

I don't know what took Jean and Françoise to Sétif, a long way to the east of Oran, but I know they lived there before moving to Algiers because that is where my mother was born. Jean was a lowly *fonctionnaire*, a government office worker, and he may have been posted there. In May 1945, the town was the scene of bloody events that would mark a turning point for the Algerian nationalist movement. A demonstration attended mainly by Algerian men who had served in the French army in the war and who were demanding full civil rights was brutally repressed. This led to widespread disturbances in the region and over a hundred *pied-noir* settlers were killed. The French authorities' retaliation, aided by *pied-noir* militias, involved weeks of indiscriminate killings of Muslims. The death toll remains disputed but estimates vary between 6,000 and 30,000. By the time this happened, the Adamos had moved to Algiers and I never once heard the massacre of Sétif being referred to. I only found out about it in my thirties, when I read accounts of it in books about the Algerian war.

When being asked questions about my background and not wishing to go very much into the complex story, I sometimes just use several names as shortcuts: the often misspelt and mispronounced Barbanneau giving the French ingredient, the Sanchis from the province of Alicante, sometimes understood as Sanchez, adding the Spanish flavour, and the Italian-sounding Adamo putting a final colourful and complication-free touch to the mix.

The multifarious triggers of memory

I saw the name on a small packet on the cold shelf of a deli in this small Scottish town: *sobrasada*, which instantly made me think of what I had known in my Algerian childhood days as *soubressade*. The shock of recognition was so great because in all the years since then I had never again come across this, either in France or in England. The label actually said *Sobrasada de Bellota, Cured Ibérico Spreading Chorizo*, and naturally I had to get it to check that it was indeed what I had known. *Chorizo*, I know, is ubiquitous enough but this version, an especially soft, moist paste easily spread on bread, is not. And there it was, exactly as I remembered it from all those times it had featured as a first course in meals at my Adamo grandparents' apartment in Bab-el-Oued. My uncle Christian was particularly fond of it and would make me *tartines* thickly spread with it. I loved it. Christian was a single man who lived with his parents and he played the young uncle role to perfection: constantly teasing and joshing me but always with good humour, warmth and obvious affection. On Sunday afternoons he sometimes took me for a ride on his motorbike along the coast road to the west of Algiers to the stadium of Saint Eugène to watch a football match. He once told me that Albert Camus had played as a goalkeeper for the ASSE, the local amateur team, but I found out later that Camus had indeed played as a goalie in his youth but for another club in Algiers. I had no idea at the time who Camus was.

The Multifarious Triggers of Memory

By the time I was ten years old I used to stay at my grandparents' flat during the week. I was told the reason was that it was nearer my college but I think it was because my mother was finding it difficult to cope with her job as a schoolteacher as well as looking after my two infant younger brothers with my father absent most of the time, working in the Sahara. Christian would let me have his bedroom while he slept on a couch in the small vestibule. I liked staying there as it was a calmer, more convivial atmosphere than home where my mother always felt harried and preoccupied, and if my father was home, often bad-tempered. The place was run with benevolent authority by *Mémé* Adamo from her tiny kitchen, lined with small multicoloured Moorish tiles. (I would come across similar motifs many times in my life that would always evoke images of that kitchen.) She would give me small chores to do. I was responsible for grinding coffee beans in one of those square wooden grinders operated by turning a metal handle, which resisted at first and then became easier and easier to turn, until the sound changed when there were no beans left in the funnel. I then had the very delicate and highly satisfying task of gently pulling out the little drawer that had collected the ground coffee and carefully, very carefully – "Don't spill it, it's precious", she would say – emptying it into a tin, all the while the pungent aroma invading my nostrils. It was a favourite daily task and here again, although I have rarely ground coffee beans since then, even with an electric device, all my life I have chased a trace of those sensations with every packet of coffee I have opened. The flat was on the second floor of a three-storey building and just above a corner grocery shop run by a Mozabite family – the Mozabites were a Berber tribe, originally from the Sahara, who were often shopkeepers. Daily shopping was carried out in an ingenious way, and sometimes entrusted to me. It involved tying a long rope to a large basket, called a *cabas*, placing a shopping list and a purse in the basket and lowering it from the balcony so it dangled in front of the always open door of the shop. Soon enough, one of the shopkeepers would grab the basket, fulfil the order, take payment from the purse and shake the rope or shout out to signal that the *cabas* was ready to be pulled back up. I felt a definite sense of pride in finally lifting it over the balustrade of the very narrow balcony and taking it to *Mémé* in the kitchen.

As I write this, I can't help thinking how much pride, with both its positive and negative side effects, played a part in everyday life in Bab-el-Oued. I used to hang around with my cousin Jean-Claude Guardascione who lived in the same street. He had two older brothers and the whole male clan of that family, including the father, was steeped in a typically Italian quasi-religious cult of male pride. Offence was easily taken, voices always quickly raised, creative insults instantly crafted, retribution exacted – or, most often, exacted in appearance only, with all sides intent on saving face. All the while, Nadia, the constantly agitated mother, loudly imploring God, "What have I done to the Lord to deserve these men?" In similar vein, only with a different God, was another friend's family I came to know well. Samuel lived in the flat below my grandparents and we often played on the building's side terrace on the same floor. His Jewish family were as loud and garrulous as the Guardasciones, and certainly as proud of their own heritage. They were as open and generous as they were noisy and argumentative, and they always made me feel welcome in their home, that is if they noticed my presence in the semi-permanent chaos. This gave me an early insight into the Sephardic way of life – by contrast, it is both understandable and incongruous that in all my Algerian years I never had an opportunity to come anywhere as close to a Muslim family and their way of life. Even before the start of the nationalist uprising, the two communities, *pieds-noirs* and Arabs, lived side by side but did not mix.

Christian worked as a technician in an optician's shop in the centre of Algiers and he was very proud of his job and of his skills. He often brought glasses to repair at home and he would show me his set of tiny tools and glass-cutting and polishing instruments. He would laugh at my vain attempts to hold his special magnifying device on my eye but would still let me have a go at trying to fit the minuscule screws in spectacle frames. For years he would remain a constantly cheerful presence in the flat, until suddenly in early 1960, following the dramatic events of the 'week of the barricades', the first *pied-noir* insurrection against the French government, he was suddenly not there for several weeks. I knew he could not have been arrested as he had not been an active participant. His only involvement had been, like thousands of others, to go on demonstrations of support for the insurgents. These were marches from Bab-el-Oued to the centre of the city, on which he had actually brought me along on several occasions. Not much was spoken about his absence, as these things were shamefully kept under wraps in those days, but I eventually gathered that he had suffered what was then referred to as a 'nervous breakdown'. He spent a long time in a specialist clinic, he told me later, undergoing a '*cure de sommeil*'. Were long periods of induced sleep really used as therapy? I would not be surprised, given the times, if electric shock had not also been involved. He came back a changed man, no longer jolly but a passive, faded version of his previous self, often voicing paranoid thoughts.

After the exile to France, he still lived with his mother, by now a widow, until well into his forties. At first, he found work at the optician's counter of a large department store but his ongoing paranoia meant this did not last long. In my student days in Paris, I used to see him when I visited *Mémé* Adamo in her flat in an eastern suburb. I noticed before the meals that she used to add water to the bottle of red wine that would go on the table. She explained, "Otherwise, it interferes with his medication…", but I think it was partly because he drank too much. By then, he had become a uniformed employee of *Electricité de France*, and after lunch and his siesta, I would watch him set off on his blue moped to do his allocation of meter readings. The tedious repetitiveness and simplicity of this job seemed to make him cope better with the paranoia – although, as I soon learnt, it was better to avoid talking of our Algerian past. I had thought he was going to end up a long-term bachelor living with his elderly mother but good luck was to strike. After a few years of therapeutic meter reading, he felt confident enough to go to some *thés dansants* on Sunday afternoons. These were, unbeknown to me at the time, rather prim functions usually held in dance halls with old-fashioned small orchestras, attended mostly by divorcées or widows of a certain age and grey-haired aspiring charmers or just lonely single men on the wrong side of fifty like my uncle. There he met a single woman of the same age who lived on her own in an old-fashioned apartment in the 10th *arrondissement* of Paris that she had recently inherited from her father, and they soon got married – and, yes, they lived a happy (or at least uneventful) life ever after… Her name, like his mother, was Françoise.

On the shoulders of short men

Just before his breakdown, in that momentous last week of January 1960, when Christian took me along to cheer the young *pied-noir* men of Bab-el-Oued march fully armed towards the seat of government in their Territorial unit uniforms, he put me on his shoulders so that I could see above the heads of the clapping crowd that lined the street. He was not tall, but it meant I was just high enough to see the scene clearly at least for a few minutes. This was not in fact the first time that I had witnessed a dramatic event from a man's shoulders. Two years earlier, on 13th May 1958, my own father had similarly carried me aloft in the vast crowd that gathered on the Forum esplanade in front of the government headquarters. I was nine years old, but after the last few years of a conflict that had become an integral part of everyone's daily life, achingly aware that something momentous was happening. I was experiencing for the first time the visceral excitement of being part of a crowd moving in unison for a shared purpose – the fact that the purpose in this case, as I realised much later, was on the wrong side of history has not diminished its lasting impact. After all these years, when I recall that day, I can still find echoes of the exhilaration I felt as I was carried by my father, a rare enough event, in the midst of that huge crowd. From my vantage point I could see the many tricolour flags being waved, the banners proclaiming *Algérie Française*, and hear the repeatedly rising sound of patriotic anthems. I was thrilled.

The protest had been called because the latest French government (they changed frequently during the Fourth Republic...), after four years of a war they could see was against the weight of history and in the long run unwinnable, was preparing to open negotiations with the FLN. To the *pieds-noirs*, still bathed in ignorance or denial of the reality of their circumstances, this was inconceivable. In Algiers, local politicians and army chiefs, as well as discreet acolytes of de Gaulle (who was then officially retired from politics), organised the opposition to the Paris government. On the morning of 13th May they sent out cars with loudhailers to criss-cross Algiers and call on the population to surround the government building that afternoon. The *pieds-noirs* did so in their thousands, feeling it was a matter of survival. In times of crisis, the appeal of simple solutions, however ill-conceived, is irresistible. Their aim was to put an end to the constantly changing governments that they thought only half-heartedly conducted the fight against the FLN and to install instead a real leader who would do so with vigour and determination – and who better to do this than the man who had already 'saved France' once? Oblivious of France's recent disastrous departure from Indochina, the *pieds-noirs* were imbued with the misconception that Algeria was not a colony, that it was *their* country.

It was a day of mass delusion. A delusion reinforced by the strange sight of a sizeable cortège of Arab Algerians from the Casbah joining the protest, waving French flags and even displaying *Algérie Française* banners. Even after all this time, I have never fully understood this unlikely show of support. Perhaps it was a last throw of the dice on the side of France by Arab veterans who had served in two world wars in the French army, who were not wholly behind the FLN methods, and who hoped that de Gaulle would at last bring in real reforms and equal civil rights. Doubtlessly they represented a minority view in their community but it was enough to make the *pied-noir* crowd delirious with joy and a new conviction that the terrible times they had lived through in the previous four years would now come to an end. It was a day of misplaced hope too.

On my father's shoulders, I felt bathed in this optimism, infused with a feeling of relief that childish dreams of peace and everyone living happily together could really come true. We were in the midst of a *happy* crowd. Happy when the government building was overrun with only token resistance from the gendarmes guarding it. Happy when local leaders and army generals appeared on a balcony to declare their opposition to the Paris government. And happy when they proclaimed that only de Gaulle could save the situation and ended their speeches with a cry of "*Vive l'Algérie Française!*" In stark contrast to the happiness of that day, that historically disastrous slogan would continue to resound with all its bloodletting consequences for the rest of my Algerian childhood and beyond.

De Gaulle was indeed called to power in what amounted to a coup, legitimised *a posteriori* by a French political establishment fearing that it was the only way to stop a full military putsch. He came to Algiers and, from that same balcony in front of another huge crowd in celebratory mood, he uttered his fateful "*Je vous ai compris*", which every *pied-noir* understood as meaning "I have understood what you want, Algeria to remain French." Soon after, at the end of another speech, he even allowed himself to proclaim the unambiguous "*Vive l'Algérie Française!*" For the *pieds-noirs* the combination of these few words would acquire a mythical meaning that would not only reinforce their delusion of a French future for their homeland but also be at the root of their profound sense of betrayal. They felt de Gaulle had made them a solemn promise. When just over a year later, in December 1959, he spoke of the Algerians' right to self-determination, they could only feel he had reneged on it. From then on, the *pieds-noirs* would stumble towards their tragic fate, blind to the reality that one million Europeans could not continue to impose an unacceptable status on nine million Algerians, that French Algeria was an oxymoronic nonsense.

De Gaulle, in the end, was doing the right thing but he had come to it in the wrong way, using deceit and manipulation. By then, I was ten years old and, though it may be difficult to understand for anyone who has not lived through times of conflict, I was aware enough of what was going on to be deeply affected by what people around me were experiencing as a betrayal. I wish my sensitivity to unfairness and injustice had been acquired from a just cause – from the Algerian national liberation cause to name but one – but I grew up on the wrong side of those particular tracks… The ill-founded nature of that first experience did not diminish its potency and durable impact.

Although I have learnt to keep this under control, for a very long time I lived with an obsessive need to challenge systematically what I perceived to be any wrong, however small, being done to me. I was always loath to let go of things, to smooth the path of relationships for example, but instead expected and demanded at least explanation, and preferably admission and reparation. This always looking for an explicit putting wrongs to right when I found myself in England in my twenties was not exactly congruent with the prevalent culture. It certainly did not contribute to making me an easy person to live with. Character flaws have deep roots.

What can never be shed

In my Scottish exile, my face has become incongruously tanned. Partly because I spend more time outside than when I had to sit for hours in front of a computer in Oxford, partly because there has been quite a lot of sunshine in this particular corner of East Lothian, which seems to enjoy the benefits of a micro-climate. On video calls I have to insist to my colleagues that I really am not in some exotic hotspot. The thing is, of course, that I always have a head start. I am a long way from Bab-el-Oued but I still carry the easily browning skin of my Spanish and Italian ancestors in my DNA. I still have the skin pigment of someone who spent years under the North African sun. It's made me reflect that there are other physical attributes that have persisted, or rather physical ways and manners that have survived, little diminished by decades of living in England. I am still prone to using gestures when speaking and I am told my face is "too easy to read". And it goes beyond the physical. Those facial expressions are not just easily read but are in fact all too often misread or, to be more accurate, measured by different yardsticks. A minor look of dislike can be perceived as hatred, a hint of disagreement as an absolute denial, a mild disapproval as total rejection. Perhaps an exaggeration, but the drift is clear.

Tone of voice can similarly be heard through a kind of cultural filter, so the degree of emotional intensity is amplified. In my early days in England, in my twenties when I worked as a teacher, I took part in a training course during which I made a contribution to a small group of participants that I felt had been well received. At the end of the session the headteacher leading it, a person much in the public eye at the time and someone I admired, came up to me for what I thought, with the overconfidence of youth, would be words of appreciation. Unsmiling and rather looking down on me, all she said was, "Do you always speak with such intensity?" I had to get used to the strange, dislocating feeling of always operating on two levels, of having to be conscious that what I meant and what was being perceived would not be the same.

I learnt early that when being in a new culture, mastery of the language is but an infant step when it comes to communicating. There is so much more that can stand in the way. I know this is falling into the realm of generalisations but there is no way of avoiding the fact that a native French speaker interacting in English with native English speakers has to get used to the dominance of the implicit over the explicit, of allusion over statement, of deflection over directness. A source of frustration at times, but also a lesson in how to create a less abrasive, more conflict-avoiding exchange. In many ways a pleasant contrast to what I had known in my years in both Algeria and France.

I have probably exaggerated the continuing prevalence of my Mediterranean traits. Like the glass fragments buffed by sea and sand that I collect on the beaches of the Firth of Forth, long immersion in British society has rounded off many sharp corners – and perhaps, like the glass, has even made me more opaque! My obsession with wanting to right every perceived slight has perhaps reduced to only a trace of thin-skinned defensiveness, sometimes even reasonably well-controlled… So is the gesticulating, I hope (too many wine glasses knocked off tables). Many years of working in the urbane and polished world of publishing have seen the intensity of expression somewhat tamed, though I don't think I've ever managed the hiding of emotions on my face, and these continue to be often misread. Although accusations of being "too literal" still fall on my head at home, I have become a fairly competent decipherer of the unsaid. None of this has come easily as it can't be other than a process against the grain – the fate of every immigrant. In my post-Algerian years, first in France and then, after escaping further to England, consciously or not, I was making every effort to shed my *pied-noir* skin. But as the subsequent decades have shown me, there remains much that can never be completely discarded.

The madness of crowds

There is something I still wish I could wholly discard from that period. It is a memory that recurs to this day like a bad dream. I am in the midst of a marching crowd again, an angry one this time. I am 13 years old and because I am not on anyone's shoulders, all I can see are the backs of adults walking ahead of me. In the fast-moving mass of people, I have lost the friends with whom I had started out. There is a lot of noise – the crowd is singing, shouting slogans, the perennial "*Algérie Française*" and, more relevant to the day, "*Libérez Bab-el-Oued*", free Bab-el-Oued. There are helicopters circling above us. I am not really afraid because I am among men, women and children of my tribe. And then, as we are all still moving forward, there is gunfire that sounds very close, several rounds of automatic rifle fire (I am already familiar with that), there is a tiny moment of hesitation in the pace of the crowd, and then people shouting, "They're firing blanks, they're just trying to scare us" – and so for a few seconds the forward movement resumes. Until I realise that what I have right in front of me are no longer the backs of adults but people turning around and trying to flee whilst another burst of gunfire can be heard. Someone has grabbed me and pushed me against the doorway of a building and as the running-away crowd is now thinning I can see that not far ahead of us there are bodies lying on the road and on the steps of the Grande Poste building. As the gunfire stops, some get up and flee, many remain motionless on the ground. And now, even though it is all at an end, I am petrified.

Later, much later, I will find out that on that day, 26th March 1962, a squad of French soldiers holding a barrier across a street near the Grande Poste opened fire on the advancing *pied-noir* crowd, killing scores – estimates vary between sixty and eighty – and injuring about two hundred. For years the French authorities went to great lengths to cover up the whole event, but it now has its own entry in French Wikipedia, known as both '*La fusillade de la rue d'Isly*' and the more forthright '*Le massacre de la rue d'Isly*'.

This marked the tragic culmination of a two-year macabre dance between de Gaulle and the *pieds-noirs*. With each forward step towards an ineluctable independence taken by the former being met by the latter with a rebellious and deeper clinging to the delusion of keeping Algeria French. And each time, as a child grown up beyond his years, on the streets of my native city, I, like all children there, witnessed and, in a very minor way, took part in episodes of those misguided uprisings.

The first open sign that de Gaulle, unlike the *pieds-noirs*, had understood the now fully-blowing historical wind of change came as early as September 1959 when he publicly stated that Algerians had a right to self-determination and envisaged that they might one day choose separation from France.

This was the time when Christian, still in his prime, took me along to watch the young men of Bab-el-Oued marching towards the centre of town in the hope of rallying the army to take a stand against the Paris government. During that week the heady mix of righteous anger, always to the accompaniment of patriotic songs and flag waving, washed over me and filled me with skin-tingling exhilaration and pride. I could only see things in simple, childish terms. There had been a betrayal and these men were standing up against it. I fantasised about being older so I could join the local Territorial units, put on a uniform, brandish the tricolour and hold a gun. (Fifteen years later, after my second exile to England, I would abandon French nationality rather than having to put on an army uniform and hold a gun for national service...) I followed events daily, the takeover of the government building, the fact that only some army units sided with the insurgents and, as a result, their eventual failure. The photographs of their surrender made a huge impression on my young mind. After a week of rebellion that had involved death and injury, they had negotiated an 'honourable rendition', marching out of their last redoubt in the government compound as a group behind their leader and their flag, a stage-managed display of defiant pride, even in defeat. These final scenes, after a week of heightened excitement and misplaced hope, provided my first experience of the alluring beauty of sacrifice, of the powerful, if noxious, appeal of martyrdom. It filled me with that strangely exquisite mix of pain and pleasure that can be felt in failure, a passing solvent but one that leaves behind a twisted yet bewitching taste for it – irrespective of the worthiness of the cause.

Just over a year later I was to encounter that same feeling with renewed sharpness. The now inescapable cycle continued. De Gaulle moved forward, in step with history and decolonisation, and the *pieds-noirs* and elements of the army went deeper and deeper into blind denial. After a referendum that approved the policy of self-determination for Algeria, in early April 1961 the French government opened negotiations with the FLN and de Gaulle explicitly mentioned the possibility of an independent Algeria, an 'Algerian Algeria' (a tautology to counter the *pied-noir* oxymoron), echoing the slogan of the Arab crowds in their pro-FLN demonstrations. In Algiers, the reaction did not take long.

On 21st April 1961, four generals took control of government buildings and the radio station and started a putsch which they hoped would topple de Gaulle. The *pied-noir* population of Algiers once again indulged in a joyous delusion that their saviours had appeared. Tricolour flags festooned every balcony, people gathered in their thousands on the Forum esplanade, as if it was a repeat of the events of 13th May 1958, but this time to banish the betrayal. After a few days, however, it became clear that the coup had not had enough support among the army to succeed. De Gaulle made one of his most powerful speeches to rally French public opinion in his support. Ordinary called-up soldiers who were serving in Algeria listened to him on transistor radios and refused to follow orders from the professional army officers sympathetic to the putsch. On 26th April, on a sunny late morning, along with a group of other boys my age, I witnessed, this time live and with a soundtrack, another stage-managed 'surrender with honour'. A large *pied-noir* crowd watched, many in tears, as the paratroopers that had been the vanguard of the attempted coup marched towards the trucks that would take them a long way from the city for disciplinary action, singing Edith Piaf's *Non, je ne regrette rien*. And in doing so, joining my childhood pantheon of unworthy heroes.

My later rational and justified rejection of the *pied-noir* cause has brought a coming to terms with the whole episode but cannot dissipate the acute poignancy of that moment in a young boy's mind. I can never hear that song without troubled and contradictory feelings.

The strange case of the absence of regrets

It is so ubiquitous it has become a cliché but I cannot understand people who say, "I have no regrets". I instantly want to counter with, "Regrets, I have plenty...". Or ask, how can you live a life of constant choices and not regret some of the ones made or some of the ones unmade? Is it really possible to be convinced that everything one has ever chosen has turned out right? Or even just to believe that there is no alternative life one can think of without a twinge of regret? Added to this, the statement implies either a life of unblemished saintliness – I have never done anything bad that I should regret – or one of heartless disregard for others – I don't care enough about the wrongs I have done to others to regret them. I realise that the affirmation of no regrets is a form of defensive denial but it still brings me up short. In defence of the statement, it could be said that it is a way of not falling into the trap of too much looking back and being immobilised by regrets, which I accept could happen – the fog of regrets obscuring the present. There is always the risk of getting stuck in the past by dwelling on it too much (and yes, touché, this is inescapable in this piece of writing…).

I have a bagful of regrets, both personal and political – a whole gamut of wrong choices, a heap of hurt caused. Regrets for many things done, many things undone. I have found that in not fighting off regrets but acknowledging them, part of the associated pain can be metabolised enough to be absorbed and made more bearable. That the actions regretted can become an integral part of a more complete self that is easier to live with. Absorption rather than closure, a much called-upon concept I do not find particularly helpful. Closure can mean that the wound has been dressed, the initial pain has gone and after a while the tissues are growing and closing the gap, but there will always be a scar and there is no closure for that. It needs to be accepted as a part of who one has become.

As well as real-life regrets, there are some that can only take form in the realm of imagination, in thoughts of lives unlived where causes for regrets can be eliminated. Imagination playing its distracting role, coming up with comforting alternatives, allowing time travel and a mental creation of other universes that can be shaped as one desires. Sometimes I indulge, in this 'lives unlived' territory, in a daydream of a whole life lived in Bab-el-Oued in a parallel universe where there was peace and reconciliation in an independent Algeria. Where some political messiah figure had guided the *pieds-noirs* to drop their privileges and their racism and accept a place in an Algerian Algeria where retribution had been abandoned by the FLN. Where I still lived a life in near proximity to an extended family, a life bathed in the extrovert warmth of a reformed *pied-noir* culture. A ludicrous daydream. But a pleasurable one of a simpler life, with no exodus to France, no exile to England, no escape from Brexit to Scotland – not that I am dissatisfied with at least the last two of these, far from it, but there is something very enticing about the thought of one's early years continuing seamlessly into a whole life. An escapist fantasy I know, but some people, albeit very few in our contemporary societies, in some places, can still experience this. It is not a rejection of my real life, just daydreaming, a form of creative regret. A fanciful small experiment in personal branching histories...

In real life, anything like this would have had to happen before too much blood had been spilt, before too many atrocities had been committed in the name of each cause. For that, we would have needed a Mandela-like leader on the nationalist side and a similar figurehead on the *pied-noir* side – I can't think of a parallel model well-known enough, maybe a more successful version of Yitzhak Rabin? Or someone like David Trimble, or one of the paramilitary leaders who eventually made the Good Friday Agreement possible in Northern Ireland? Maybe de Gaulle should have played that role but he was too contemptuous of the *pieds-noirs*, dismissing them as culpable backward colonialists when in fact most of them were just misguided *petits blancs*, modest drones in an unfair system.

Instead, all that happened was a limited attempt by a philosopher – nothing wrong with that but it just did not have the necessary reach. In the early years of the conflict, Albert Camus, shocked by the growing bloodletting in his beloved native land, tried to bring the two communities together but his attempts were misinterpreted and promptly rejected by both sides. A source of great regret.

Childish pursuits

One of the more pleasant sights in this small Scottish town is that of children going around on their own, without parents nearby. Now that summer holidays are over, I notice that they walk or cycle to school and that there is no sign of the awful school-run traffic that plagued the streets of North Oxford. Prior to that, I saw groups of them everywhere, at all times of day, walking in the streets, playing in the park, meeting on the beaches. I have even seen quite young ones playing on the swings in the park with what appeared to be the presence of slightly older siblings as the only supervision. It is a great contrast with what I had observed in England, particularly in recent years. Scottish children do appear to be encouraged to spend more time outdoors and be allowed to be more independent.

Set against that, I cannot say that my own track record as a father of three boys has been exemplary. There were the mitigating circumstances attached to living in south London for a while but these certainly did not apply to the easier streets of North Oxford. My own mother once referred to me as a *papa poule* – a hen-like father – which she did not mean as a compliment. I hoped the description had more to do with the contrast I represented with the behaviour of my quasi-absent father but as is usual with critical remarks there was a grain of truth in it. I was probably an overprotective parent, possibly overcontrolling. However, it is difficult to gauge the impact of parental influence among so many other factors. One is soon lost trying to discern one's way in the still mysterious, quantum-like territory of the interaction between nature and nurture. I think that apart from beach holiday times, in the case of the two older boys there was a greater inclination towards indoor activities. The youngest, with the limitations of a disability which meant some of the usual childhood outdoor pursuits were too difficult for him, turned to an early interest in reading, for example – although he soon took up riding and then sailing enthusiastically.

Thinking about this has made me recall two features of whatever they got involved in, which I am sure are common to most childhoods, and were certainly shared by all three boys. The first is how engrossed they could become, how much time and attention could be expended on what was of interest at that particular point. Often there was intensity, even passion, and always a high degree of persistence. I should qualify that the latter could transfer after a few months or so from one subject of interest to another. The other aspect was the variety of these interests. Again, nothing unusual in that but a contrast to my own childhood overwhelmingly dominated by one overarching event, leaving little room for other interests. From books to fantasy games, from folk music to playing the keyboard, from Lego to video games, from sailing to theatre, the range was varied and enormous. And, of course, there was the football phase. All of which was far from familiar to me.

I only really discovered these kinds of subjects of childhood fascination on the verge of my teenage years, when, fresh from the chaos of the *pied-noir* exodus, I first encountered my French peers in a *lycée* in a small provincial town in the west of France. I always think of them as *les blouses grises*, even though only the boarders wore these thin grey overalls, perhaps better described as long smocks with buttons down the front, the sort that some shopkeepers in old-fashioned hardware shops in England still wear to this day (except those are usually light brown). At breaktime, though there was only a minority of boarders in the throng of pupils in the courtyard, there was enough of a sprinkling of these grey garments for me to think of grey as the dominant colour of the whole environment. The weather was often grey, and the building, resembling nineteenth-century army barracks, was always grey.

As a new boy appearing in the middle of term, the first question I was often confronted with was, "Which football team do you support?", to which I had no answer. After that I was mostly ignored for a period. They all seemed taller than me but any minimal attempt at bullying was met with such blind, fierce anger, so obviously unthinking of consequences, that it was soon abandoned. I got a few detentions and they thought I was odd and possibly disturbed. I did not speak of my recent past. They did not know I was a *rapatrié* (that's what the papers called us, the repatriated, even though for many it was their first visit to France) because I did not speak with a pronounced *pied-noir* accent (that they might have heard on the TV news). Even with those who began to tolerate me and gradually admit me into their circle, I found that I had little in common. They spoke of famous football players and cycling champions I hardly knew anything about beyond their names, of films starring Brigitte Bardot that they wished they had been allowed to watch, films that had completely passed me by – all run-of-the-mill topics of boys of that age at that time. Despite this, I did eventually make friends but I kept silent about my Algerian past.

CHILDISH PURSUITS

I recognised the intensity in some of their interests, such as their commitment to and enthusiasm for football teams, but my experience of similar feelings had been for patriotic symbols and slogans and for an undeserving cause – and this was an unbridgeable distance from their world. Mine matched theirs in intensity and passion but not in innocent pastimes. I don't claim any special status for this, it has been commonplace in all childhoods in urban conflicts from Belfast to Beirut. Still, for my relatively innocent fellow pupils who only had a superficial knowledge of the Algerian war it would have been difficult to even imagine what people of their age got up to on either side of the conflict.

In the early years of that conflict I was mostly an observer, imbibing the ideology of my tribe, but the last two years were a time of more active involvement. Even after all these years I find it difficult to write about that period. Not that I did anything terrible, at least not on an individual basis. I occasionally had my hands on guns but never fired one. Instead of wishing to be older as I did at the time, I am now thankful that I was not. I saw too many people around me, only a couple of years older, who became drawn into the fighting in a much more damaging way.

Quite a few of my fellow *lycée* pupils would have heard of the OAS because of its attempts to kill de Gaulle. They probably would have known that it was an extreme right-wing terrorist organisation largely reviled by French public opinion. All true in many ways, but the OAS had also been most of the people around me, in Bab-el-Oued especially: my cousin's elder brothers, some of my uncles (not Christian, by then mentally unwell), other young men who were more distant relatives certainly as participants and everyone else as supporters. In Algiers, it had been the type of organisation that, like the IRA or the UDA in Northern Ireland, could not have existed without a high degree of support in the local community. The *Organisation Armée Secrète* was founded in early 1960 after the debacle of the insurrection of the 'week of the barricades'; it grew massively after the failed putsch of the generals in April 1961, and then rapidly gained the wide support of the *pieds-noirs*. It was a simple and straightforward allegiance – not many would have thought of themselves as right-wing extremists, much less fascists, in fact in Bab-el-Oued many voted for left-wing parties. You just had to believe in the impossible and unjustified chimera of *Algérie Française*, and then it was easy to see the OAS as the last and only defenders of that cause.

So, most nights I and other boys sneaked out to collect paint pots and brushes to scrawl those three letters and slogans on walls along what were the busiest streets during the day. We were given this task because the men thought the army would not open fire on young boys for breaking the curfew. By early 1961, my parents had moved to a new flat in El Biar, a residential area on one of the hills above the city centre, but I still stayed at my grandparents' flat in Bab-el-Oued during the week. I had groups of friends in both places. It did not take long for local men to enlist us for these nightfall outings and other tasks. A main one was the distribution of leaflets, which meant we always knew early on what demonstrations or other mass actions were planned and so could be early attenders – which is how we found ourselves among the crowd in the front part of the cortège in the Rue d'Isly on 26th March 1962.

After the French government signed a peace agreement with the FLN in Evian in March 1962, and declared a cease-fire to start on 19th April, the OAS launched its last-ditch campaign of resistance in Bab-el-Oued, which had become its stronghold in Algiers. De Gaulle gave orders to crush the rebellion by "all means necessary". Tanks and armoured vehicles encircled the *quartier* and fighter planes strafed buildings indiscriminately. My school was closed, so I was in El Biar, but my grandparents and Christian recounted later how they had to lie on the floor as bullets hit the outer walls of their flat. Nothing came as a surprise any longer, but they were clearly traumatised. My grandfather in particular, the patriot and veteran of Verdun, retreated into a silent bewilderment that would never be dispelled. The whole area was sealed off as French troops carried out street-by-street searches of all buildings. The blockade lasted a fortnight. In other parts of Algiers, support for the population of Bab-el-Oued quickly gathered pace and our little group of boys in El Biar was called upon to do deliveries via the small tunnels of the sewers. We carried rucksacks full of food and medical supplies but also well-wrapped heavy packages that we were told to handle with care and never to open. Some, from the feel of them, were rolls of plastic explosives. Others, probably ammunition. We felt both very scared and very proud.

The OAS then called for a mass demonstration to gather in central Algiers and march towards Bab-el-Oued to break through the blockade by sheer force of numbers. Indeed, tens of thousands turned out, men, women and children. The leaflet had called for a peaceful march. My friends and I joined a cortège from El Biar and found ourselves towards the front of the main march by the time we reached the city centre. The crowd was so huge that we got separated and I experienced the last moments on my own, as already described.

Many, many years later, I discovered on the internet a video of a contemporaneous newsreel, which includes a live audio of the short period just before, during and just after the bursts of gunfire that killed and injured scores. From the more reliable accounts of what happened, it seems that a platoon of inexperienced young army recruits who were guarding a barrier panicked when they saw the crowd marching towards them and spontaneously opened fire with sub-machine guns. One of the most affecting features of that newsreel is the sound of the officer in charge of the platoon shouting over the noise of gunfire, "*Halte au feu! Halte au feu!*" Stop firing! It takes twelve minutes for his order to be obeyed. Periodically I have returned to it, but not very often. The images of the many bodies lying on the road and on the steps of the Grande Poste, a vision which I witnessed live for a few seconds only but which has remained imprinted on my mind, are too much. Looking at them again gives rise to a sense of relief that I was lucky enough to escape unharmed, tinged with a troubling, vague feeling of guilt. Maybe because I can only look back on the most exciting years of my childhood with shame and, yes, plenty of adult regrets. For me now, all the real gore and the sham glory of war-torn French Algeria is encapsulated in those tragic moments.

Scorched earth

It's festival time here, not the big one in Edinburgh, but our own local version called 'Fringe by the Sea'. The town is full to bursting not just with the usual holidaymakers but also with people who have come specially for the many shows and events put on during this ten-day period. There is an air of shared jollity all around. Because of Covid, event marquees have open sides, and music and laughter and snatches of interesting talks or stand-up routines can be heard as you pass by. It puts smiles on people's faces and it all adds up to a sense of ambient gaiety, with the various venues dotted around the town centre. On the final Sunday morning there is an event of spectacular entertainment with more than a touch of serious content. A huge, 10-metre-high articulated puppet made of materials recycled from refuse is paraded along the seafront road. This is Storm and she is meant to highlight what we are doing to the planet. As she stands and starts slowly moving to the sound of loud music, everyone gasps. I am enjoying being among the benign crowd, swathes of people of all ages following the strange, bedraggled giant, some behind her on the road, others running alongside on the beach. Everyone is having fun, but in an awed sort of way, no doubt unable to entirely ignore the message. Wildfires, after all, have been burning ferociously in several parts of the globe.

For me, perhaps because of being so engaged in this attempt at gathering pieces from the clutter of my memory, what this brings to mind are images of my native city burning night after night. A time, far away from this well-meaning throng, when I knew not just the madness of crowds but the despair of crowds too.

The killings of 26th March were a turning point. Most people realised we were entering a last and losing phase. The OAS itself seemed to have accepted that and, insanely, called on its supporters to adopt a scorched earth approach, to destroy as many public and official buildings as possible. The *pied-noir* part of the city descended into a sort of trance-like anarchy. A rational move would have been to prepare to leave but most people did not. They stayed and despaired. And set about to destroy much of their environment, and revel in it. For a couple of months, every evening after nightfall, people in our block in El Biar would come out onto their balconies to watch the spectacle. It was a family affair, although there was a notable absence of young men, who were otherwise occupied – boys too were late to the show as they often had 'deliveries' to make. As they waited for the first explosion, people began hitting saucepans with wooden spoons, three shorts and two longs, to accompany their shouting of '*Al-gé-rie Fran-çaise*'. This became known as a '*concert de casseroles*'. A great cheer then marked the start of the nightly series of bombs. There were often scores of them in a single night. Huge flashes lit up various parts of the city and people shouted from one balcony to another their takes on what building had been hit. The atmosphere was similar to that of a crowd watching a 14th July fireworks display. Each explosion brought renewed cheering as if a favourite team had scored a goal, people celebrating it as a victory when each one in fact sealed their defeat. After a while there were fires burning throughout the city, lighting up the night sky over the bay of Algiers.

There was a strange beauty to this terrible spectacle, the tragic beauty of hopeless, desperate acts. I remember standing on our balcony with my mother and two younger brothers, bursting with conflicting emotions. Still hanging on to naive thoughts that the extremity of what was going on could bring a change to our fate, and at the same time drifting into the pleasurable hurt of acceptance of defeat. I was learning very young that there is a certain allure to failure, a kind of addictive nobility to loss.

One up, one down

Even now, when I travel through France, I look out for them and want to notice every one of them, take each one in as I pass by. Not difficult as they are everywhere, not taking up whole streets or making up whole estates as they would in England but scattered among other houses of a different kind. Whatever part of France you find yourself in, it does not take long before you come across this ubiquitous type of house. Detached, square, fairly large, usually set back from the street in the middle of a sort of plain lawn or gravel-dominated garden that the French seem to specialise in. They are always on two levels, the bottom part made up of natural-shaped irregular stones of various sizes and the top part rendered white or cream. The ground floor has a garage door. There are exterior steps leading up to a usually over-ornate wood and glass front door on the first floor. To the side of which, and this is the key feature, is always a long balcony with black wrought iron railings that goes along the full width of the front and at least one side of the house. Sometimes the balcony is quite wide, you could call it a terrace, wide enough for a table and chairs. French windows open onto the balcony from what is probably the main living room. The French call these modern detached houses '*pavillons*', and I have baptised this particular type a 'two-tone *pavillon*' in recognition of the contrasting look of their ground and upper floors.

It's an architectural model you would never find in the UK. You might find the odd similar ones just beyond the French borders, in Belgium or Germany, but it is a particularly French sight. Not one, I admit, that would attract the attention of tourists, and for good reasons, not distinctive or creative enough, and too recent to be of historical interest. But I never fail to notice them. Those travelling with me can't understand my interest. They know my taste is now common to my current peers: what we all like are period houses, characterful late Victorian or Edwardian piles with original features, preferably detached (ha!) with a mature garden... They can also understand that at another extreme, I like the more innovative glass, wood and brick creations of contemporary architects. Both are a long way from these bland non-entities built largely in the 1960s. They are not identical, each has a few distinguishing features, a wider balcony, one going along the left rather than the more usual right side; there is some variation in size, but they follow the same overall pattern. And they all look solid and safe. I am touched by them. It took me a while to work out why, because the origin of that feeling was not conscious, but I am now sure that I must have first noticed them when we arrived in France after our exile in June 1962. Out of the bloody chaos of the previous few months in Algiers, they must have represented the ultimate in peaceful normality. The homes of ordinary families, leading ordinary lives in ordinary towns. Not that I was fully aware of this at the time. I was too preoccupied with the aftermath of our loss, still too vibrating with anger and an unabating sense of injustice. But deep down, they must have left a mark as symbols of a hankering after a normal life.

Later, much later, well after I had left France in my early twenties, the sight of one of them sometimes triggered fantasies of an alternative life, of a life unlived that I found myself enticed to imagine. Not that I was necessarily dissatisfied with my then current life. Just as an exercise in imagination, a glimpse of a theoretical life which I found comforting. Probably because the pieces of the life imagined can be arranged in a satisfyingly neat set-up. Had I not gone to university in Paris and, after the events of 1968, not moved to England, had I stayed in the nearest university to where my parents had settled in France, I might have ended up living in one of these houses, in a small provincial town, teaching philosophy in the local *lycée*, married to another teacher, and spending summer holidays in a second-home villa in the nearest seaside resort. (French high school teachers, as a couple, could well have afforded this in what is referred to as '*les trentes glorieuses*', the prosperous three decades from the end of the war to the mid-seventies…).

Recalling these fantasies makes me realise that my inclination for tidy imaginings of what life could be started early. In my primary school days, a friend and I used to walk up to Notre Dame d'Afrique high up on top of the hill above Bab-el-Oued, not to go into the famous basilica but just to stand on its forecourt from where you had an amazing view over the whole of the city, a white jewel glistening in the bay. I liked looking at our area, spot the roof of our school and its playground, the little square where we went roller-skating, the street of the daily market we were sometimes sent to for errands, and feel good about the orderliness of it all from this distance above. The straightest way up was along the narrow alleys of an Arab quarter, and at the beginning of the war, though it was something of yet another walk of fear, we carried on doing it. The feeling of reassurance that emanated from the tidy and peaceful view from above was all the more satisfying. Later, it became too dangerous to go that way.

Had I been able to look down from a similar height above my French grandmother's house in Frontenay, where we found refuge and which was to become our home for a few years, it would have been difficult to locate the roof, so very small was it. At first we stayed, all five of us, in the tiny house itself. Mamie, as we knew her, kept her own bedroom, my parents had the only other one and I and my two younger brothers, by then seven and five, were in the small sitting room where each night makeshift beds were set up. There was a garage behind the house and a small barn attached to it. A sliver of garden ran the length of the whole building. The garage was full of furniture and old junk, but Mamie said my father could try to create some living quarters in the small barn and he soon set about doing this, mostly by himself. He made one large room downstairs and a mezzanine room, half the size, up a staircase on the left wall. On the right-hand wall of the large room was a small kitchen area, in the middle a table and chairs, and at the back, behind curtains, my parents' double bed. All of us boys slept upstairs on what we called the balcony. My father had managed to clear enough of a slice of the garage adjacent to our barn to install a bathroom and toilet. The whole arrangement was tiny, crowded and very basic.

After living there for about a year, we found out that one of these 'two-tone *pavillons*' was being built on the other side of the road, almost opposite Mamie's house. It was a large one that I would get to know well. It had all the usual features in abundance: wide garage and terrace-like balcony, very decorative wrought iron balustrade, utility rooms and cellar on the ground floor, large living room, four bedrooms and so on. And it transpired that it was being built for my father's sister, my aunt Monique, and her husband Jacques, who already had a two-year-old daughter and were expecting a second child. The three great-aunts, Henriette, Germaine and Madeleine, and their respective husbands had clubbed together to fund the construction. The plot of land had remained in family ownership when my great-grandfather died a few years earlier and his farmhouse was sold. I am sure the plan had been mooted before our so-called 'repatriation' and was understandable – all the great-aunts were childless, and Monique had become a quasi-daughter to them all. Nor was it unusual for a French extended family to help in this way. Nonetheless, the contrast could not be starker. It mystified me at the time, and it was only much later that I pieced together enough of the story to throw some light on the background to this.

Jack the lad – part one

My father's name, Jack, is pronounced the same way in French as the more usual Jacques, not with the English initial '*dg*' sound but with a soft '*j*'. His friends and family called him Jacky. There are things I know about his life, and then things I can deduce or suspect. I am pretty sure that as the first child born to the clan, he would have been doted on by the three aunts, who by then must have known they were unlikely to have children of their own. As a boy in those days, he must have continued to occupy a privileged position in the family even after his sister was born and this would have been enhanced when his own father died in 1940. They must have fussed over him in the same way they did over me as a young boy during my summer holidays in France, except that in his case it was full time. Then in 1943 when he was sixteen and a pupil at the technical college in Niort, under German occupation, he did something that would alter the trajectory of his life. Nothing heroic, just a small act of juvenile defiance. The Germans were using a building in his college to administer the issuing of food-rationing tickets. This was only lightly guarded, and my father and a few friends managed to break in and steal a large quantity of ration books, which they passed on to people connected with the resistance for distribution. The German authorities worked out that the theft had been committed by students at the college and when serious enquiries started, my father and his friends were advised by their contacts to join a nearby *maquis*, a small group of resistance fighters living hidden in the countryside.

They had the support of local farmers and were constantly on the move from woods and caves to barns and other hiding places. Their main resistance activity was to set up bombs on railway lines to attack train convoys bringing supplies and munitions to the occupying forces. Occasionally they tried to ambush passing German army cars or trucks. My father has only rarely spoken about that period and never in any vainglorious way, just providing matter-of-fact answers to my few questions. By a strange coincidence, for the last twenty years he has lived in an area where his old *maquis* operated. I only found this out when, by chance, I came across a roadside plaque dedicated to some of his comrades fallen in an ambush in that spot. I can only speculate about the family's reaction to my father's deeds. I do know from stories shared later on that they were de Gaulle supporters, listening to BBC broadcasts, and certainly not collaborators. I also know that my great-grandfather gave shelter and supplies to the resistance. But I suspect that Mamie and the doting aunties can't have been very pleased with sixteen-year-old Jacky's self-chosen disappearance into a highly dangerous environment. I think they felt it was an utterly foolish thing to do and it was perhaps the first crack in their devotion. They did not see him again until the end of the war in 1945. Their reunion was brief. He had just turned eighteen and was immediately called up to do his national service, soon being sent out to Algiers.

There, he fell in love, first with the city, the climate and the people, then with my mother. To his surprise, he found it easy to get a job in a laboratory despite not having any qualifications. Unlike in France, the few technical skills he had gained during his curtailed schooldays seemed to suffice. All the easy-going charm and outward confidence acquired during his emotionally cosseted childhood served him well in a *pied-noir* society highly receptive to these attributes. He had no difficulty in making many friends among the more hip of the young men and women of Algiers. I have seen photos of him in his courting days and I am sure his dapper sense of dress also helped. I wonder if it was a gift passed on by the aunties. By the time he and Gisèle married in 1948, there was no question of going back to France. Well, they did cross the Mediterranean soon after, but only for a short holiday riding a Vespa along the Riviera – again, there is a glamorous photo. I suppose it may have been a sort of honeymoon. By the time they came back and Jack managed to buy his first second-hand sports car, he must have been certain that his future lay in Algeria.

Back in Frontenay, I suspect the family would have been appalled. It was not a personal rejection of my mother; they simply hated that Jacky had decided to stay away from them.

Suitcase or coffin

The rift was a silent one. At least for me, I never heard any words spoken about it. But it was real enough. In all our years in Algeria I don't remember my father once going to visit anyone in his family. My mother took us for holiday visits, and she was made welcome, or we, all three boys, would be sent on our own and be spoilt as is usual with grandchildren. If he had hopes of returning one day and impressing the family with a record of success and fortune, the eventual outcome could not have been worse. Far from the prodigal son's return that he may have imagined, he came back having lost everything, home, job and almost all possessions. There was a friendly but awkward welcome from Henriette and André, who came to pick us up at Bordeaux airport. I had assumed it would be them who would put us up as their house was large enough but they took us straight to Mamie's. My two brothers had been sent a few weeks ahead of us and were already there. I realised later on that for André, a local dignitary with mayoral ambitions in his village, hosting a *pied-noir* family might have damaged his chances.

The whole of France seemed to be embarrassed by the mass arrival of destitute *pieds-noirs*. They had after all been painted by the press as well-off colonialists. What people saw on the news disembarking from ships in Marseille and other ports were distressed families wearing almost all they possessed. The vast majority of them were artisans, shopkeepers, low-level public service employees, schoolteachers, people of modest means at the best of times, and often poorer than their counterparts in France. The very small minority of rich landowners had long secured a safe passage out of Algeria for themselves and their wealth. French public opinion was sick of the 'Algerian problem'. Now that an agreement had been signed with the FLN, anything that reminded people of the almost eight-year-long conflict that had cost the lives of so many young Frenchmen was understandably unwelcome. I could sense this on the drive from the airport in the way that André and Henriette would curtail any allusions to what we had recently lived through with instant changes of subject and falsely cheerful diversions.

Later I would learn that it did not take long for open antagonism to surface. The *pieds-noirs* had been widely depicted in the news as supporters of OAS terrorism, which indeed was true, and this had become a commonly-held view. There was never an opportunity to talk about context. Just like in the car journey, when anything that was close to the subject of our loss came up during one of those habitual long family meals, usually voiced by my mother who in her raw grief could not help it, there was a flurry of distracting talk and sudden offers of second helpings and more wine. Certainly, I never heard a word of sympathy or compassion for our predicament. We were family, and were welcome as such, but only as such. There was a definite feeling that we were the authors of our own misfortune and that the less said about it the better.

In wanting to ignore the subject, the family was not alone. When tens of thousands of *pieds-noirs* started arriving in overcrowded ships in the French Mediterranean ports, a government minister dismissed the scale of what was happening by referring to those disembarking as holidaymakers taking early summer breaks in metropolitan France. Another minister added to the cynical ludicrousness of that comment by declaring that "summer had arrived early in Algeria" and *pieds-noirs* were "escaping the unpleasantly hot weather". Had he chosen to face reality he could have spoken of another kind of heat. During the previous few weeks, he could have seen people in the depths of anger and despair setting fire to communal pyres in the streets below their flats, pyres made up of all the possessions they had no prospect of taking with them. Those who had cars set fire to them too. He could have seen the women "holidaymakers" escaping the "hot weather" queuing up for hours for a ship, wearing several coats on top of one another to save room in the family suitcases. On the quayside he could have seen the old men "going on holiday", silent and looking dejected, sitting on battered cases, some of them wearing their medals, others clutching their framed *Légion d'honneur* certificate, and many with shiny tired eyes, staring at the hillsides of their white city, knowing it would be for the last time. He could have seen that people were so keen on their holidays in metropolitan France that shipping companies were taking the rescue boats from their ships so that over a thousand desperate people could be boarded onto vessels meant to carry a maximum of four hundred.

After the orgy of indiscriminate killings, by both FLN and OAS, and the scorched earth destruction that followed the 26th March events, the *pieds-noirs* realised that their choice was now reduced, in the words of an FLN slogan painted on many walls, to *'la valise ou le cercueil'*. The choice was either packing a suitcase and leaving or staying and ending up in a coffin. I am sure that my father's family had no inkling of that stark choice. They certainly did not want to hear about it. Jack, probably aware of this, retreated into a sullen silence. He must also have realised that there was nothing left for him in the family's old reservoir of indulgence. This now flowed out towards his younger sister Monique and her 'perfect son-in-law' husband, going by the more conventional homonym, Jacques. My mother treaded carefully, having picked up quickly on the deflecting tactics. She tried to control her emotions and keep up a front of dignified and contained sorrow. Still treated as a grandchild or nephew, I continued to be the recipient of unalloyed warmth and approval from Mamie and all the aunties and uncles, with Jacques and Monique if anything overdoing the attention and kindness, but all this only served to sharpen my already acute sense of injustice.

Different welcomes

Recently a Conservative MSP accused the Scottish First Minister of being anti-English, which she later retracted. There have also been mentions in some English media of antagonism being shown in Scotland to people speaking with English accents. I am sure a few isolated examples could be found but we have never come across it. After over fifty years in Britain, I can pass for English at least in short daily exchanges (the longer the conversation goes on, the quicker I can be tripped up by a misapplied stress or slight mispronunciation) and my partner, though half Scottish, speaks with a definitely English accent. Neither of us has detected any negative reactions to this, at least not in these parts (nor in all our trips throughout Scotland over the last twenty-five years). In this small town, I have been struck by how friendly everyone is. Most people on the town's narrow pavements seem to show an unusual (for us, compared to Oxford or London) consideration for others. On my morning walks on the beach, strangers will invariably smile and issue a greeting as we pass. All this, in spite of a recent influx of English people wanting to settle here.

Not long after we moved, we asked the local electrician, who had to come to our flat to fix something, if there was any feeling of resentment against the number of English moving to East Lothian. His reply was that no, there was not, because Scotland needed more people, but he added that the welcome was not extended to a certain type of loud, arrogant, entitled English, "The ones who don't respond to a stranger's friendly hello", he said. He also said, unprompted by any of our questions, that there was a greater sense of community in Scotland than in southern England. It is not easy to define this, but I have certainly felt it here. I know it has something to do with the size of the town, but it is not just that, because I have had this same feeling of being more at ease with my new environment in the middle of Edinburgh. My third and last exile, from an England disfigured by Brexit to a more enlightened Scotland, has started well.

So did my second one in August 1969 when I arrived in Brighton from Paris and when it felt wonderful to escape a France full of asperities for the softness of England. It was not my first visit but this time I had all my possessions with me. I was meant to be coming for a year only as a French assistant in a school in Hove, but I was already thinking that I might try to stay on. It did not take long for my already keen infatuation to turn into a blossoming love affair with the country. The seed had already fallen some years ago on the fertile ground of my frustrated early adolescence.

My first trip to England was on a school exchange in autumn 1963. I had no high expectations as it was very much a school activity, to do with our English lessons and more or less compulsory, but anything that took me away from the rigorous routine of the *lycée* was welcome.

In fact, it turned out to be a series of revelations and shocks – almost all of them pleasant. I think the only exception was a rough crossing of the Channel in one of those old, rather dingy ferries that used to ply the Calais–Dover route prior to the tunnel and the advent of plush modern vessels. But arriving in the Shropshire countryside was indeed coming into a green and pleasant land. A place of gentle hills, and green, so green everywhere. That colour, in all its brightness and varying tones, has for some reason dominated the images left on the screen of my memory, infusing everything with luminosity so that all the other colours have become oversaturated too, and looking a bit like a Wes Anderson film, unreal and enchanting. I was staying with a family who lived near a village a few miles out of Newport, and David, my *correspondant*, and I had to catch a country bus, vivid green of course, to get to the school. Sometimes his mother would drive us there in the most unusual car I had ever seen, a Morris Traveller – I would become familiar with them and even own an old one myself years later, but cars with "a wooden frame at the back", as I would explain to people on my return home, were unknown in France and felt, well, quite unreal.

And then the school itself was out of an imaginary world too. Far from the drab mix of nineteenth-century prison and army barrack of the Lycée Fontanes in Niort, the Adams Grammar School was smaller in scale but much grander in style, an imposing stone and brick building, with two wings graced with elegant Georgian windows, a small clock tower perched in the middle of the roof, and manicured lawns in front. However, the bigger shocks were in the school itself. First, I saw teachers actually talking to pupils, and I don't mean telling off or talking in the course of a lesson, but frequently engaging with them as fellow human beings in corridors and playgrounds. Even more astonishing, they seemed to address them by their first names. Sometimes it was to remind them to come to Chess Club or some other after-school activity, like Drama Club or the school choir.

All of this was utterly unfamiliar to our little group of French pupils. Our French *lycée* was a place you trooped into at 8am and hurried out of at 4 or 5pm, generally having gone back home for lunch between 12 and 2pm, to listen to a succession of hour-long lessons, with the odd hour of PE. The only after-school activity was playing matches against other schools if you were selected for the football, rugby or hand-ball (yes, it's a thing, and very popular in France) teams. Teachers came into the building for their timetabled lessons only, delivered them to silent classes of thirty or so boys busily taking notes, and then went home, again preferably without having had any individual interaction with any of the pupils. They had no other duties or roles in the school. A small cadre of *surveillants*, usually post-grad students doing it to earn a living while working on their doctorate theses, were employed to enforce discipline or supervise classes of absent teachers.

Our English peers at the grammar school did have to wear a uniform, including shirt and tie, something which we would have considered an outrageous imposition, but paradoxically discipline throughout the school seemed to be far more consensual than in the *lycée*. Another thing we could not envy was the religious content of assemblies, which we watched with incredulity. But in that ritual and in other things like the after-school clubs or the belonging to 'houses' (which took quite a lot of explanation for us to grasp), we could see that the school forged a sense of community that was completely absent in our usual environment. I think we were all touched by that. I certainly was, profoundly. The whole experience had the quality of being transported into a make-believe world. I know this is an anachronistic and stretched parallel, but I think it had something of the quaint, charming appeal that my own children, many years later, found in imagining the world of Hogwarts.

Beyond the school, there was another sort of magic. After the first few days, we discovered that in Newport, unlike in Niort, girls did not live on another planet. That was another welcome shock. Adams Grammar School was for boys only but unlike at home there seemed to be quite a few opportunities to make contact with girls. Or perhaps it would be more accurate to say girls were definitely more approachable there. Of course, a group of French boys in town must have been an interesting novelty, but I did not feel that it was only with us that they were open to chatting and laughing. Waiting at the bus stop and the bus journeys themselves were always lively affairs with a lot of joshing and banter between boys and girls that appeared to be completely usual. It was a long way from the off-hand distance and froideur that the *lycée* girls in Niort felt obliged to keep up at all times. I realise this may put cracks in the widely-held myths in Britain about the French propensity for sexual dissoluteness, but this was the reality of pre-1968 France.

The peak of this feat of easy exchanges was reached when we had a Friday night dance at a youth club. It was held in a church hall, which in itself was surprising enough, but then this was again a completely new experience. Youth clubs were unknown in France. When David's mother dropped us off at the entrance, we could already hear the pop music pulsating at some volume out of the hall. Inside was packed with a mass of dancing young people, their shiny faces lit up by multicoloured flashing lights. I had never seen anything like this – or heard anything like the songs being played. It was a time when rock and pop music had burst onto the scene in Britain but not quite broken through in France. I could not have had a better introduction to the thrill and energy of it all than being among these, to me, rather outlandish boys and girls who seemed to be so free to enjoy themselves together. This music turned on a switch inside me that would never for the rest of my life be turned off – a fate I know common to most people of my generation. A new band was telling us to twist and shout, and everyone did. And the music played on, urgent tune after fast and urgent tune, and everyone carried on dancing. Until, near the end, when one of the girls in the group we had formed took me by the hand and gestured for us to go outside for some air. Given the ambient noise, we had only exchanged a few words by then, and all I knew was that she went to the local girls' high school and was called Valerie. I can't remember how she handled 'Jean-Luc' but I am sure I did not care. There, in a dark spot against a front garden wall, under a tree, she drew me close and kissed me. A real kiss, that felt like it went on for a long time. I was stunned with delight. I was fourteen and this was my first kiss. I learnt later the English called it a French kiss.

Later I was struck by how, in one forward, daring move, she had taken an incredible shortcut through the strict conventions of French teenage courting, ignoring the many elaborate steps to get to that longed-for point: the initial periods of message-sending purely through eye contact, the following each other at a distance, the meeting through friends if you were lucky, the waiting for a slow number at a party, where if you could bring yourself to take the risk the kiss might at last happen. Obviously, they did things differently here.

After the thrill of the kiss itself – which unsurprisingly turned out to be an adieu, Valerie had to go back home; our group left a couple of days later and I never saw her again – I was suffused with a lasting sense of gratitude for how easy she had made it feel, for the impulsive, well-meaning generosity of the act. I held on to it as a precious gift. Not only had it unleashed a wave of rapture at the time but it also left me with a new sense of confidence, with a feeling that it was a portent of much more pleasure to come.

All this was the pre-history of my love affair with England.

Double dose of adolescent spleen

Not that the good times exactly continued to roll after our return to Niort. At least not immediately. The first youth club would not appear until a couple of years later and even then it only provided worthy activities, from drama to table tennis, and certainly not dances. In daily life there remained a wall, albeit an invisible one, between boys and girls. They mostly existed in separate universes, very occasionally awkwardly overlapping. This only happened during the few parties that started to be allowed to take place in the homes of some of the more liberal-minded of my friends' parents. If you were lucky, the boy holding the party for his birthday had a sister or a cousin who could be persuaded to bring along a posse of her schoolfriends and the room would at least have two largely unmixing opposite-sex gaggles, exchanging glances. The boys tried to look cool and the girls giggled. Some icebreaking did occur when a suitable piece of music got everyone dancing energetically. I remember that, without any conscious irony being shown, the Rolling Stones' '(I Can't Get No) Satisfaction' never failed to achieve this. Other favourites were the Beatles' 'She Loves You' or the Kinks' 'You Really Got Me'.

Then, once the fast and pounding music had succeeded in making the invisible wall begin to crumble, everyone waited for the slow numbers, almost invariably from the repertoire of sentimental French pop songs produced with this very purpose in mind, to see if the sustained exchanges of looks were to lead to the hoped-for sealing step, the kiss. This was not given loosely, by the girl at least. No random and repeated experimentation: when you kissed, it was with one person only and, from that moment, it meant you were 'going out'. The relationship might only last a few hours or a few days, or at most a few weeks, but it was certainly meant to be exclusive. I know my British peers will have very different recollections, but that's the way it was in France. Oddly, in the teenage slang of the time, these parties were called '*boums*', a misnomer if ever there was one as they were always such sedate affairs, certainly with no explosion of dissolute behaviour. In most cases, the parents had only surrendered the sitting room or the garage and were still around somewhere in the house. In rarer cases they had gone out for the evening but were always back early.

While we still lived in Frontenay I had to catch an early commuter train to Niort, one of those red and cream short trains, known as *michelines*, that seemed to run on every bit of railway line in France. There were a few other boys and girls on the same train but they kept well apart, and I never found there the fun and banter of the green country buses of Shropshire. When I turned fifteen, I sometimes did the journey on my moped. After a long period of hankering after one, thinking of it as an absolutely essential key to personal freedom, I managed to acquire a second-hand blue *Mobylette*. These, ubiquitous in France in those days, along with the equally common black *Solex* with a little engine on the front wheel, have become treasured triggers of memories of the 1960s for millions of French men and women of my generation. But in winter, the trips ended up as miserable as the train journey – not only miserable but actually painful because of having freezing hands on arrival, which hurt even more as I held them against the classroom radiators, a probably stupid but irresistible thing to do. The cold was still new to me and so, most of the time, it was back to the train. As there was only one return train in the early evening after the end of lessons, I had to extend my day at the *lycée* and spend an hour-and-a-half in a study classroom with the *blouses grises* weekly boarders, under the supervision of a morose *surveillant*. Of course, the boarders had it much worse than me, with only the prospect of a canteen dinner and a cold dormitory ahead. They would give us forlorn looks as I and a few others left the room early to catch our trains. I could well understand why some of them came up with creative ways of distracting themselves.

The most enterprising was perhaps the setting up of a secret bar in one of the wooden lockers fixed to the walls of the room. This had been rigged up and was 'managed' by a boy whose desk was conveniently located just below his own locker. Unlike most of the other boarders who came from isolated farms, he was the son of a café owner in a village a fair distance from town. No doubt this is why he had been able to obtain one of those optic devices that hold bottles upside down and dispense measures of alcohol behind bar counters. He'd adapted this, attaching a small plastic tube that he could pull from the locker to beneath his desk so he could discreetly do the serving from there. The list of drinks changed from week to week, but mostly consisted of a variety of fortified wines, such as vermouth, but also occasionally, particularly near the end of term when he liked to offer something stronger, a cheap brandy. The favourite means of collecting the drinks was a small medicine bottle, passed around from desk to desk. I suspect the boy sourced his supplies from his father's stock. There was a charge for each drink but it was moderate and he had many takers. They called it *'l'apéro'* (short for *'l'apéritif'*), as they had no doubt heard their parents call this time-honoured French practice. The surveillant can't have been unaware of the trading going on but as long as there was not much noise in the room to disturb his own work on his thesis he did not care. In fact, the alcohol helped with that, as the mostly sweet drinks on offer were not exactly stimulating, more like positively soporific, and as the study session progressed many of the boys drifted into a happy torpor – their own semi-comatose version of Happy Hour! It was not so much that they were into drinking per se, unlike what I would later discover young people in Britain tended to be. It was more a small act of defiance against the mind-numbing tediousness of their boarding life.

My own defiance against the general petty-mindedness of the *lycée* discipline and the leaden teaching style increasingly got me into difficulties. My troubled Algerian years had made me more mature and perhaps more assertive and daring than most of my fellow pupils, certainly more familiar with the concept of rebellion and more able to articulate reasons for that rebellion. I had grown up with political arguments, of the wrong kind admittedly, but it did give me a certain grounding. To the *surveillant général* and the deputy head in charge of discipline (interestingly called *le censeur*), I had become a leading troublemaker without particularly wishing to be one. This meant that both the *surveillants* and the teachers were increasingly looking out for the smallest infringement of rules or the slightest sign of insubordination on my part. Standard punishment was detention on Sunday morning: two or four hours depending on the seriousness of the offence, stuck in a silent classroom, having to do a piece of additional and usually pointless homework. 'Stuck' being the appropriate word, as this punishment was called in French '*heures de colle*', *colle* meaning glue. When landed with the longer version on a Sunday morning, some claimed a newly acquired religious fervour and were escorted to Mass in a nearby church, which took up an hour or so. It made a change. I became quite proficient at imitating my mother's signature on the form we had to bring back to school to show that parents had been informed of the misdeed and the punishment.

Infractions could be of a trivial nature. As the Beatles, Rolling Stones, Animals and other British groups made more and more frequent appearances on French TV screens, a few of us started letting our hair grow. Long hair was not only in breach of regulations at school, but widely disapproved of in society at large. This led to ridiculous cat-and-mouse situations with the enforcers. Teachers hardly cared or probably did not even notice, given that their preferred modus operandi was to address the class as a group and not focus on individuals. We became adept at brushing back fringes, sticking long sides behind ears and turning up shirt collars at the back. But the *surveillants* patrolling the corridors and playgrounds presented more of a risk. The most dangerous time of day was the morning when we tried to enter the school without being noticed. By then I had made quite a few friends and was enjoying a degree of support. Before I walked through the gates, taller friends (one of the few times when it was advantageous to be short) would form a group around me so that the scrutinising *surveillant* by the gate would not be able to see the length of my hair. It didn't always work. I was sometimes sent home or in one case ordered by the *surveillant général*, the boss *Gauleiter* himself, to have an immediate haircut – "But Sir, I haven't got any money and there's no one at home." "Well, here is five francs, go down the road to the barber's and bring me the money back tomorrow. Either that or another four hours." The *lycée* authorities did not quite know how to handle me – my results were good but I was troublesome. Usually, troublesome pupils indulged in random, pointless acts of disruptive behaviour and combined their rebelliousness with poor academic standards. They found how I behaved more of a challenge to the established order. I was a bit of a rebel all right, but a rebel with a well-argued cause.

Unfortunately for the well-being of my family, I was becoming a bit of a rebel at the dinner table too. Whilst my mother had learnt to control her bitterness at our exile from Algeria when in the presence of the extended family, she had no qualms about expressing it during a meal when it was just us. Instead of 'a' meal, I should say every meal. This venting went on for years. I understood all too well the pain of loss as I felt it too and to a large extent shared the sense of injustice involved in our fate. But as my knowledge of what had happened in Algeria widened and I became more aware of the larger historical context, instead of simply listening and occasionally echoing her sentiments, I started questioning the righteousness of the *pied-noir* cause. Sometimes, with all the forcefulness of the newly enlightened, I pointed out that for us to have believed in the possibility of an ongoing *Algérie Française* in the world we lived in had been a chimera, a preposterous delusion. This did not go down well, but rather stoked my mother's grievances. I would later feel guilty, but also angry and frustrated at not being able to get through – as I would have seen it. The clash I suppose was unavoidable. I was increasingly trying to find comfort in a rational, intellectual approach, whilst she was still, understandably, in a phase of raw emotional distress. My father, if he was there, would stay silent and broody for a while, his anger slowly building up, to finally erupt either in fiercely ordering me to go to my room, or just storming out to get his car keys and leave the house when he could no longer put up with my mother's diatribes and tears.

Mother, martyr and matriarch

My mother was in so many ways admirable. She could also be, not to put too fine a point on it, a terrible curmudgeon. She was our saviour but also an unextinguishable source of radiating negativity.

I have kept a photo of her and my father in their twenties walking arm in arm in a street of Algiers, probably taken by a street photographer, the type that captured the moment opportunistically and gave out a voucher for the picture to be bought from the shop that employed him. They clearly noticed the camera as they are both smiling slightly. They look like a happy young couple walking in the sunshine, lightly dressed. Looking smart and confident passing a small palm tree on the pavement. He is wearing what today would be called light chinos, and a white shirt. She is wearing an A-shaped pleated skirt in a pattern of pale-coloured squares and a short-sleeve blouse that could also be white. Somewhat surprisingly her hair is blond, which emphasises the matt tan of her skin, against which shine strikingly light-coloured eyes. These were in fact a beautiful blue-green. They both look carefree and full of promise.

They were clearly in the first bloom of their relationship. It must have been a source of joy for her to have met my father and marry him after the disappointments that the Second World War had brought. Though she was from a modest background, her brightness had allowed her to study medicine but she had had to give this up when the war came. I am not quite sure why, as she was quite evasive when asked, shrugging it off as an unavoidable consequence of the war. By then, her older brother, Lucien, was a prisoner of war in Germany and she implied that she needed to support her family. There is so much that I don't know. As with my father's early life there are patches of knowledge, other things I can realistically surmise, but still large areas of her life that have remained a void. Either because I did not think of asking – another great regret – or because, like my father, she was reticent or vague about them.

I had always thought, given the mores of the time and place, that her love affair with my father would have been her first, that is, the first that led to a sexual relationship. However, after her death, going through her vast collection of photo albums, my brother Patrick and I found a letter that would reveal something we had never known. It was quite a long letter on flimsy paper, the ink of a fountain pen faded but still readable. It was from her best friend Denise, written in 1945, when our mother would have been twenty-two. It was a warm letter, offering sympathy and comfort after a painful disappointment in love. What transpired was that my mother, Gisèle, had had a serious relationship with a British (possibly Scottish, going by the name) army officer, serving in Algiers with the Allied troops towards the end of the war. A poignant passage revealed that he had made a proposal of marriage that had clearly been enthusiastically accepted. He had then been posted back home, leaving with a promise to send for Gisèle soon. A long silence followed, during which she waited in hope, only to be shattered by the short letter of rejection that eventually came. Denise's own letter included reassurance that Gisèle should not regret how far she had committed to that relationship as it had been right to seize the opportunity in such troubled times. And a confident prediction that with the end of the war there would be plenty of chances to meet other eligible young men. She added that her experience would make it easier to do that. I don't know how much of this came to pass but it did take another three years for Gisèle to meet Jack.

My mother had a good knowledge of English, though she did not speak it well – her pronunciation was execrable, as is not unusual for a French speaker. Her having been jilted in English had not in the least put her off the language. She was always keen to use it whenever she could. She was far from happy when my exile to England became permanent but only because she would have preferred all three sons to be closer to her, not at all because of any negative feelings about Britain. In fact, she liked visiting and having to use the language. After our discovery of Denise's letter, I wondered if it had been because it brought back memories of her first significant love affair.

My first encounter with the English language was a great contrast; it could not have been more mundane and yet has remained with me to this day. Perhaps because it was a rare instance I remember of my mother doing something in a properly attentive way with me as a young child. We were having a colder than usual winter in Algiers and my father had bought one of those slim, square Valor paraffin heaters that must have been newly launched at the time. Having provided it, my father in his usual way then left it to my mother to deal with its functioning. It was an object of fascination to me, something my mother must have noticed as she asked me to help her when she first set it up. This involved taking off the front panel to fill the small tank and lighting the flame. I was tasked with unhooking the panel and holding on to it, while my mother carried out the other tasks, talking to me the whole time in an unusually cheerful mood. We were discovering something new together and it felt good. Whilst she was pouring out the paraffin, I was examining a label stuck on the back of the panel and realised the words on it were not French. My mother told me it was English and started to read out a few sentences, and then tell me what they meant, and we both laughed. The text was utterly banal, stilted safety instructions, and she must have been creative in her translations. Anyway, it sounded ludicrously funny and we laughed more and more, as she read on in this strange-sounding language which I was amazed she knew. Notwithstanding all this, I soon came to hate the Valor heater because of the pervading odour of paraffin and its cumbersomeness. It was difficult to move and wherever it was placed it constrained my movements in such a small flat.

Yet, that feeling of shared joy at the reading of the label joined forever the only other memory of a moment of intimacy with my mother. I must have been four or five at the time. I was ill in bed and she came in to give me a spoonful of syrupy medicine. She then sat and stayed with me for a while and gently stroked my hot forehead. That's it. My only retained childhood memory of a display of physical affection from my mother.

In her defence she was a busy and preoccupied parent. She had a full-time job as a primary school teacher and, when my two younger brothers were born, had to look after three young children at home. She was probably suffering from the full blast of disenchantment with my father who was increasingly absent, working in the Sahara. When he was in Algiers, he would often go out and certainly did nothing to help with domestic or childcare tasks. Unsurprisingly, there was a lot of tension and often open conflict in the relationship. I don't know whether this was at the root of her very bad asthma, but it must have made it much worse. Her attacks were frequent and became more and more acute. I have a memory of her being taken away by ambulance in what was referred to at the time as an 'oxygen tent'. I saw her on the stretcher, oxygen mask on, and a transparent plastic contraption over the top part of her body. At my grandmother's, where we were looked after while she was in hospital, I gathered from overhearing adults' conversation that she had nearly died.

There was an advantage to having a preoccupied mother. It allowed me a high degree of independence early on and often staying at my grandmother's only enhanced that. Even at the height of the Algerian war, I was able to be out on the streets a lot, with few restrictions, in striking contrast to today's overprotectiveness towards children. It was an unintentional trade-off, less affection but more freedom. There was still more of the latter in my teenage years when my mother was even busier and more preoccupied. When we arrived in France, my father, devoid of formal qualifications as he was, could not hope to find the sort of job he aspired to in civil engineering. He drifted into a lackadaisical search for opportunities, mainly by contacting old friends from his schooldays. This proved mostly fruitless and for long periods he was unable to earn anything. We were only kept afloat by my mother's salary. She was the strong matriarch, the breadwinner, the responsible one. But it was her peak period of dissatisfaction and she did not hold back from venting this.

Mother, Martyr and Matriarch

In a classic case of 'child caught in the middle', my sympathy was torn between the two. I could see that her grievances were largely justified but found the way she expressed them almost too painful to bear. It was always a vicious cycle of her going overboard on some minor complaint, being met by father's silence or curt defensive response, only for her to escalate her litany of complaints in an increasingly offensive and contemptuous way, until my father lost his temper, shouted and left. All through these repeated altercations I had a not entirely coherent but insistent feeling that there could be another way. One where she would calmly come up with constructive steps to mend aspects of his behaviour, to address his failings while allowing him to save face. One where he could find the words to respond with equanimity and control his temper. I am aware that this sounds like childish, naive wishful thinking. But in a strange transfer between two different spheres of life, there are principles and practices coming out of these personal conflicts that have actually proved incredibly useful in my professional life – for example, offer steps for improvement rather than crude criticisms, don't humiliate your adversary, find a way out of disputes that allow for face-saving, stay calm. (Unfortunately, I can't claim to have always been able to apply the same principles in my private life – another sore regret.)

Thinking of the lengthening list of regrets, I will add a major one laden with a heavy dollop of guilt. There was no trace of irony in using the term 'martyr' as a descriptor for my mother in the heading for this section, at least in its non-religious, ordinary sense. When I think back about that period, I am assailed by pangs of shame and embarrassment about the fact that none of us, not my father, not we three boys, did anything to help with domestic chores. My mother, on top of working full-time, did everything. Beyond a bit of occasional tidying up in our bedroom, we never did any laying or clearing of the table, any washing-up or drying, any cleaning, any laundry, nor any cooking. And no, we were not asked. But this does not excuse us or alleviate the burden of guilt. Men and boys in those days, especially from the Mediterranean culture of my mother, were not expected to do any of this, but how can we not have realised how much she was doing, how can we have been so blind? Why did I not offer?

Later, when all three children had left home, there were two periods in my mother's life that were easier and more enjoyable. I like to think of them as her rewarding halcyon days. Although, because life can't be otherwise, they were not without difficulties. In her mid-career, she became an *inspectrice*, a school inspector, whose job was to assess the performance of teachers in a local area. Even though she never made this explicit, I think she appreciated it not just as a professional achievement but also because it established her as a person of status and influence, a *notable*, wherever she was posted. This counted for a lot in a French society still dominated by hierarchies and power relationships – what you were and who you knew mattered. She was posted to Réunion, an overseas French territory in the Indian Ocean, a relatively small world where such things mattered even more. She found the climate and lifestyle reminded her of Algeria, without the war. She loved being able to pick mangoes and papayas in her garden and to spend time on the beach at the weekend. She managed to pull strings to get my father a part-time job in the local technical college as a teacher in construction skills. This meant that for the first time in many years they were financially comfortable. He joined the local yacht club, an ideal setting for his latest charm offensive to become a known and well-liked character in their small community. Which possibly made it easier for her to put up with his failings and peccadilloes. Her professional life may not have been all that easy as she insisted on carrying out her inspections with great thoroughness and not enough of the 'flexibility' the local teachers were used to, but the mellow lifestyle was enough of a compensation for her to stay for nearly ten years.

The second period was in her retirement in France, in the seaside resort of Royan where they had bought a tiny villa close to the beach of Vallières. By then, she was mostly on her own as my father had stayed on in Réunion and made only brief occasional visits. She became part of a large social scene, centred on a group of ladies who did not so much lunch as spend hours on the beach, gossiping and engaging in ponderous and leisurely sea-bathing. Their other main activity, especially in the non-beach months of the year, was to plan almost weekly themed dinners. These were elaborate affairs, extended multi-course feasts with bacchanalian amounts of food and drink, attended by twenty or more guests depending on the size of the host's dining room. I have no first-hand knowledge of these occasions, but I have seen the photos. The dozens of mostly embarrassing photos, which we found when ploughing through the extensive album collection (to know what we could dare to discard without too much guilt...). Not that there was any evidence of carnal misbehaviour among these late-middle-age, conventional people, just a lot of ludicrous dressing-up. And often of a cringe-inducing variety when based on themes that today would be considered culturally insensitive. Often these seemed to be inspired by a recent holiday in some far-away country – worldwide 'third-age' organised travel being another regular occupation. I will leave it to the imagination to conjure up images of what an event post-sojourn in Kenya or Egypt could look like. However, there is no doubt they all appeared to be enjoying themselves.

Gisèle, a confident cook and an eager organiser, was a leading light at these jolly soirées and I know she derived great pleasure from them. I have kept a few of the photos as evidence of her having some happy times in that phase of her life. She was also one of the most assiduous travellers among her friends, never missing an opportunity to join those organised trips to the four corners of the globe. Although when I spoke to her about these, I got the impression they were more of a distraction from living mostly on her own than for the joys of travel. The latter certainly did not feature prominently in her accounts, which usually consisted of litanies of complaints about perceived flaws of the various countries, the uselessness of the guides, the poor quality of the food and the uncomfortable coach journeys on pot-holed roads – so much so that my brothers and I came to dread asking, "How was your trip?" Still, she kept going, well into her late seventies. In between her foreign trips, she also managed to try out a variety of adventurous pursuits, the most outlandish of which was probably paragliding.

Despite all the setbacks, my mother embraced life to the end with an unquenchable appetite. That, and her resilience, is what I try to hold on to whenever I think of her.

Jack the lad – part two

My father never grew up. He stayed resolutely immature all his life. He did not have a mid-life crisis; he had a whole-of-life crisis. You would not be wrong in choosing a sportscar as his leitmotif. Or an extremely large motorbike that my father, being short and slim, had no hope of pulling upright if it fell sideways – and he did possess one for a while. He remained a boy throughout his life, a charming, cheeky boy, but a flighty husband and a quasi-non-existent father. Maybe the interruption of a more normal emotional development caused by the war was at the root of this. After running off to the *maquis* at the age of sixteen, he never really returned to his family, as straight after the war he was called up and sent to Algeria. He did not get a chance to wean himself gradually from the cocoon of the spoiling aunties and grow naturally into a young adult. The break had been too sudden. So, he turned his life into a pursuit of indulgence and the easy fix of superficial approval from groups of people around him. Algeria, being in those days something of a pioneering country, was a propitious environment. It was a society, at least among the Europeans, where you were expected to make your own way irrespective of family connections, class or, to a large extent, formal qualifications. What would be called 'people skills' today, along with confidence and initiative, were more highly prized. Jacky had plenty of those and they enabled him to carve out for himself a professional path he could not have hoped for in France.

The one time I can remember him as a proper, serious grown-up was when, as a child, I went with my mother to stay with him in the Sahara during the school holidays. It was soon after oil had been discovered near Hassi Messaoud and my father was in charge of one of the major road-building programmes in the area, based in the oasis town of Ouargla. This was a tough assignment, working with tough men in a harsh environment, away from home for weeks at a time. I have an image of him meeting us at the airport looking, as usual, immaculate in white shirt and sand-coloured light trousers and wearing aviator Ray-Ban sunglasses that were *de rigueur* among his colleagues. The peak of his Sahara glory days was when *Paris Match* magazine did a long feature on "the men helping to bring oil and prosperity to France", showing lots of photographs of men working in the oilfields and on the road-building, describing them in dithyrambic terms as quasi-heroes. Jack appeared in a couple of the large colour photos, by the roadside near an enormous macadam-laying machine, holding blueprint plans and pointing to something, looking slim, tanned and dashing, almost frail compared to the brawny workers surrounding him, and yet very much in charge.

During our holiday stays in Ouargla, he did not particularly change his benign indifference to me but there were moments of fatherly behaviour that, being rare, have remained imprinted on my memory. He once gave me a beautiful desert sandstone rose that he had found. I was fascinated by the intricate arrangement of its crystallised sand petals, which looked as if they would crumble at the lightest touch but were in fact as hard as stone and their edges as sharp as a blade. Another exciting desert discovery he produced one day was a petrified tree slice that he had come across on a dune by the road. He explained this was proof that the Sahara had not always been a desert, which to my child's mind was an amazing revelation. For years I treasured these two strange objects, but they did not find their way into the suitcases of our exile. My father seemed to find it easier than in Algiers to do things with me, a few of them leaving strong impressions, like showing me what a scorpion looked like and how dangerous it could be. I also remember him taking me in the Land Rover on two successive days to the same spot on a road out of town to show me how small dunes could be made to shift right across the road by the wind.

The oil- and road-workers were welcome guests in Ouargla, as local people felt they were bringing jobs and greater prosperity. The Bedouin chieftains often organised open-air celebrations for the Europeans and one of these gave me my first experience of a *mechoui*. Under a star-studded purple sky, against a backdrop of the oasis palm trees and the distant dunes, dozens of people, many in traditional blue robes and golden turbans, gathered around an open fire on which a young camel was being spit-roasted. Cooks poured olive oil and scattered herbs and spices on the turning meat, which made it crackle and spit, releasing powerful aromas in the night air. When it was cooked, and the fire doused down to make it approachable, you took a tin plate and simply grabbed a chunk of tender meat, making sure to use your right hand. To a child, this was heaven. I much enjoyed all these rare interactions with my father but as they happened in this other-worldly desert environment, they seemed all the more unreal. When back in Algiers, reality returned, and I had to get used once more to the in-and-out-fleeting father.

In my early thirties, I had an oddly triggered emotional memory that was not immediately easy to decode. It was the first time I had a car with the kind of central divide that is now common in front seats, and as my lower left leg leant against it as I drove away, I had a diffuse but strong feeling of well-being rising in my body. It took me a while, but I did recall that I had once experienced this feeling in my childhood, when I would have been seven or eight. My father had just bought a new sportscar and, in a rare attempt at creating a moment of father–son bonding, he took me for a ride, just me, exceptionally sitting in the front seat. I remember the smell of the leather seats and the shiny veneered wooden dashboard, the sense of being in a low, enclosed safe space, but even more acutely a sharp feeling of happiness as we sped along the coast road, my leg leaning against the upholstered central divide.

At home, his presence was not so benign as there was increasing conflict between him and my mother. There was something about their tense exchanges that would have been noticed as highly unusual by most people. Even at the height of their arguments, they maintained what appeared to be a degree of formality. This was because they always addressed each other as '*vous*'. I never once heard them at any point in their whole lives using the more familiar '*tu*'. The normal pattern in France, at least in those days, was that you said '*vous*' to each other when courting, but that the first kiss, and therefore the immediate assumption that you were 'going out', ushered in the use of the more intimate '*tu*'. Why this did not happen between my parents in 1948 remains a mystery. I did ask a few times. My father gave evasive answers along the lines of, "Well, it's always been like this", and my mother never went further than saying, "We did not switch to '*tu*' in the usual way and then it stuck." The use of '*vous*' between husband and wife is not unknown but is a rarefied practice confined to the tiny number of surviving members of the old nobility or to the pretentious denizens of the Parisian *haute bourgeoisie*, who no doubt regard it as a sign of sophistication and social superiority. Jack always aspired to the trappings of a lifestyle that was really beyond his means, but he was not a snob. He mixed easily with everyone, irrespective of social background. Neither he nor my mother could have imagined that this would be of any help in their getting on in society. In fact, it was more likely to single them out and expose them to mild ridicule. I am convinced it was a choice made by my father, as it would have been up to the man in those days to switch, post-kiss to '*tu*', and my mother just went along with it. Given what I now know of his whole life, I wonder if the use of '*vous*' was another sign of immaturity, of not wanting to face up to the reality of a relationship. Opting instead, unconsciously, for an idealised image of a wife – one who is put on a pedestal and kept at a distance. Using formality as a shield because unable to have proper intimacy. Then, when his own behaviour gave rise to criticism from her, the idealised image was broken and he could only flee. (I am sure he said '*tu*' to his passing paramours.)

If as I suspect this use of a certain formalism was a protection, it would fit in with other aspects of his controlled self. In many ways he was a very fastidious man: being always attentive to what he wore, taking meticulous care of his cars, producing clean and precise technical plans for his work. He loved to use India ink in fountain pens with fine nibs, and of course he had small and beautifully neat handwriting. If I had been able to keep a couple of objects as mementoes of his life, I would have picked a propelling pencil and a slide rule, both in matt, light-grey brushed metal.

Returning to France, destitute, in June 1962 hit him hard. He was in his mid-thirties, he had lost almost everything and his professional life was in ruins. His career did not recover. Competing against people with proper diplomas, he never managed to get a position in civil engineering equivalent to the one he had had in Algeria. After a while he resigned himself to accepting a few short-term, much lower-level jobs as works site manager. Unfortunately, the last one of those ended dramatically when a crane's counterweight fell and nearly crushed him to death. Luckily, the only lasting damage was that he lost the use of a lung. After that, he tended to rely on often unsuitable opportunities and sometimes commercially dodgy projects usually obtained through friends and acquaintances. Wherever he was, he seemed able to embed himself in groups of people who helped to sustain him, to find him temporary but always renewed breaks – and occasionally, it has to be said, to take advantage of him at the same time. At one point, when my mother was posted in the south-west of France, near Cahors, he even became a Freemason. Somehow falling on his feet was a repeated if effortless achievement throughout his life.

The most glorious example of this, when he was in his mid-seventies, was a remarkable stroke of good fortune. By then, although not divorced because they belonged to a generation who generally did not, Jack and Gisèle were living separately. My brothers and I started to be concerned that our father, having stayed behind in Réunion when my mother retired and returned to France, would find himself without support in his old age. We knew that whatever relationships he was having there were bound to be transient. He himself must have become conscious of his potential isolation and he started to re-establish contacts with old schoolfriends in Niort and Frontenay, with a view to coming back. Whilst recalling memories of their village with one of them, Jack spoke of his teenage sweetheart Anne, whom they both knew, and his friend said, "Funny you should mention her, I have been in touch with her recently, she lives in Paris and she is a widow now...." Jack soon returned to France, tracked Anne down and set about courting her in his consummate, but in this case deeply rooted and I believe genuinely-felt, way. It must have been a whirlwind romance, no time to waste at their age, for they were soon living together.

They had known each other as children in Frontenay and started going out when they were both fifteen. Their early romance was interrupted when Jack left for the *maquis* and they completely lost contact after that, but it must have been significant enough for it to have been rekindled so easily. Anne had twice been married, to a banker and a diplomat, and was the mother of six children, all grown up by then of course. She had an apartment in Paris, where Jack reconnected with her, and a large converted barn in the countryside near Niort, where they settled. She had enjoyed a comfortable life financially. She was cultured and sophisticated, and a talented artist. Her bold, colourful paintings and large abstract sculptures in both stone and carved wood were displayed around the house and the extensive grounds. She was always elegantly dressed in the slightly sober way of a Parisian *bourgeoise* but she was warm and genial.

After some initial reticence on the part of my brothers and me, because the memory of our mother's troubled times with my father were still fresh, we soon came to enjoy her company whenever we visited for family lunches. Anne loved the jolly conviviality of a large group of people around the table, enjoying her delicious food and the fine wines Jack proudly fetched from their well-stocked cellar. Typically, he had become good friends with a champagne producer who had a second home nearby, and he bought ample supplies directly from him. When they didn't have family or friends visiting, they travelled around France, especially in the wine regions. Jack still had the inevitable sportscar and they would take part in social rallies of similar cars that combined old-fashioned touring and gastronomic enjoyment. I watched in awe, this late blossoming of a life of comfort and indulgence that lasted a good fifteen years or so.

But what was most striking was the ease with which Anne handled my difficult father. She was adept at preventing rather than remonstrating. At being firm but in a positive and cheerful way. There was no doubt that she was very much in charge, but it was a benevolent dominion, considerate and good-tempered. Whilst pleasing to observe, it was also sad, bringing up thoughts of how different life could have been had Gisèle been able to act in the same way.

Unsurprisingly, for my brothers and me, there was something moving about these rare, joyful, lengthy family lunches we had on the terrace of their beautiful house. They were fleeting glimpses of what a reasonably happy family life could have been.

Awakened by the Master

Coincidentally, the years of my father's glorious apogee coincided with the period of our having the house in the Charente, and over that time I was able to attend a few of those lunches, making what seemed like pilgrimages to a retrofitted normality. On the car journeys there, through familiar countryside, I could fantasise that I was on a regular visit to aged parents, or if members of my own family were with me, for them to see grandparents. Not that Jack, having mostly avoided being a father, had ever shown any inclination to be a grandfather. But imaginary nostalgia can be a powerful, mind-invading, drug-like emotion.

Their house being close to Niort, I would sometimes make a detour to indulge in a bout of more real-life nostalgia and do a drive-by tour of the old haunts. The cafés where we had perfected our table football skills had changed looks and names, but the school had not lost its appearance of a grim Napoleonic closed institution. I always ended my circuit by passing the house of someone who had changed my life. I now know the *lycée* turned out to be a locus of both repression and salvation. The latter, as is often the case, came from one particular teacher, who to me became much more than a teacher of French literature. We did not call our teachers 'masters' but I now think of him as a true '*maître*', in the broadest sense of the term, an opener of eyes and minds, an example to follow, a mentor. Not that he ever acted as one, at least not in the traditional fashion – there was no arrogance, only eagerness to share knowledge. He taught us – I even hesitate to use the word teach, it may be better to say that he introduced us – to intellectual curiosity and especially its rewards, that the more you know and understand about the world, the more likely you are to enjoy it and have a good life.

Audier was like no other teacher. He was a maverick, inspiring figure in a landscape of convention and boredom. A tall, gaunt, pale-faced man with shiny dark eyes and closely cropped hair, and a lingering smile on his lips, he had the keen, ascetic looks of a bright young priest or a scout leader – though his personality could not be further removed from either of those roles. He used to burst rather than walk into the classroom, striding up to his desk, arms waving at the pupils to sit down. He would turn to face the class before they had had time to settle, and would launch into the lesson in dramatic fashion, sometimes with an exclamation, a word shouted defiantly, followed by a loaded silence, sometimes with a quote delivered theatrically with no preamble. He always managed to convey a sense of great urgency, but an urgency filled with enthusiasm and promise – unlike other teachers, whose sense of urgency seemed to contain an underlying threat and stemmed only from their preoccupation with completing the set curriculum. He emanated a feeling that there was so little time in which to make the most of life and that none should be wasted. He treated any attempt to play up with incredulity and impatience, a highly effective way of saying, "Why are you making us all waste our precious time with such childish behaviour?" It usually isolated the culprit rather than creating the kind of solidarity from the rest of the class that other teachers brought about with their stern pomposity and transparent delight at any chance to exercise their authority.

Audier never mocked or belittled – a notable achievement given that most of his colleagues seemed to think that dismissive criticisms, humiliating pupils and making fun of failure were effective pedagogical practices. He was the first teacher to treat us like young adults, not children. His existence was the embodiment of a kind of nonconformity which made messing around, our immature attempts at rebellion, pointless. We quickly became too interested in finding out what outrage he was going to come up with next to do anything other than pay attention. He made us feel that there was so much to say, to discuss, to take in, that not a single second should be lost in silly diversions.

Not that he did not digress himself from the subject he was supposed to teach, but it was never trivially. He often departed from the set texts to entertain, but also to provoke and truly educate with impromptu commentaries on something in the news, a television programme, a film or a book, always finding a way of making a link with the classics of French literature that we were supposed to study. Anything that raised an issue which would challenge our adolescent prejudices and make us think. In these rambling monologues, he never sought to avoid topics which to any other teacher would have been taboo: politics, religion, morals, relationships with parents, sex. We were offered Rabelais in all its rambunctious life-affirming crudity. Verlaine's poems were not commented on with prudish euphemisms, nor was Rimbaud's life sanitised, or Baudelaire's most graphic verses ever censored. For a class of fifteen- or sixteen-year-olds, for a while at least, the pettiness of the *lycée*, the stuffiness of other teachers, the difficulties with parents, the narrow-mindedness of the provincial town were forgotten, as suddenly a window was thrust open on the whole breadth of life in all its gore and glory. Suddenly, layers of obfuscating conventions were swept aside by a few well-chosen, unorthodox words, and it felt like reality ceased to be concealed from us.

For some, it was too much. There was an initial period during which everyone was enthralled, almost inebriated by his daring eloquence. But after a while, a few turned against him. For some, it was a clumsy way of practising the very critical faculties he had awakened in them. For others, it was simply because he made them feel uncomfortable. Because he expected too much of what they were not used to, independent thought. He questioned too many of their certainties, and whereas at first they were amused by his unconventional ways, after a while they felt threatened.

I could easily have felt threatened too when he first voiced his views on colonialism in general and the Algerian war in particular. Fortunately, by then I had already grown to respect and admire him. Nonetheless his views came as a shock. How could a man who always showed so much understanding, who always spoke for the underdog, against all injustice, how could this same man take the side of the FLN terrorists, how could he not see the plight of the *pieds-noirs* thrown out of their homeland? And yet... I could not help feeling, almost in spite of myself, that once again he must be right, that somewhere in what he said lay the real reason for our defeat, an explanation for our tragedy. For so much of what he said did make sense. After the few remarks that had revealed his stance and had left me in such a quandary, there had been other comments, more elaborate, perhaps especially for my benefit, for I think he had noticed my reaction, which set the Algerian war against the background of the history of colonialism and the post-war rise of nationalist aspirations, the evolution of other colonies.

There was no preaching or disapproval of my then views or my experience in Algeria. Just questions and suggestions of what to investigate further, and how. And as I found out about a whole range of facts and events which until then had remained outside my experience and knowledge, everything I had so passionately believed in was little by little disintegrating. It was as if an actor at the end of a play had been told new facts about it which changed the whole nature of the plot and made him realise that he had been among the villains, on the side of infamy, when all along he thought he had been on the side of the heroes. My first reaction was horror, a sickening feeling of a terrible, tragic waste. Had the flags, the songs, the crowds, had the suffering, the sacrifices, the deaths all been in vain, all for an unjustified cause? Defeat itself lost its perverse pleasure. Where could pride now find refuge after the ignominy of defeat if it could not do so in in the memory of having been part of a just struggle? And if there was no room for pride, there could only be shame in the first instance, and, later, only guilt. And a great void. My childhood past had been devastated by a mental and emotional earthquake that left all my beliefs in ruins.

Audier, who had already spotted me as a bit of a lost soul and having now realised he had been the catalyst of this upheaval, invited me to his house for longer conversations than were possible after lessons at school. It was an offer to listen to my bewilderment. The clearing-up of so much confusion was to be a protracted and difficult process, a long march of the mind and the emotions that would take me years, but these counselling-like talks in his study at least propped me up when I could easily have fallen, and helped me start the unravelling.

The old ways of a French provincial town

As is often the case with places of one's youth, I grew fond of Niort only long after I had left it for good. There were occasional returns that would be tinged, if not quite with a feeling of homecoming, at least with a comforting one of familiarity. True, the town had changed. It had become more pleasant as a result of its growing affluence. The centre now boasted several attractive pedestrianised streets, with benches and fountains, and baskets of flowers hanging from every lamp post. There was a general air of jolly, agreeable living. I could now also appreciate the softness of its light grey stone buildings, the medieval character of the old town centre huddled around the well-preserved keep of a castle long gone, the narrow, paved streets around the cathedral and the ancient houses with leaning facades. Near the keep, there was an impressive covered market, a classically beautiful nineteenth-century vast iron and glass structure, light and cool, which on market days would be bursting with multicoloured heaps of fresh vegetables, fruit, cheese, meat and fish. Seeing it partly through the eyes of the British people I occasionally took there, it became easier to think of Niort as a delightful town, displaying all the picturesque charm of provincial France.

But for a sixteen-year-old preoccupied with the desperate desires of adolescence, that charm had little appeal. I had come back from that school trip to England filled with a confidence quite disproportionate to the nature of the event that had induced it, that first kiss. Yet it had been sufficient to enable me to face Niort with renewed optimism, with a feeling that from now on girls could not be as unreachable as before. And at first it did appear that circumstances were indeed becoming more propitious. Invisible hands seemed to be at work, creating more opportunities to meet girls. Doors appeared to have opened on various meeting places. First and foremost were the cafés around the central square, frequented after school, and where *bandes*, mixed groups that met regularly in the same establishment, were beginning to form. Boys with sisters were assiduously cultivated as it was mainly through them that girls, sisters and, more importantly, sisters' friends, were brought into the group. There was also a film club on Wednesday nights, a mixed activity where encounters could occur in the foyer and perhaps lead to further meetings.

Best of all were the parties held on Saturday afternoons in someone's home, usually in a basement or garage which could easily be made dark. The cover of darkness was badly needed, for in spite of these opportunities, things were nowhere near as straightforward as they had appeared to be in the very different world I had glimpsed in England. The long physical separation between boys and girls had left us with an awkwardness that could not simply vanish now that we were allowed to meet. And it was not just that we were ignorant of one another's ways. Our embryonic relationships took place within a rigid framework of traditions and customs. Looking back, I believe we ourselves were unconsciously constrained by moral straightjackets that had surreptitiously been slipped upon us by parents and teachers, magazines and films, by all the exponents of conformism, the guardians of convention. One thing I did discover at the time was that the higher up the social scale, the more encumbered young people were by these strictures. The weight of hypocritical morality was evidently heavier on the pupils from the *lycées* than on young people who had already gone out to work or were studying at the technical colleges.

In today's world of online dating and casual sex, I know that what I am describing will come across as incomprehensible, or at the very least as quaint, but these were the old ways. And especially the old French ways, the non-mating rituals of French youth before the social earthquake of May 1968. Thus, in secluded corner seats of cafés discreetly, in deserted alleys of public gardens secretly, in the back rows of cinemas silently, in the dimmed lights of parties self-consciously, and rarely, behind the closed door of my bedroom nervously, I went through this extended initiation into the confounding complexities of what at the time, in that milieu, passed for discovering sexuality. Finding out what was expected of the boy, what could be hoped for from the girl, learning the elaborate hierarchy of physical approaches and gestures, experiencing the strictly determined and always incomplete escalation of intimacy. The tentative initial move of holding hands, the emboldened daring of the first kiss, the significance of the subsequent switching from *vous* to *tu* – bearing in mind that with everything being made so difficult, one kiss was enough to seal the fact that you were 'going out'. Until then, the paths for boys and girls, however tortuous and however much they were required to play different roles (boy made move, girl responded or not), had at least been parallel. Now they diverged. Unequal demands were made, different values applied, depending on whether you were a boy or a girl.

What should have been a natural and joyful fulfilment of common desires was instead played as a dismal battle of wills, during which boys had to prove their assertiveness and girls display suitable resistance. Double standards already reigned supreme. 'Going out' immediately subjected the girl to stringent rules of faithfulness and exclusivity. No question here of the English girls' habit, which I had observed with astonishment, of having several boyfriends at the same time. Any transgression would land the girl with a reputation of being a bit of a *salope*, an 'easy' girl to be treated accordingly (for it was understood that boys were boys and would *naturally* take advantage of 'easy' girls), and not someone with whom you 'went out'. The boyfriend suffered the shame of being 'cuckolded' if the girlfriend happened to transgress – they did actually use that word – and he would be the butt of his male friends' taunts. In a ridiculous and clumsy parody of their elders, we were playing the preposterous games of possessiveness, acquiring twisted notions of jealousy, not knowing them to be harbingers of future misery.

Although I had by then become accepted among the so-called well brought-up boys and girls, perhaps because of my Algerian past I did not really feel that I truly belonged. I found the ways and trappings of this milieu too tame, too predictably proper. After a while I could not bear to comply with all the posing, the slavish conforming to fashion, the judgements based on appearances, on looks and clothes. Instead, I took up what in some ways was my first form of travel, my first attempt at escaping – I became a bit of a social explorer. All I had to do was to cross the road.

Another world across the road

Several times a year, funfairs were set up in the large central square. They offered the usual range of attractions, big wheels and ghost trains, dodgems and shooting stalls. On the street edge of these fairs were long, open-sided wooden huts that were set up as amusement arcades. At one end was a cash desk behind which sat a fearsome looking *patronne*, at the other a jukebox belting out rock-and-roll, and between the two, against the back wall, an alluring array of pinball machines, all garish colours, flashing lights and incessant pinging. In front of them, completing the scene, a line of wooden table football stands, four players bent over in absolute concentration at each of them. Between the fairs, these huts were not always taken down and so, for all but the coldest months of the year, they remained at the bottom of the square, enticingly open until late in the evening, just opposite the row of fashionable cafés on the other side of the road.

More and more often I dared myself to cross over in order to explore the disreputable world of the leather-jacketed youths who hung out there. They were young people who had left school at sixteen to work in factories, garages and shops, to become apprentice mechanics, carpenters or sales assistants. They still lived at home and the ones with the better jobs could afford the large British motorbikes parked outside under the double row of plane trees. All of them could afford the one essential item of uniform, the black leather jacket, that set them apart from respectable youth. These were young men playing the serious game of looking tough and menacing to the sounds of Elvis Presley, Bill Hailey, Gene Vincent or Eddie Cochrane. And the girls, fewer than the boys but often looking older, girls with dyed blond hair and lipstick, pointy bras under tight sweaters, miniskirts and high-heeled shoes, looking provocative and sexy, whether pouting or chewing gum. Girls I saw being pulled into the darkness between the huts, girls I saw pressed against trees, in passionate clinches, boys' hands wandering freely, girls I saw disappearing into the night on the back of motorbikes, with a different boy each time. It was the sort of vibrant and exciting environment where it was easy to become inebriated on a potent mixture of sharply heightened desire and basic envy. A place of aching pleasures and sweet agonies that kept drawing me back.

Strangely, I gained a certain respect from being able (or at least better able than others) to work out some of the English words of the songs being played on the jukebox and as a result I was, if not exactly accepted, at least tolerated. English being an unexpected key to this new world probably increased my motivation to become better at it – language as a way of escaping. After a period of assiduous attendance and rock-song deciphering, I managed to get to know some of the boys but I could not overcome my shyness with the girls. As a result, they teased me, and I did not know how to respond. The more they realised this, the more flirtatious they were, deliberately brushing past me at the jukebox, joining me in a game of pinball, standing hip to hip, leaning against me pretending to be tired, close, so pleasurably close and at the same time so painfully unattainable. Yet it appeared simple for the other boys. It was as if they just had to decide to pull a girl away and she would willingly follow – certainly more straightforward than among my *lycée* peers, though in reality just a cruder version of the same poisonous stereotypes behind it all.

I was of course never more than an observer, tolerated but always on the fringes of the group. Still, having got a taste for this kind of social venturing, I replicated it among the young men from Frontenay, especially at the weekends. They were the sons of farmers and shopkeepers, most of them a couple of years older than me, at that age when, a little in limbo before being called up for military service, young French men were expected to be carefree and have fun so as to be ready on their return to settle down to a job and married life. In that period, they all shared the same practical ambition, that of owning a car, for a car was the key to having fun. A few managed to scrape enough money together to acquire a second-hand one that would then be resprayed in a racy colour, covered in go-faster stickers, to become an object of immense pride, an infallible status symbol. Especially on Saturday nights. The routine was always the same. They would meet in the café opposite the old church, all cleaned-up and after-shaved, to have a drink before going off to whichever village dance they had chosen for that night. I had become accepted enough to be taken along if there was room. They piled into cars and drove, fast, in a state of high eagerness. It was entertaining to notice how these boys fell into well-defined types. There were one or two successful seducers, usually the star players of the village football team or the owners of the snazziest cars; at the other extreme, the unsuccessful fat boy who, to compensate, had become the clown of the group. In between, the sullen and short-tempered ones who could be relied on to start the fights; the younger ones, unsure and nervous, who could not hold their drink and would miss everything because of it; the quiet, relaxed or bored ones, who already had steady girlfriends they were going to meet at the dance.

The dances were held in village halls or specially put-up marquees. Inside, it was always packed. At the start, there were quite a few older people from the village, local dignitaries and people connected with the organisation putting on the dance, the local fishing or football club. For their benefit, the band played old-fashioned tunes, waltzes, foxtrots and tangos. Some of the young women joined in, trying out a few steps in pairs, or self-consciously being whisked around the dance floor by a father or an uncle. Meanwhile the young men congregated by the bar to fortify themselves with a few more drinks, to exchange news and banter with groups from other villages – needless to say, everyone hunted in packs. Then the older people drifted away and the evening proceeded along unchangeable lines. The band would move to faster, more modern tunes. The young men were all on one side of the dance floor, nearest the bar, but now facing the women on the other side, nearest the cloakroom. Whether subtly or blatantly, silently or boisterously, they all eyed one another in preparation for what was to come. Women danced together, serious looks on their faces, in a relentless and almost mechanical display of their jiving skills, showing off the steps so often rehearsed at home with younger sisters. A few mixed couples, those who were already 'going out', also ventured onto the dance floor, leaving only the predatory men still observing and drinking.

Then came the most crucial moments of the evening. The band started playing the first set of slow songs. Immediately, the place was in a whirl. During the last of the fast songs, most of the women had briefly disappeared into the cloakroom for a final brushing of hair and applying of lipstick, and now they were lining up, ready for the coming scramble, pretending not to care, but all chatting and giggling had stopped and there was not a single pair of women left dancing together. The men moved in a fast and pushy shuffle, trying to appear not too hurried, to look as if they were casually moving around the dance floor on their way somewhere, but in fact going as swiftly as the crush would allow for the girl they had noticed or, if she had already been taken or said no, for an acceptable alternative. Having 'secured' a girl, they had four or five slow songs to make their moves, just as regulated as everything else, though again requiring few words, just a gradual physical approach – dancing a little closer by the second song, cheek to cheek by the third and, if all going well, kissing by the fourth.

During the next set of fast songs, the men returned to their friends to recount tales of easy successes and weigh up chances of further progress. Slow songs sent them scurrying back to the girls to press ahead towards their next aim. They would buy the girl a drink, hoping it would later help her to agree to going out to 'sit in the car for a while'. There, there would be fumbling kisses and clumsy touching that went no further or, depending on the girl, that led on to clumsy, hurried and uncomfortable sex in the back seat – a squalid little escapade that for some would end in unwanted pregnancy and reluctant marriage. But whatever happened, the men would come back with triumphant looks, giving meaningful winks to their friends before lighting a cigarette and downing another drink. By then, those who had not managed to find a dance partner were gathered round the bar, in various states of drunkenness and frustration. Finally, the inevitable would happen, the pent-up aggressivity would erupt into a fight. Sometimes because of a girl, because someone had unwisely tried to be too pushy in asking a girl already committed to dance, sometimes for a more trivial reason or no reason at all, simply because a boy from another group had been staring at someone who had responded in the time-honoured fashion, "You want my photo?"

At the end of these evenings, tired, slightly drunk, acutely conscious of my failure to be anything more than an observer, I would sometimes be overcome by a wave of disgust. Disgust at the squalor of the scene, the crush of sweating bodies, the sickly smell of cheap perfume and hairspray, the spilled drinks and cigarette smoke, the atmosphere of impending violence, the stupidity of the violence when it came, and the wretched return in the back of a crowded car recklessly driven. But also, self-disgust at my own willingness to take part, time and again, in the same sordid exercise.

Lesson drawn, with help...

Eventually an opportunity did come my way, but one that led only to a false start... She had been standing next to me at the start of a slow song and had accepted my offer to dance, made on the spur of the moment. I had not particularly noticed her before but there was something attractive about her pronounced features and, when we danced close, I found her plumpness voluptuous and soon having an effect on me. I knew straightaway that she would be different from the other girls I had known. Looking back, it may be that I was aroused more by the idea of having finally found an 'easy' girl than by the reality of what I was being so readily offered. Aroused more by the erotic power of a certain notion of transgression than by the actual experience. But all I could think about in the moment was how difficult it would be for me to get hold of the keys of a friend's car. Then as we came to the end of a dance, she said she had a car. I could not believe my luck. After that, it was easy to suggest going for a drive. We went a couple of miles and turned into a country lane where she parked and switched off the lights. At that moment I knew that the time had come, and started to show all the impatience of inexperience, not waiting for any words to pass, kissing in the front of the car. She seemed both amused and excited by my haste. She stopped me, in a gesture not of refusal but of promise, and said, "Let's get in the back."

The car was in fact a small van and in the back there was just about enough room to lie down. I was taking off my shirt, at the same time pulling down her skirt, desperately hurrying, with only a slight hesitation when her thighs, fully revealed, seemed to me no longer plump but fat, a hint that I no longer found her as attractive as I had in the dance hall, yet carrying on, undoing my trousers. Then "Wait", she said, as she took out a blanket from under the front seat and spread it on the hard floor, before adding what turned out to be the fateful words, "I always come prepared." The arousal I had so thrillingly felt all evening now suddenly vanished.

The rest had been pretty dismal. I went through the motions of making up for my predicament, all the while thinking it will be all right in a moment, it's got to be all right in a moment. But of course it wasn't. She had said nothing and tried to be helpful but when she saw that it was of no avail, a slight look of annoyance at having wasted her time came over her face. I just wanted to get away, ashamed of what had happened.

The full horror of what had happened – or rather, *not* happened – only struck me the following day. I went around constantly preoccupied by what I feared might be a terrible condition. And I could not think of what to do about it. I certainly could not talk to either of my parents. I knew I would not get much comfort from my male friends. I had heard all their stories of sexual prowess, about the times they had struck lucky and had performed wonders. I could not even ask my best friend for advice as I knew very well that my best friend had never 'done it'. And those who had were not going to admit to any failures – at least not to such a crucial one. For in all the scores of conversations, tales, stories, jokes, anecdotes, reminiscences, even confessions, about sex that I had heard, I could not remember a single one when the protagonist, boy or young man, had said I could not do it that time, I was too tired, too drunk, put off or whatever. As far back as I could remember, they always, always did it if they were given the chance, and it always worked. On all the occasions the subject came up, boys, young men never, ever spoke of losing it when there was an opportunity to have sex. How could they otherwise claim to be men?

Fortunately, Audier was there. He had noticed my distress and when I sat down in his study, he soon brought the conversation round to what could be the cause of it. There was something soothing and conducive to revelations in that space. It was a small room. The window was open but the shutters were half drawn, letting in just enough diffused sunlight to give the atmosphere a dusk-like quality, not too bright and not too dark, a serene light spreading its tranquillity to all the objects it fell upon, the large desk, the two deep, comfortable leather armchairs, the bookcases lining the walls. As if in deliberate contrast to this, was evidence of Audier's extraordinarily diverse interests scattered on his desk. Freud, Jung and Reich in the same pile of books, next to Montesquieu, Hegel and Marx, all of them with bits of annotated paper sticking out; an illustrated volume on the films of Jean-Luc Godard; magazines, the left-wing weekly *Le Nouvel Observateur* predictably, but also *Planning Familial*, which campaigned for access to contraception and at the time would have been considered by 'respectable' society as nothing less than subversive; newspaper cuttings, with passages underlined and comments scribbled in the margins; some black and white photographs of rural scenes; piles of essays in the process of being marked. All signs of a rich intellectual life, which in a strange way put me at ease.

I sat in one of the armchairs, facing Audier behind his desk, sitting against a halo of light coming from the half-shuttered window. He did not broach the subject immediately but started instead with a topic we had been discussing at school, honour and duty in the plays of Corneille and Racine, how the same themes could be found in the plots of classic American westerns, how they played a part in real life, in the conflicts of men, as they had in Algeria. As always, it was an unconventional discourse ranging across time and contexts to highlight links and draw lessons. Then, as neutral subjects were exhausted and there was a pause in the conversation, Audier casually mentioned how he had seen me looking worried and downcast recently. Was it to do with how I was getting on with my parents? He was aware that my new understanding of the Algerian war was likely to cause problems at home. I said it was not that. Was it to do with girls? Yes. I began to talk, avoiding the real issue to start with, pretending it was simply to do with the frustrations of not having opportunities to experience full relationships, using euphemisms and evasions. But Audier's gently probing questions kept drawing me out a little more. Whenever I gave an equivocal or imprecise answer, he would fix his gaze on me and remain silent, but his lingering smile became a little more ironic, as if to say, "Come now, you don't think I'm going to be taken in by this...".

And so the truth came out. Slowly. Piece by piece. Not very articulately. With a great deal of embarrassment. Helped along by Audier playing the role of midwife to a mind giving birth to an inadmissible worry. Then he set to work on the problem, a bit like a doctor now, reassuring the patient on the nature of the ailment, relieving the immediate pain, and clinically asking a few precise, no-nonsense questions. "Were you aroused when you danced with the girl, when you were kissing in the front her car, when you were still attracted to her?" I had a brief flash of detachment from the situation, stunned at the thought that this was my French literature teacher speaking, then checked myself to reply as firmly and definitely as I could, wanting to appear mature and collected, unaware that in those few moments was condensed the equivalent of months or even years of growing up. "Then I can assure you that there is nothing intrinsically, physically wrong with you." As my anguish began to dissipate and at what I thought would be the end of the examination, Audier, still doctor-like, went on to get behind the symptoms, at the real cause of the complaint. Having shown his sympathy, he was now firm and challenging, pressing me with quick-fire questions, leaving no room for avoidance or excuses, ruthlessly pointing out contradictions, exposing hidden prejudice, and finally giving his diagnosis, which, in a departure from the doctor-like manner, sounded more like the verdict of a well-meaning judge on a first-time offender.

"The first thing you have to acquire, to do with your sexuality, is a sense of humility. You need to banish from your mind the idea that you have to prove something at the point of your penis, to your partner, to yourself or, and I should say least of all, to your male friends. And if they are at that infantile stage at which unfortunately too many men remain stuck, then leave them there, ignore them and what they say, treat it for what it is, at worst lies, at best delusions.

There are, as far as I can see, two reasons why you could not make love, one perfectly valid and easily avoidable, the other which you should perhaps be concerned about. The valid reason is that you cannot force yourself to be attracted to someone, and your initial attraction was a superficial one, to do with excitement, circumstance, and not with the young woman herself. You should have sensed this early on and not even attempted to make love. That was a mistake of impatience. The other reason, to be challenged, is I think the reason why you were put off. Because of what she said, because you realised that she had just been looking for someone to have sex with, that she probably did this regularly, you suddenly despised her, and from the hypocritical height of your moralistic pedestal you looked down on her as a '*salope*'. You were happy enough to be titillated by her forwardness, to be excited by the prospect of easy sex, but when you were faced with the reality of it, the fact that you were one among others, perhaps many, was too much for your precious little male ego, and suddenly she was no longer worthy of your virginal penis... But it was you – and here he addressed me by name – who was not worthy of her freedom. Why do you, deep down, deny her the right to do what you would like so much to do yourself? What is it that makes it right for you and wrong for her? Why is it, for you, something to boast about to your friends and for her, something that makes her a 'slut'? Ask yourself these questions. Review all your values and if you can't back them up with rational arguments, cast them out of your mind. Free your mind of all notions that create one moral law for men and another for women, particularly when it comes to sex. Then, you will be ready to make love, with someone you find attractive, someone you like whether it is her first time or her hundredth, preferably in pleasant and comfortable surroundings, and as long as you take your time – and perhaps we shall have to talk more about this – there is no reason why everything should not be fine. You are not impotent, you are just too impatient. You chase after something that should be allowed to come to you naturally, and in your haste it is easy to make a mess of it. If you find the limitations of Niort, of the circles you frequent, too restricting, and I know only too well that they are, then take advantage of the coming holidays to travel. Get away from friends, family – and fantasies – and face life on your own for a while."

Just as I was about to leave, Audier took two books from his shelves and gave them to me. "These are presents to wish you luck. They should provide inspiration, one for life, the other for your travels." One was André Gide's *Les Nourritures Terrestres (The Fruits of the Earth)* and the other Jack Kerouac's *On the Road* and they were to remain cherished symbols of that particular turning point in my life.

I have wanted to possess a leather armchair exactly as the one I sat in that day for the whole of my life and so far, for one reason or another, I have failed to get one. Currently, we are in limbo, in a temporary home, looking for what may be our last house, the one where I hope finally to be able to fulfil that desire. Speaking of things not done, I am sure any lifetime has in it a series of letters never sent – significant letters to friends, lovers or even parents – that were intended, drafted many times in one's mind, or even scribbled down, but never posted. Letters on to-do lists never ticked off because of hesitation, embarrassment, or the relentless demands of daily life. I have plenty of those in my own life, but one of the things I am most glad about is that in my thirties, after my exile to England, I wrote, and actually sent, a long letter to Audier telling him what he had meant to me.

In limbo – flux and uncertainty

That letter and the generous and elegant response it elicited, with a few significant others from the long gone past when people still wrote letters, is at the bottom of a cardboard box I have just retrieved from storage in France. I say 'retrieve' because, along with a stack of other boxes, it was part of what was left there when the farmhouse in the Charente was finally sold, unfortunately in the time of Covid. Lockdown and travel restrictions meant we had to rely on a trustworthy young man from the local area to pack up all that we wanted to keep and take it even deeper into the French countryside for safe keeping in a friend of a friend's half-empty house.

Not many months after that, still in the ongoing time of Covid, the house in Oxford was sold, and here too it was mostly down to strangers to sweep up all our possessions into boxes – the only difference this time being that we actually witnessed the thorough emptying of rooms, the wholesale erasure of almost all signs of our life there for twenty-five years. All neatly, or in some cases bunglingly, packed away in forty-eight hours. Nothing left behind. It made me think of my first departure, that hurried leaving of the El Biar flat in Algiers, when almost everything was left behind. And I recalled that, because I still cared for childish possessions even after what I had lived through, I was upset that my Dinky Toy cars did not make it into the few suitcases we could take with us. Perhaps as a result, every piece of Duplo and Lego, a large assortment of soft and wooden toys, and dozens of children's books have made their way from Oxford to Scotland – even though the three boys are now well into their thirties... There was a certain amount of trimming in the weeks preceding the move but Covid put the brakes on this too, as charity shops were closed, and there was a limit to how many offerings we could put out on the pavement each day. So, in the first few months in this rented flat we moved through narrow valleys between cliffs of stacked-up removal boxes – and spent hours sifting through them, with the aim of paring down the overall number. Giving away has become easier with the end of lockdowns but selecting between what to keep and what to jettison remains as tricky as ever. Each box is opened in a quandary, chuck or treasure?

There is something both moving and pathetic in going through a lifetime's possessions – well, in this case not *a* lifetime because there have been several discrete portions with a lot lost along the way, but still leaving an enormous amount of 'things'. We are torn between keeping objects that define us and a desire to cleanse, to become lighter, to make a fresh start (however inappropriate the concept at our age). In fact, part of the discarding side of the exercise has an ending in mind, a wish not to leave too much for others to sort out. Each of us has their own insecurity, which can imbue the smallest thing with enough emotional stickiness to ensure it goes on the 'keep' pile. We both tread cautiously, careful not to push the other into abandoning something they might regret, which is considerate but does not help progress. Fortunately, our tastes are similar and there are few instances of 'surely you don't want to keep that horrible thing'.

In line with the times, we are in favour of recycling, reducing and reusing but much of what we keep is not exactly for practical purposes. There is a gap between the desire to do the right thing and the need for familiarity, for evidence of personal history, for symbols and signifiers of our lives. The gravitational pull of these is strong. All these possessions that we can't abandon are objects that we need to keep circling in orbit around our self. Never mind that many of them are clothes we will never wear again, letters and diaries we will never read again or books we will never open again. We fear there would be too much disturbance if they were not there, surrounding us, mostly unseen and untouched for long periods, but defining the little universe of which we are the centre. They help keep a certain emotional equilibrium.

For someone haunted by the search for permanence and stability, it is odd that I have accepted two dislocations almost at once. How can I have thrown everything up in the air? Relinquishing my adopted home ground of Oxford, a cultural hive, and giving up my small domain in France, my rural refuge, my fantasy of an alternative life. In part at least, it was because one had lost its shine and the other had become too difficult to keep. Both of these reasons were to do with Brexit, that dark shadow of populist insanity that descended on England in 2016. And there was the natural, inescapable reason of advancing years. The lure of Scotland had been present for years, and was now increasingly hard to resist. Scotland, its beauty and its sense of community, its rejection of the Buffoon-in-chief and Brexit, was a haven within reach.

Unfortunately for us, and not for the first time for me, our individual fate has coalesced with a societal trend – in this case the Covid-induced exodus from cities – and the small coastal town we have chosen seems to be a favoured destination. Not only that, but the place is so nice that no one wants to leave and houses for sale are few and far between. So, we live in a time of both escape and uncertainty. A time of flux that should make me unsteady, and yet, as we settle in, there is something that leaves me in no doubt. As I get used to walking in the strong winds of the Firth of Forth, I feel I have never been surer of a suitable consonance between location and time of life. This is the place where I can see myself sliding into what I hope will be a not too brief adagio of old age.

On the road

Recently, it has been more a case of experiencing the discordant notes of troublesome travel – again, the fallout from living in the time of Covid. Because of lockdowns and associated restrictions, I had not driven to France for nearly two years. Even lately, after some relaxations, there always seemed to be a perfect storm of potential impediments brewing: queues at petrol stations, still complex and ever-changing testing rules, climate crisis protestors blocking roads in Britain, French fishers threatening to blockade access to Calais. By chance I managed to evade all these obstacles and travel just before the surge of another variant. But the fun of these motoring trips had faded, if not disappeared altogether. I used to enjoy them, in spite of the long hours of driving, as they gave me an excuse for indulgent stopovers complete with gastronomic delights. This time, to minimise risks, I made the journey in just two long stretches from Scotland to my brother's house in La Rochelle, and my one stop was in a nondescript business hotel near the tunnel offering only microwave cuisine. In addition to the weariness of it all there is now the inescapable pang of guilt as you fill up the tank, leaving a bad mark on your conscience, an awkward feeling of 'here you go again, contributing to the destruction of the world'.

It is no wonder that I started asking myself if the lure of travel has completely dissipated. The relentless miles even gave rise to the thought that I have perhaps reached the stage of life when at least a big part me would like to stop moving, to stay put. This was the strangest of feelings given the place of travel in my life. Now that I am put off by the very thought of driving long distances, the harm it is causing being drummed into me from all sides, it is odd to think that there was a time when the prospect of an unfolding grey ribbon of road meant freedom. As a doubly-troubled teenager, travel was more than just that, it was my salvation. Audier had been right on this too. In a way I was lucky that as the son of an often-absent father and a preoccupied mother I had known a lot of freedom as a child, even in a time of conflict. I suppose by then, in spite of all the family friction, they had convinced themselves that I was 'sensible' and they did not try very hard to contain me within the confines of a small French provincial town. So, when I turned sixteen, I took advantage of school holidays to go on trips abroad. Strange as it may seem today, the key form of travel for a penniless youth in those days was hitchhiking.

Now the practice has almost disappeared, perhaps because of the ubiquity and cheapness of other means of travel – and also because of safety concerns, though I am not sure these are based in reality. Perceptions seem actually to have reversed. In those days the perceived danger was the risk of being harmed by the driver, whereas now it is the appearance of some of the characters still hitchhiking, rarely bright-eyed young people with rucksacks. Sadly, it makes me hesitate and often break the long-ago promise to myself on many long waits that when I was older and had a car I would always stop. I do remember it all. The initial embarrassment of standing conspicuously by the roadside on the edge of town, the boredom of long waits, the annoyance at expressions of mockery or disapproval on faces glimpsed in cars roaring past.

But then there was also the little thrill of success each time a car drew up. That delicious flutter of expectation on getting in, wondering not only how far the lift would take you, but also how much was to be discovered, how much was to be revealed, to be guessed, from unfinished conversations, from telltale details observed in these moments of permitted intrusion. The silent drivers were the exception. Normally it was easy to indulge in games of investigation and be rewarded with enough fascinating trivia from other people's lives to make the journey interesting. I sometimes wonder if this is the source of an enduring fascination with eavesdropping on strangers' conversations in restaurants or in cinemas. A more surprising legacy after all these years is that images occasionally still pop into my mind, like frozen frames from an old film, of landscapes gazed at during long hours waiting on deserted roads in the heat and silence of a foreign land. Not necessarily significant moments, just flashbacks of random times in those youthful wanderings, like broken shards of a half-forgotten picture. It was easy to become addicted. I looked forward to every trip as a potentially picaresque adventure that might surpass the previous one.

Not that it was always an easy ride. There were moments of lonely helplessness in the midst of foreign crowds, usually saved by the spontaneous fellowship of other young people. One such time was a stormy night in the town of Nis in what was then Yugoslavia, at the end of a long day travelling, tired and hungry, feeling incapable of the simplest decision. Where to eat. Where to find somewhere to sleep. Suddenly immobilised by incertitude. And then, just as weariness might have overcome me, the hand of friendship was extended – a chance meeting with a group of young people ready to offer help and instant companionship. They came towards me, smiling, with curious but friendly faces. Using bits of different languages like disparate pieces from children's construction games, we built makeshift bridges that would, for our few hours of togetherness, span the differences in our backgrounds. I showed them on a map my journey so far and where I was going and felt the selfish pleasure of providing something different in their lives. They took me to a nearby beerhall, a large room, dimly lit, dingy but filled with the jollity of the crowd inside and the old-fashioned sounds of the small brass band playing in a corner. As we drank cheap beer and ate cheap food, I felt my tiredness evaporate and a warm glow of happiness rise inside me. Nothing so gratifying as the pleasures of small comforts after a period of adversity. Later they took me to a loft above some stables, where I spent the night on a dusty wooden floor. They came back early in the morning to point me on my way, walking me to the edge of town and wishing me luck with what I took to be traces of envy in their eyes. I was to know many such friendships, quickly formed and too quickly lost, which each time left me with a feeling of abandonment – only relieved by the prospect of other encounters on the road ahead.

Many of these were with other travellers – in youth hostels or by the roadside, it did not take long to come across other young people, travelling on their own or in pairs, looking just like I did and trying to live out the same experience. I remember a particular occasion, also in Yugoslavia, when to my stupefaction I was given a lift in an army bus. When I got in, the only other people were the driver, a couple of smiling conscripts and a German hitchhiker with the largest rucksack I had ever seen. This was already unusual enough but the rest of the journey soon became quite extraordinary. As we progressed, we picked up every single hitchhiker on the road (no shortage of those as it was on the way to Greece, a favoured destination at the time) to the cheers of those inside. The back of the bus filled up with a motley collection of young travellers, long-haired and scruffy, in marked contrast to the uniformed soldiers with their crew cuts. But everyone was happy, not least the driver who seemed overjoyed by his growing popularity each time he stopped for yet another lucky hitchhiker. The rucksacks piled up on the spare seats, someone played a mouth organ, the soldiers chatted to the girls, the driver shook his head in good-humoured amazement at his own temerity in breaking the rules, and the locals in the villages we went through watched in astonishment this most outlandish sight in a passing Yugoslav army bus. That evening in Skopje, we all ended up in the same youth hostel, elated. It was as if a special bond had been created in our shared, unusual experience, which for one night at least gave our separate journeys to Greece, Turkey, Lebanon or India a single purpose, a search for a feeling of fraternity. It is a tragic irony of history that thirty years later, the city where we celebrated this would be at the heart of one of the bloodiest European conflicts since the Second World War.

But at that time it was part of a well-meaning wave of aspirations for 'peace and love' among the youth of the western world. A great flow of like-minded young men and women took to travelling as no previous generation had been able to do – they came from the four corners of Europe, as well as North America and Australia. They were like unarmed modern-day knights-errant, looking for adventure, looking to escape the stifling conformity of their elders. Keen to discover the world, conscious that it was a more peaceful world than the one their parents had known at their age, conscious, however hazily, that their fathers had been made to kill one another. Yet to us then, it seemed so simple and so good to love one another instead. We brandished the idea of peace as if we had invented it. We were infatuated with it. Our enthusiasm may have been naive but it was no less vibrant or less genuine for that. The symbol of peace flourished on our jackets and peace became a sort of password to friendships. Often unable to go much beyond this in words because of language barriers, we would sit around someone playing a guitar and join in singing the most known English or American folk songs. Eyes shining with the tiredness of the road and hopes for the future.

Although it could have been described as superficial, what we had in common actually went deeper. From different countries and speaking different languages, we were all children of the post-war mood of hopefulness. Teenagers of sixties' affluence, we listened to the same music, read the same books, and nurtured the same dreams. And each and every time our encounters made us aware of this, it was an exhilarating revelation. It gave us hope that everything could be so simple – that love and peace could be the panacea. We were the lucky victims of an epidemic of optimism that had swept over Europe, and we carried the germs of that optimism wherever we went, cheerfully contaminating the local youth. But what we did not know is that we were privileged travellers in a short-lived period of grace. Within a few years, distant and not so distant wars would put paid to the illusion of peace.

At last...

I start this section with a certain amount of trepidation and hesitancy as writing about sexual experiences can be a minefield, difficult to find the right words for, and in many cases inappropriate anyway. But I proceed, telling myself I have already strayed into this territory with an account of my fumbled near-loss of virginity – and at least I can balance that misadventure with a more positive outcome, with a story of luck that has all the elements of a fairy tale: a chance encounter with an adventurous, more experienced woman, under the sun of a Greek island, with a temple to Aphrodite even featuring as part of the story. Sometimes, everything falls into place. How could this stay in the background?

Also, and this could come as over-sentimental or self-indulgent, I feel it is a way of paying my respect to someone long disappeared from my life. I mean it to be a small act of remembrance for a good person. A small show of a gratitude still keenly felt after all these years.

In the youth hostel in Athens, the morning after my arrival in the city, I went to sit in the sunshine on the small balcony overlooking a narrow street that reminded me of Bab-el-Oued. She was already there, sitting on the floor against the railings, blonde and suntanned, wearing shorts and a T-shirt, reading a book. When I sat opposite her to write my diary, she looked up and smiled. Familiar noises were coming up from the street below, some shouting, music from a radio, cars honking, the mixed sounds of a bustling

Mediterranean street. I smiled back and the ritual questions were asked, where do you come from, where are you going... It was easy to talk, it happened all the time between travellers. She was on her way back home to Denmark after a failed attempt to reach Australia via India. I tried to make the most of my own trip, which by comparison was of modest scope. I spoke of the good times along the way, warming to the subject when it came to stories of hospitality and instant friendships. I told her how moved I had been by the kindness and generosity of a Greek peasant family who had shared what little food they had and welcomed me into their tiny whitewashed house. She, of course, had experienced all this before and probably took it for granted, but perhaps she liked the freshness of my appreciation, my enthusiasm. She was amused by a self-deprecating account of my embarrassed discomfiture one night when in an unlit room I had grabbed for myself a plate of scrambled eggs that was supposed to be left in the middle of the low table for everyone to dip into. There was a lot of laughter and I sensed that she quite liked me, even though I was a few years younger than her, still not quite seventeen to her twenty-one...

The story of her own journey was of byzantine complexity involving among other things a romance with an American man in Istanbul who turned out to be a shady character and who then disappeared, apparently presumed kidnapped. She had then had her passport and most of her money stolen by some of his 'friends' and had been made to leave by the authorities. It seemed she had delved unwittingly into some of the nefarious secret worlds of Istanbul – smugglers, dealers and, she claimed, spies. It all sounded too incredible for real life but I would have no reason later on, when I got to know her better, to disbelieve anything she ever told me.

We soon gave up on diary and book and decided to walk around Athens.

We went up to the Acropolis, gently making fun of the swarms of more conventional tourists. But later, walking through the crowded streets, we became irritated at being accosted and pestered. Hanne's blond hair attracting young men on one side and my own long hair, in a society unused to it, causing a couple of approaches by other differently-motivated young men. By the evening, we were fed up with the hot, dirty and crowded city that had made us feel so conspicuous but happy in each other's company. We ate in a cheap taverna, talking more intimately about ourselves over the meal. Walking back to the hostel, she said, "It would be nice to go to bed together now."

That night, lying awake on my bunk in the men's dormitory, I kept thinking how easy and natural it had been to get to that point, how different from the rigmaroles I had known in Niort. The next day, we found a way of getting out of Athens. We both had three days before having to catch our respective boats, hers to Brindisi, mine to Haifa. Hanne had been told of a small island, Aegina, only an hour away from Piraeus. It was cheap to get there by ferry and it would be cheap to stay there, sleeping on the beach. We were both pretty broke but, as all young foreigners in Athens at the time, we had heard about the easiest way of earning a few drachmas. So, along with most of the youth hostel's newly-arrived travellers, off we went to the local hospital where we queued up to sign a form stating, among other things, that we did not suffer from a venereal disease... I had to lie about my age, saying I was eighteen and had forgotten my passport. We then waited for what seemed like hours, sitting on benches in a small, hot and airless room, crossed every few minutes by a nurse carrying a bottle half-filled with dark red blood covered with a layer of thick cloudy yellow liquid. The sight of it was really off-putting but the nurse was quite oblivious to the effect it had on the people waiting. Several left before it was their turn. I began to feel squeamish and had to fight off dizziness. I reminded myself of the ultimate purpose of my being there – diverting myself with the thought that not many first sexual experiences can literally have been paid for in blood.

That same afternoon we caught a ferry to Aegina where we arrived early enough to find a beach and have a swim in the warm sea. In front of us, the sun still shining in a clear blue sky, behind us a hill covered in dark green pine trees, on our left, a short distance away, a cluster of white houses, a small fishing village with a couple of outdoor restaurants near the jetty of the small port. I hoped the beauty of the scenery was a good augury for what was to come. It felt as if we had been flicked off the course of our separate destinies to find ourselves temporarily stranded on this dot in the Aegean Sea, with nothing to do but fill with love this brief parenthesis in our young lives. I think that, for her, it was a welcome relief from the complications of her troubled journey. For me, it was the idyll I had been dreaming of, the golden prize of the road, for once reality exceeding expectations.

The sleeping on the beach part was not quite as straightforward as we had hoped. When darkness fell, we found what we thought was a discrete spot only to be almost immediately moved on by a jobsworth municipal warden doing his final rounds. We then happened upon a large beached fishing boat, and tried to settle in that, hidden away below deck. Not only did it turn out to be exceedingly hot and uncomfortable, we were soon disrupted by entertaining goings-on above us. Two French girls, obviously making out with a couple of Greek lotharios, were giving a running, not always complimentary, commentary to each other in French, which we were able to follow quite clearly, blow by blow. Fortunately, as we tried to stifle our giggles, it was not long before we overheard their decision not to go any further with their frolics and leave – a rare time I was grateful for French girls' usual reticence.

Once the noisy foursome was out of the way, we too made our escape. Backing onto the beach was a small hill with a wooded area around the ruins of a temple (the next day we would find out that it was dedicated to Aphrodite, which sounds made up but is not...). We climbed over the fence and found a secluded spot under the pine trees, where we spread our sleeping bags. And there, in the warm and fragrant night, with the sound of cicadas in the background, the sea shining in the moonlight, I gave up any pretence of previous experience and was led by knowing, helping hands and lips into the blissful pleasures of sex, into manhood.

Writing this, I am made aware again that a sense of gratefulness, felt for the first time then, has never left me. I always feel there is something truly munificent about that sweet invasion being desired. I have never stopped being awed by this miraculous act of complete acceptance.

I felt lucky then, and I still feel lucky to this day, to have had Hanne as a first lover. She was both passionate and delicately considerate. Not least of all, I realised later, she gave me, lovingly, a much-needed first lesson in being attentive to the other's needs.

After a while, we took a break from our lovemaking. I felt ravenous, with a hunger I had never known before. We hurried along the beach to the village. For a long time after that, I was often to walk that short distance in my mind, from the crushed sleeping bags to the terrace of the restaurant, remembering how I had felt strangely detached from myself, as if the old me was still there looking at the new me, who was suddenly stronger, taller, fitter, and immensely happier. Brimming with a feeling of being fully alive, at last.

The 'Duke of Zellidja Award'

"I really enjoyed reading your diary entries about your little adventure on that island in Greece...", said the crusty but eminent Sorbonne professor sitting next to me at the awards celebratory lunch. He said it in a rather tremulous tone that starkly contrasted with the bored and detached manner of his previous questions about my experiences of working in a kibbutz. The reason he had read my journal of that trip to Greece and Israel was that he was a member of the jury panel for an award called *Bourses de voyages Zellidja*. (There is, unfortunately, a connection to colonialism here: Zellidja is the name of a lead mine in Morocco, from which a French entrepreneur, Jean Walter, made the fortune that enabled him to set up the award in 1939.) The nearest I have been able to compare this scheme to in Britain is the Duke of Edinburgh's Award, hence my slightly facetious badging of this section. In fact, it was very different. (It is still running today, albeit in a slightly modified form.)

In the *lycée* equivalent of the lower sixth, you could apply for this travel scholarship by putting forward a project to travel abroad on your own, spend a month in situ, and write both a journal and a study of a topic of your choice. If your project was selected, you were given a very modest and deliberately inadequate sum of money and a rather grandiloquent letter of recommendation to help you wangle various forms of help in your travels to make up for your lack of funds. The letter was impressively headed *Académie*

Française, under whose auspices the scheme was being run, and laid out to look like an official diploma with one's name handwritten in a fancy script, followed by an explanation of the scheme – translated into several languages on the verso – which included this passage:

> *Xxx has committed himself to travel on his own, to undertake a study project in a distant land, to use only a modest sum. He has accepted to face all the physical, moral and intellectual difficulties of this adventure. He is preparing himself for his life as an adult.*

Somehow, the French version sounds less declamatory... (An example of the undeniable phenomenon of something that comes across as reasonable, if somewhat earnest and occasionally abstract, in French being transformed into pretentiousness or pomposity as soon as it is put into English.) I have kept the 'he/his' because in those days the scheme was open only to young men. I applied because I had been encouraged to do so by Audier and also as a way of being allowed to venture a lot further afield than my parents had tolerated so far.

The kibbutz at the time appealed as an interesting experiment in creating a new model of collective social organisation and it was relatively easy to get work in one during the summer. Given their evolution since, my no doubt naive study would make sad reading today, but it was deemed good enough to win the scheme's third prize that year. Given the somewhat prurient comments of the old professor (who, by the way, must have been younger than I am now), I suspect it was the daringly frank nature of my journal that tipped my submission into a prize-winner – the study was diligent but dull, whereas the journal was a full and direct, unself-censored, fervent account of events and feelings. This was quite a departure from anything that would have been expected in those days of written work to be handed in to a teacher at school, but I felt it was in the spirit of Zellidja: a candid account of opening oneself up to the world, of the joys and tribulations of learning to be autonomous and self-reliant, of starting to become an adult.

One immediate advantage of being among the top fifty reports was that you were given an opportunity to do a second and usually more ambitious trip in the summer of your last year at school. After much procrastination, I came up with the idea of going to Liberia, the only country in Africa not to have experienced European colonisation, a journey which will deserve its own account later. It turned out I wasn't alone in finding it difficult to choose a topic and a destination for this second trip – it was a common experience among the Zellidja laureates, probably because for seventeen/eighteen-year-olds in their last year at school, there are so many other priorities and diversions. I recall the story of a boy who, almost up against the deadline, hit on the idea of selecting a destination at random, limiting his choice to France (which was allowed). He laid out a map, took a pin, shut his eyes, swivelled the map around a couple of times and then brought the pin down. It landed on a small obscure town in the middle of the Auvergne. His topic, just as quickly chosen, would be 'How the desertification of the French countryside [already in the news even then...] is affecting a small town in the Auvergne'. He promptly wrote to all the local dignitaries, from the mayor to the priest and everyone in between, offering to do any job in exchange for bed and board (this is where the fancy letter of recommendation headed *Académie Française* came in useful). The doctor replied saying he could come to do menial tasks in his surgery and garden. Rural doctors were quite well off in those days and when the boy arrived, he found there was another helper staying in the large family home: a German au pair. Needless to say, the two young people fell for each other and after less than a month they eloped and set out together on what was to be a year-long, round-the-world adventure.

Part of the enjoyment of being involved in this award was meeting a cast of exceptional characters with sometimes hardly believable stories. Stories which, unlike the above stroke of first love in the Auvergne, could easily have had terrible endings. I have forgotten most of them but there are a couple that have survived the passage of time. A boy had put forward a project to study 'The growth of wine production in Sicily' and successfully travelled to Palermo. However, this topic was a fig leaf, or perhaps I should say a vine leaf. He fancied himself as a budding investigative reporter and his real goal was to uncover a story of Mafia involvement in the wine trade. Unsurprisingly, he lasted less than a week. One early morning, a couple of mean-looking men in dark glasses came to his digs, asked him nicely to pack his bag and put him on the ferry back to the mainland.

The other outlandish tale which has stayed with me is that of another eighteen-year-old, who aspired to study anthropology at university and had managed to spend time with an Amazonian tribe in Brazil. He had been well received and had managed to take copious notes and photographs in his four weeks. Then, as the day he was meant to set out on his long journey back home approached, things got rather complicated. It transpired that, in that particular tribe, if the Chief's eldest child was a girl, she was entitled to choose

The 'Duke of Zellidja Award'

her husband, and the exotic-looking young Frenchman turned out to be her favoured choice. Polite explanations of an unavoidable need to return to one's family and to attend university were conveyed to justify having to pass on this kind proposal, regretfully of course – all this communicated by sign language and facial expressions (a good time to be French...). Equally politely but unambiguously firmly, the response from the Chief and the assembled elders was that the honour could not possibly be refused and that the young betrothed would have to remain as a 'guest' until preparations were made for a proper consecration of this special union. The 'guest' had no choice but to comply.

In the weeks that followed, he endeavoured to do so in a way that showed appreciation for his fate in order to reassure his hosts, who he had noticed were keeping him under close observation. Part of the preparations involved his having to go through an initiation process to become a full member of the tribe. As things progressed, he began to feel less and less under scrutiny until, one day at dawn, he was able to make his escape. With the minimum of possessions in a small satchel, he took a dugout canoe and paddled his way downriver towards the main artery of the Amazon. After a while he could hear and soon see a posse from the village in pursuit, and moving at a much faster pace. Just as they were getting near, his luck suddenly changed – he saw a couple of men standing on a wooden makeshift pontoon by an old motorboat. He knew straightaway from their appearance, their equipment, and their guns, that they were gold prospectors – usually, he had been warned, disreputable characters to be avoided, but given his predicament he did not hesitate to shout at them and ask for their help. Prospectors in general were not well disposed towards indigenous tribes and these two were immediately ready to point their guns at the pursuers. They were persuaded to fire just a couple of shots wide of the target only when our laureate told them they would be rewarded for taking him away quickly in their boat. This was another occasion when the letter of recommendation came in useful, this time in getting the French Embassy's help in repatriating the young man, who by then had been officially missing for several weeks. I should add that this did not put him off embarking on his degree in anthropology.

I was to hear many more tales of adventurous travels from fellow Zellidja laureates, but in a way what is more significant than the outlandishness of some of them is the common thread of how meaningful, indeed life-transforming, the whole experience of travelling on one's own with a self-chosen purpose was for us all.

I visited the website of the current Bourses Zellidja scheme as I was writing this and was deeply moved by the short testimonials of recent laureates, setting out in touching, modest terms what they had gained from their travels. No matter how far they went or what topic they studied, or how successful it was, you can tell from their comments that the experience had filled them with a sense of achievement and given them lasting strength and confidence.

The late Duke would have approved, I think.

In Graham Greene's footsteps

We had been trekking in the bush for several hours before we reached our destination, an isolated village in the middle of the regional Chief's dominion. His young son, probably about my age, was my guide and translator, along with a couple of helpers. He might have resented being given this particular mission, as while not exactly unfriendly he remained tight-lipped. Or maybe it was just his nature, as he had an impassive, round face that never seemed to show much emotion. It was dusk when we arrived and I was dizzy with heat and exhaustion. The sound of drumbeats announced our approach and as our bush path emerged into clearer ground, I could see ahead of us the cluster of mud houses and, in front of the first one, across the path, our welcoming committee. Five ferocious-looking (the word that came to my seventeen-year-old mind at the time) men stood at attention, in traditional gear, holding impressive long spears, and stared silently at us. As we came to stand in front of them, the central figure took a step forward and launched into what sounded like a fierce proclamation, stamping his spear on the ground repeatedly as he spoke. "AKABE TAKUTA OKIDE MATOBA KAWOKE AMA TOWA...", he went on for what felt like long minutes – sounds I can only transcribe, regretfully, as onomatopoeic nonsense, as, naturally, I could not understand any of it. Then two of the others went through a similarly spine-chilling routine. Eventually there was a longer pause and, somewhat shaken by then, I nervously asked my silent guide, "What did they say? What did they say?" And the boy turned to me, still impassive, and said: "They say 'Hello'."

So, it turned out that I too had an encounter with tribal elders, albeit of a more benign kind and on another continent. Without having some of the scope and extreme incidents of the tales I have mentioned, my second Zellidja trip with its more unusual destination was certainly more adventurous than my first. Most people to whom I mentioned it did not even know exactly where Liberia was. 'Somewhere in Africa' was often the only response. This was long before Liberia gained notoriety when the terrible civil wars of the 1990s were in the news. Until then it was a country that was not much heard of in the wider world, on the west coast of Africa, between Sierra Leone and the Ivory Coast. Located between a former British colony and a former French one, it was one of the few places in Africa that had remained uncolonised by European powers. Its origin as a country lies in a 'repatriation' project run between 1822 and 1866 by an outfit called the American Colonization Society (ACS). This was created by an odd combination of abolitionist Quakers and rich slavers with the common aim, if for different reasons, of 'returning' freed enslaved people to Africa. Philanthropy providing a codpiece for highly dubious motives. So, they picked an area of the west African coast that had not yet been claimed by Britain or France and funded the first settlements there, the largest one later to become Monrovia, the capital, named after American president James Monroe. No one had bothered to consult the indigenous population and the arrival of the culturally very different freed people was not exactly welcomed by the local tribes. There were even a few skirmishes initially, but US dollars helped to smooth things over sufficiently for the dual elements of the population to coexist. The Americo-Liberians, as the former enslaved people became known, settled mostly on the coast and ran the country as a self-perpetuating elite backed by American money, and the tribal chiefs were paid to supply cheap, and at times what could be called indentured or slave, labour to the conglomerates that soon came to exploit the country's natural resources. The extreme diversity of the indigenous population – sixteen ethnic groups, speaking different languages – greatly helped the dominance of the Americo-Liberian elite to last until the 1990s.

When considering Liberia as a destination I read about Graham Greene's travels there in 1935, which had been motivated precisely because Liberia was so different from other African countries. Not that he appeared to have enjoyed the trip very much. He had been bored by the long, arduous forest treks and later wrote of a "slow footsore journey". I looked up his *Journey without Maps* (1936) and was nearly put off, but there was still enough oddity and mystery about the place for me to persist. My Zellidja letter of recommendation got me a working passage on a cargo ship from Bordeaux to the alluringly named Tabou in the Ivory Coast, which on the map looked quite close to the Liberian border. Everyone on board, from the crew members I had to work with to the captain who invited me to eat at his table along with the half-dozen paying passengers, thought I was crazy – or rather that my parents had been crazy to let me go. For ten days or so, I was subjected to a pretty constant stream of horror stories from the inevitably racist crew, whose lack of much actual 'on land' experience did not appear to stop them being experts on West Africa and West Africans...They enjoyed dangling the spectre of cannibalism in particular and warned me that Tabou was a hotbed of the practice – that there had recently been an attempted murder there linked to it. I just dismissed everything I heard, but in this case I had a surprise in store.

Our ship arrived off Tabou late in the evening. As there was no proper harbour, the ship anchored a short distance from the beach and a wooden platform was tugged next to it to transport goods and the few disembarking passengers to the shore. It was a precarious operation. They dealt with goods first, both unloading and taking on cargo, all of which seemed to go smoothly enough. By the time the platform came back for a Senegalese family we had picked up in Dakar and myself, it was dark. Everything was wet and slippery. The waves were getting bigger and the platform shifted constantly and banged loudly against the side of the ship. We were lowered on to it by a small crane in a makeshift contraption made up of a sort of palette on which we stood enclosed in a protective net of ropes. It looked very scary. Several goes were needed to bring down all six people and their luggage, and those already on the platform had to hold on for dear life as it was buffeted by the waves. Then we were towed towards shore, with just one more obstacle to surmount. About a hundred yards from the beach, there was a line of a permanently rolling wave which the platform was meant to cut through head on, but the tug must have mishandled the manoeuvre of letting go of the platform and we ended up approaching the wave sideways. All six of us slid into the water.

Fortunately it was not very deep and local onlookers, after getting over their surprise at the sight of a drenched young French boy on their beach, helped us retrieve our luggage. A group of them took me to the local judge, a

Sorbonne-educated young Ivorian, who welcomed me into his home, no less curious than his compatriots about my presence in Tabou. Later, as we sat over a meal and I tried to reciprocate his interest, I asked the judge, "...and what sort of cases do you have to deal with?" "Well," he said, "we have an awkward case at the moment that cuts across both our national law and the local customary law. Traditional people here in the bush still practise a form of ritualised cannibalism, which they believe allows the spirit of their dead relative to live on, and two cousins have fallen out badly over the allocation of parts of their common grandfather's body. The disagreement has escalated and threats of murder have been made. Nothing terrible has happened so far, but I have been brought in to resolve the dispute before it gets worse... Not an easy case for me." I never let on that I had heard a heavily distorted version of the story from my racist fellow crew members but it was very hard not to show my surprise at coming face-to-face with a complex reality, having dismissed it all as a fabrication.

Discovering Monrovia was another shock to my sense of reality. Many of the capital's streets in those days had the appearance of a shanty town, but a shanty town on an attempted grand scale. Houses made of makeshift materials, wood and corrugated iron, were built almost on the scale of American Southern mansions, which made them all the more susceptible to a look of faded dereliction. It was as if destitution had to put on an air of pretence. They had been erected by the first Americo-Liberians to arrive, who were going by the only architectural style they had known. They now housed the less fortunate of their descendants or, more likely, the servant classes brought in from the interior. The more successful Americo-Liberians had their own quarters, in more substantial villas, most of which still aspiring to pay some sort of homage to the enormous houses of the South. The aspirations of this elite extended to being assiduous purchasers from the Sears mail-order catalogue, as I discovered when I was taken into some of these houses by my host in Monrovia, the French Embassy's commercial attaché, a single, middle-aged man called Bernard. Sadly, the not always fully functioning infrastructure meant that some of the gadgets and sophisticated equipment were often no more than mere symbols of wealth.

Here too, reality was not always what it appeared at first. After we returned from a crowded house party that Bernard had taken me to "so that I could meet interesting people", he asked me how I had got on. Excitedly, I told him that I was really pleased because I had met and become quite friendly with a young man who was actually "the son of President Tubman!" "Ah yes," came his blasé response, "...but which one?" The supply of official and unofficial-but-recognised sons apparently ran into double figures. Although I gained some understanding of how the system worked, I did not get very far, unsurprisingly, in penetrating the top echelons of the Monrovia elite. Mostly they seemed to react to my interest in Liberia with amused surprise and soon put an end to our exchanges. And, indeed, why should they have indulged this out-of-place white boy asking too many questions.

I moved on from the strangeness of this otherworldly city to an equally odd and self-contained universe in the middle of the dense forest area of the interior. Through an introduction from Bernard, I was invited to stay with John and Betty, a middle-aged American couple living on the vast Firestone rubber plantation, the largest in the world, at that point anyway. John was a middle-ranking manager and Betty was involved in what she referred to as "religious work" there. It was the first time in my life that I experienced people saying grace before a meal. And, indeed, they were very gracious to me, displaying all the generous hospitality typical of their Southern background. However, no amount of this could erase sharp feelings of dissonance at the sight of a place that looked like a harsh workcamp.

John and Betty lived in a well-appointed, air-conditioned bungalow in a cluster of similar dwellings dotted about on a couple of small hills in the middle of the domain, overlooking the forest. These were the homes of the American managers, all white. Out of view, but not far away, were the dozens of closely lined-up wooden cabins in which the black workers lived. I was not offered a proper visit to these but was told that each one was meant to accommodate twenty or thirty workers in basic bunk beds in what looked like very bleak surroundings. Hundreds of men were brought in from their distant villages to live and work on the plantation for several months at a time before returning to their families, to be replaced by another lot. This system ensured employment was precarious and the workforce came from diverse ethnic groups, thus minimising the potential for organising for better conditions. As John and Betty conclusively and pithily said to me, following too many questions on my part, "Things run really smoothly here." I wanted to talk to them about how the whole enterprise worked, they wanted to show me the full-size golf course that had been created on the estate for their entertainment. Not for the last time in my life, I was experiencing the dilemma of being in the company of very nice people whose attitudes and actions I could not approve of.

It was my curiosity about where the men came from that took me further into the bush. By chance, I met Pete, an American Peace Corps volunteer, as we were squeezed together in a collective taxi. I told him I was keen to see how people lived in the deep bush, away from the small town we were both staying in. Luckily for me his aid work meant he was friendly with the region's tribal chief and the latter agreed to lend me one of his sons, who I was to know as Chris although he probably had another tribal name, to take me for a short stay in a typical remote village. This is where we were given the colourful welcome described above, the elaborate nature of which was not of course for my benefit but to show respect to the Chief's son. The semi-mute, impassive Chris represented local power. I, on the other hand, naturally became an object of curiosity. The isolated village had most probably not seen any aid worker, and therefore any white person, for several years. Babies in arms and toddlers aged two or three were brought to me by their mothers to touch my skin, and cried or laughed, or both! A few looked at their fingers to see if my strange colour had come off.

There were many women and children in the village, as well as a small number of older people, but very few men of working age. I was told they were away working but it was not easy to get anyone to elaborate. Unsurprisingly, I saw no trace of organised resistance to the regime there or anywhere else I travelled through. I did see plenty of evidence, because it was really in full view, of how the clientelism functioned – local chiefs becoming prosperous organising the supply of cheap labour to the large companies. It would take another twenty-five years of festering before conflicts and civil war would erupt in a devastating way and put Liberia on the front pages of world news.

Starting out on my way back to Tabou, I got a lift in a crowded open-backed lorry. There must have been thirty or forty bodies pressed against one another, not counting a few animals too – I seem to recall a goat, though I could not be sure. I was the only white person there, and it brought home to me in a very visceral way what I had experienced in quite a few similar situations in the previous few weeks, whether in the house parties of the Americo-Liberian elite or amongst the mud huts of the bush village, the awkward and disconcerting feeling of being the one who is different. The memory of that feeling was imprinted on me and helped in later life understand, at least in a more empathetic way, the unsettling experience of difference.

My next mode of transport to reach the border with the Ivory Coast was even more unusual. For a few dollars I was offered to be taken along a river in a traditional dugout canoe to a border village. I sat opposite my guide and paddler, with my bag behind me, and on the floor of the canoe between us an impressive-looking machete and some recently caught large fish. Communication was minimal as he could not speak either English or French. As we moved downriver, I admired the dense forest on either side and let my left hand drift into the cool water. I had on my wrist one of those black-fronted diving watches in vogue in France at the time but not yet common in deepest Liberia. I became conscious of my paddling companion's constant staring at it and started having paranoid thoughts about his grabbing his machete and cutting it off my wrist. Just as I tried to dispel these lurid thoughts, he did lunge forward. He grabbed his machete. Then, as I recoiled in fear, he quickly cut off a bit of still-bleeding fish at his feet, gestured forcefully for me to take my hand out of the water, dangled the piece of fresh fish in its place and pointed so that I could see a swarm of small fish feasting on it... He had spotted a few scratches on my left hand and had clearly been worried that blood could attract these flesh-eating little beasts. Had I not needed it so badly for the rest of my trip, I would happily have given him my watch. But maybe he would not even have been interested...

I have to confess to pangs of retrospective fear when I think back on this whole trip to Liberia. I was scared at times as described above but I do not remember having a real crisis of anxiety at any point – but maybe that is down to the naivety and optimism of youth. I know these are different times but in hindsight it does seem to have been a fairly foolhardy undertaking. But then I feel somewhat guilty about these retrospective doubts as the reality is that I never encountered anything untoward during the entire journey. Plenty of persistent curiosity, sometimes mocking curiosity, but never in a nefarious way. Plenty of generosity and practical help too. And always, tolerance of my presence, however odd it was.

From the vantage point of over fifty years later, I can see that my Zellidja experiences were some of the peak moments of my life. That early sense of achievement did carry the risk of a legacy of raised expectations, instilling the illusory hope that life would carry on in an upward curve. But that in itself was a useful lesson as life soon reclaimed its zig-zag course, and the acquired resilience did at least help me cope with it.

In the time of fear – part one

There has been no shortage of fear in the last two years. It did not appear suddenly, in one fell swoop, but has gradually crept in. It followed the geographical spreading of the pandemic, and then became a pervasive presence in our collective perception, a permanent background fear of catching the marauding virus. The fear ebbs and flows as the virus subsides and then rears itself in a different form, but it has not disappeared yet. In fact, out of the last twenty-four months, only the first two could have been considered free of all restrictions and therefore thought of as normal. In these dislocated times, I find it is even more of a comfort to be living by the sea, with easy access to the open air and unlimited horizons, where you can easily convince yourself that the almost permanent winds will blow away the airborne nasties. I never forget that these remain around in shops and streets but the seashore feels like a welcoming safe space that is never further than a few minutes away.

My now daily routine of an early morning walk along the beach, whatever the weather, has become a sort of secular rite that sets me up for the day. And it never fails to stir, invigorate and sometimes just delight – whether it's a biting easterly wind making my face tingle with cold or a spectacular sunrise throwing its copper-like reflections over the shiny films of water left by the receding tide. On the way out, I walk as close as possible to the edge of the sea to get the full effect of the sound of rolling waves, accompanied by the odd cacophonous noise of seagulls. I revel in the fact that these are natural sounds only. And most mornings, at some point, when the seagulls go quiet for a bit, I pick up another sound, amplified over the water, the sound of laughter. Then I spot them, the few behatted heads of women wild swimmers. It was the most striking thing about discovering them from the beginning, how happy they were, what a good time they were having. This was no ordeal to be overcome, it was something embraced with enthusiasm and joy.

Apart from the daily sight of the enticing beauty of the sea itself, I suppose it was the sound of that laughter that finally made me overcome my fear of the cold water and take the plunge as it were – though I have not managed an early morning dip so far. After a few weeks here I started going in, usually in mid-afternoon two or three times a week, in a solitary fashion, opposite 'the blue house' (a local marker of a rock-free area) on East Beach. It was less of a shock than I had imagined and, as is clear, there was no life-threatening blockage of my narrowed arteries. The best part is unsurprisingly when you come out, for me anyway. There is a strange sense of tingling warmth when you emerge from the water. As if your body, having received a benign electrical charge, is now suffused with a buzzing feeling of elation. And, it has to be said, a satisfying sense of accomplishment. The funny thing is that it actually leaves you wanting do it again soon. There is definitely something addictive about it. With the help of hastily acquired hat, socks and gloves, I carried on until early November – then travel and illness, and really quite bad weather, interfered. As it is a lot to do with psychological motivation – you need to want to do it, and to keep wanting to do it – I lost my nerve for a while. Then, as the first of the new year was a bright sunny day, I finally managed to break the spell and force myself in (briefly...). It was helped by the fact that I was joining dozens of others taking part in what's known locally as the annual Loony Dook. As I squeezed my eyes shut against the low sky, swimming as vigorously as I could manage, I had a fleeting image in my mind of lolling about in the warm Mediterranean waters of Bab-el-Oued as a boy, and, not for the first time, I was struck by what a long way north my life has taken me.

There are other small comforts to be found in the reassuring ways of a small town. Inevitably you fall in with how things are in the place you live in – small town brings out small-town ways. I chat daily to the friendly newsagent. I have given up my strange addiction to shopping in large supermarkets. (I used to justify it to people close to me and others by saying I was getting pleasure from bringing home, well, not the bacon, as we are a non-meat household, but let's call them the victuals, a leftover trace of some atavistic hunter-gatherer streak.) Like everyone else, I put up gracefully with the coolness of the young men and women serving briskly in the artisan baker. I am on 'ach-no-worries-you-can-pay-me-next-time' terms with the greengrocer whenever I forget my wallet. I readily pay a bit more to buy coffee as beans to be ground by the lady who calls me 'love' in the deli. (Ever since I was first called this as a nineteen-year-old visiting French boy by a bus conductor in Doncaster – yes, Doncaster, and it would have been 'luv' – it is one of those things I have never quite got used to.) The cash register people in the small supermarket often ask me, "How are you doing today?" and appear to mean it. Little strokes of goodwill and friendliness abound.

There is though one notable thing we have not yet fallen in with here. It is not an uncommon sign of these troubled times, I know, but it is very much 'dogsville' here, more so than anywhere else I have seen. I should hasten to add that the downsides of this are minimal. Maybe it is do with Scottish civic pride being more developed than in England – which I think is indubitably the case – but almost all dogs are well trained and almost all owners are responsible. The beaches stay clean in spite of daily dog invasions. The town itself has long decided to make them welcome, with every other shop having water bowls on the pavement and, most surprisingly, cafés and restaurants allowing, even inviting, them in.

We do not currently have a dog but did have for almost fifteen years. A teddy bear on four legs, a border terrier called Billy. A dog from one of the brighter, if not the most biddable, breeds, he was headstrong and characterful, and naturally became part of the family. There were not so many of them in Oxford, so there was a sense of belonging to the same club when you met another border owner with their pet. After we lost ours, we occasionally came across a lookalike, gazing with a pang of longing at 'another Billy'. When we moved here, though, we realised after a few days that there were so many of them you could literally never go out without spotting one or several. There were just too many 'Billies' to remark on, and the poignancy began to fade.

Meanwhile, we just appreciate that we get a chance every day to realise that it is impossible not to be cheered by the sight of a happy dog running around on the beach. So, in this time of fear, solace is found in all the small ways of small-town living, in the habits and conventions of both humans and dogs around us in this little corner of the Scottish east coast.

Fitting in

Returning from Liberia to take up my place as a student at the *Institut d'Etudes Politiques* (known as *Sciences Po*) in Paris in October 1967 was a culture shock all right, but I faced it by just trying to fit in. In fact, I am now slightly embarrassed at how easily I found my inner chameleon and made myself at least *look* like every other male student there. So, following the conventions of that place at that time, most days I did wear a blazer and even a tie. It was not to last very long. But it was a way of coping with feeling an outsider, not to say an interloper.

I have to say something here about the French higher education system because it was quite different from that of the UK. Access to tertiary education was much wider in France (by a factor of three) but it was very much a two-tier system. The main difference, at least in the first tier comprising the vast majority of universities dotted around the country, is that it was not selective. Apart from some degrees, like medicine, that had special entry requirements, once you had passed your *baccalauréat* (equivalent to A levels in England), getting into a university was simply a question of registering and paying a small administrative fee. No application process, no visits to choose your university, no expected grades to achieve, no interviews, no offer of places, and certainly no tuition fees. You usually went to the university nearest to where your parents lived, just as you would have gone to your local school. In many cases, you still lived with your parents (a situation which had quite a lot of implications in terms of the relative maturity of same-age cohorts of British and French young people at the time). But 'ordinary' universities were just the basic layer, where the vast majority went. Ranking above them in desirability and difficulty of access were the various specialised institutions collectively known as the *Grandes Ecoles*, the most prestigious numbering just over a dozen, with *Polytechnique* being perhaps the most famous. Many of them were on the maths and science side of things. There were fewer on the arts side, the *Ecole Normale Supérieure* and *Sciences Po* among them.

All of the *Grandes Ecoles* were highly selective but with these, too, there were major differences with the UK: access was on the basis of competitive entrance exams, not interviews, with very few places and large numbers applying. In common with other institutions, there were no tuition fees. In order to stand any chance of success in the entrance exams, you had to have attended a couple of extra years' study after the *bac* at the few *lycées* that offered this. The classes were called *classes préparatoires* or *prépas* for short. Bear with me, as all this will have relevance to events to come.

Sciences Po was meant to be the necessary step for getting into the *Ecole Nationale d'Administration* (known as *ENA*) as a postgraduate, which, until very recently, was the hothouse training the top civil servants, politicians, technocrats and business leaders destined to head up the elaborate and well-oiled machinery of the French state. But even if you did not make the *ENA*, *Sciences Po* was seen as a good way to enter journalism, publishing or politics. This is what had attracted me. But my joining it had been opportunistic. Apart from entry through the selective exam, it also accepted a few candidates on the basis of exceptionally good results in their *bac*, and this is how I managed to gain a place. I have to mention this, at the risk of sounding boastful, because that fortuitous situation had in it the seed of my limited time at *Sciences Po*. It was at the root of my feeling an outsider. I discovered that most of the other students had spent two years preparing for the entrance exam in *classes prépas* or in many cases in fee-paying institutes, crammers for entry into the *Grandes Ecoles*.

I soon realised they were indeed much better equipped for the real hard slog of studying at *Sciences Po*. They had been trained in the intellectual methodology and general approach of the school, and had become used to the level of work required. Whereas for me the relentless amount of reading and essay- and presentation-writing involved came as a shock. Even my good *bac* grades had not been the reward of assiduous revision but mostly the result of having been particularly lucky with the topic in my philosophy exam (to do with existentialism, which I had been especially interested in) and the high marks I obtained in English, which had come easily as thanks to my travels I had become fluent. No hard slog involved there.

So, not only were my fellow students older and better prepared, the vast majority were from a particular milieu, the Parisian *haute bourgeoisie*. You very much felt that the institution was there to serve a self-perpetuating elite, that it was an exclusive club, with the door ajar to let in only a few token outsiders like me, but where a privileged group still retained an inside track – and certainly behaved with a sense of entitlement and superiority. (In that respect, at least, if you think of Oxford and Cambridge, there was a degree of similarity with the British system.)

The only two people I became close to in my year at *Sciences Po* did nothing to dissolve that impression. A sort-of-love-affair with the daughter of a well-connected family from the 16th *arrondissement*, and friendship with a scion of an old-style aristocratic family, now deeply enmeshed in that same bourgeoisie, both exposed me to backgrounds that, although new to me, were not untypical of many of my fellow students. With hindsight, they have remained with me more as revealing sociological explorations than as relationships.

Marie-Christine could indeed claim that she wasn't living with her parents but that was putting a bit of a spin on reality. She had the use of the servant's bedroom (the *chambre de bonne*) perched on the top floor of the posh nineteenth-century block of flats where her parents had their vast apartment. Most of the time, she would prefer for us to go to my tiny bedroom in a hall of residence during daytime escapades from lectures or the library but once or twice she took the risk of sneaking me into her room, though I could see that she did this with great reluctance. I soon understood why. She was engaged to the son of another *bonne famille*, a relationship highly approved of by all parents concerned, partly, she admitted, because it would be beneficial to both fathers' positions. I suppose that in a very relative way I was her 'bit of rough', her experimenting (not very dangerously) with a cross-tracks fling before settling down to a quasi-ordained marriage. The whole set-up was not only unfamiliar to me but wholly puzzling, in fact hardly credible, but this was the France of pre-May 1968 (just...).

These particular ways of courtship and betrothal among the Parisian bourgeoisie were revealed further with my friendship with Charles de B. He came from one of the few aristocratic families that have preserved their privileged economic status by judicious marriages with successful commoners, trading their titles and occasionally old decrepit chateaux for an injection of cash. For some reason, Charles took a liking to me, perhaps because he could see that I did not know many people in Paris, and that my difference from his usual circle was sufficiently diverting for him to let me in to his world in a tentative way. I was asked to have tea with his mother in their plush residence (also in the 16th *arrondissement*), so that she could be satisfied I suppose that I would not be too corrupting an influence on the family's oldest son.

Once I had passed muster, Charles invited me to a couple of functions typical of his milieu. This took quite a lot of effort on his part as I needed induction into a whole convention-laden process totally unknown to me. These events were effectively formal balls, where male attendance was limited to those who appeared on leading families' lists of young men deemed to be worthy of being potential husbands for their precious daughters – and were known as *rallyes*. Occasionally, listed individuals such as Charles could top up the male contingent with duly approved guests, which explained my two invitations. Having explained the whole set-up, Charles then had to instruct me in the details of the dress code (socks *had* to be black silk) and the complex etiquette of these occasions. However much he helped with fulsome introductions and generally looking after me, I could never feel more than on the margin of these close-knit circles. Fascinating though it was to observe, I remained as much of an outsider in these *Bois de Boulogne* venues as I had been in the mud-hut village deep in the Liberian forest.

Neither the love affair nor the friendship were to survive what was to come in the spring of 1968...

'Sois jeune et tais-toi'

The events of May and June 1968, first in Paris and then throughout the country, were an epoch-defining moment for France. For me, whilst they were some of the most intensely lived times of my life, they are also some of the most difficult to write about. I can't assume too much knowledge of them, as for most people nowadays they are only vaguely remembered as a student revolt in Paris, long ago. This seems to point to much explanation being required, as it turned out to be a lot more than that – for a short period it became an almost revolutionary upheaval threatening to bring down de Gaulle's government and the whole regime, and in the end they did profoundly transform French society. On the other hand, I can't help feeling that too many words have already been expended on the subject, and details can easily be found elsewhere. There is also the pitfall, which I hope will be avoided, of sounding like an elderly man rather pathetically reminiscing about his street-fighting younger days. But I can at least bear witness as I *was* there, involved every day of those two months, and the fact remains after all these years that the whole experience changed my life – as indeed it did for many of my contemporaries.

I can certainly give a brief account of the actual beginning of the revolt because I happened to be there, on the right street, at the right time, quite by chance. And because it provides a classic example of how small events, given the right context and favourable conditions, can trigger off major crises.

Friday 3rd May 1968 was a sunny day in Paris. As I left *Sciences Po* in St Germain early in the afternoon, I decided to walk back part of the way to my student residence, along the boulevard St Germain and then up the boulevard St Michel to look into bookshops. By the time I got within sight of the little square on the side of the Sorbonne building halfway up the *Boul'Mich*, it was full of gendarmes and police vans and young people were gathering around them. As I drew nearer, the crowd was growing rapidly bigger and angrier, surrounding the vans, banging on their sides and blocking their way out onto the boulevard. People started shouting, "*Libérez nos camarades!*" The comrades in question had just been bundled into the vans. It did not take long to find out what had happened.

A little earlier there had been a meeting in the courtyard of the Sorbonne attended by fewer than a hundred left-wing activists from the *Mouvement du 22 Mars*, normally based in Nanterre, a newly-built university in a suburb of Paris. There, they had been campaigning for months to obtain various rights – all of which, by the way, would have been commonly accepted in any British university at the time, among them the right to visit both men's and women's halls of residence, and especially the right to hold meetings. The vice-chancellor (*recteur* in French) of Nanterre responded to the students' growing campaign of disrupting events by closing down the whole university – hence their decision to call a meeting in the Sorbonne itself. Given the poor attendance and the trouble-free nature of the meeting, it could easily have been of no consequence. But perhaps out of solidarity with his Nanterre colleague, or fearing that things could degenerate within the precinct of his august institution, the Sorbonne *recteur* took the most extraordinary decision to call the police to clear the courtyard.

The officers in charge of the gendarmes and CRS (anti-riot police) who turned up made the next fateful mistake. They told the people attending the meeting that if they filed out in small groups through the side door and into the Place de la Sorbonne, their identity papers would be checked and they would be allowed to go free. In reality, the women were allowed to go (an odd sign of these backward times) but the men were arrested and pushed into the police vans. They could not have chosen a worse time of day to do this – between 4 and 5pm student numbers were boosted by school pupils coming out of the nearby high schools, so a large crowd built up quickly. As the throng grew, so did the outrage. The vans were surrounded and prevented from leaving the square. Police reinforcements soon arrived and in the predictable fashion of the times set about dispersing the crowd with tear gas and fierce baton charges. What was different that day, however, is that the ever-increasing crowd of young people resisted and fought back. This was an entirely spontaneous reaction. These were young people who just happened to be there – hardly surprising, given this was right in the middle of the Quartier Latin, the student area. This was not, as the government would claim the next day, led by 'agitators' or even political activists – if students like me were present, it was by sheer accident. And I saw no one organising the resistance to the police action. It was quite simply an explosion of what the French call '*ras-le-bol*', an outburst of 'we can't take any more'. (Many years later, while living in London, I saw similarities with the start of the Brixton riots of 1981.)

There were many factors behind this 'we've had enough', beyond the sheer outrage at the duplicity of the police on that day, but with the passage of time there are two that for me stand out. An objective one to do with numbers, and a more subjective one which has more to do with perception. The first thing is simply that the baby boomers had arrived. The generation born after the war had reached university age, in such huge numbers that the non-selective part of the French higher education system could not cope. Student numbers had nearly trebled between 1960–61 and 1967–68, reaching six hundred thousand that year (more than three times the UK equivalent). And, of course, the infrastructure was not there for them. The result was packed amphitheatres where hordes of students went to listen to ageing professors give the same lecture they had been doling out for the past twenty years. In ordinary universities, as opposed to the *Grandes Ecoles*, there were no small group seminars, no discussions, certainly no tutoring, and no one had even heard of the concept of student support or pastoral care. At the end of each year, you sat exams in which up to 50 per cent failed. You then either repeated the year (thereby increasing numbers even more) or gave up completely. It was a chaotic, overcrowded, old-fashioned system which churned out, sausage-factory-like, batches of poorly equipped graduates into a job market where many could not find a suitable job.

But even more importantly, to explain that burst of anger on the boulevard St Michel, was the perception by most young people of their place in French society. France had not experienced the explosion of youth culture that occurred in the early to mid-sixties in Britain, the arrival of pop music, the end of deference and the advent of a more permissive society. There was a trickle of similarities – such as the fact that yes, pop music had made an appearance – but the point is that it was resisted much more than in Britain, widely derided and mocked by adult society. It may be difficult for a British audience to believe, but pre-1968 French society was a highly hierarchical, sclerotic society, morally repressive, and certainly un-permissive, and one which, quite frankly, was not at ease with its youth.

It was a society where, all too often, young people were treated as potential moral dissidents, potential subversives who had to be constrained and controlled. A society that treated its young people as children for as long as possible, and not as young adults, and expected them to conform to strict moral and social codes. And, crucially, if you transgressed in the slightest, say by having long hair as a boy or by wearing a miniskirt if you were a girl, you would be treated daily with at the very least condescension, derision and contempt, and occasionally insults. All things the French can be pretty good at engaging in – and to be slightly facetious, just imagine your worst experience with a rude café waiter or a grumpy Parisian taxi driver or a petty, inflexible bureaucrat who stubbornly ignores your simple and sensible request – and you will get a sense of what most sixteen-to-twenty-five-year-olds repeatedly experienced in their lives in pre-1968 French society.

There is a photograph which I think perfectly captures the feelings of young people on the streets that afternoon. It shows a young woman standing alone in the middle of the boulevard, probably facing a row of baton-wielding police a few metres away. She is sticking her tongue out at them, in a bold display of provocative disdain. But when you look closely, you can see there is enough anger for her to want to stand her ground and resist: her right arm, slightly hidden, is holding a *pavé* (a cobblestone). Behind her, on the pavement, there is a small group of students and school pupils who no doubt were about to join her in the fray. Many hundreds of young people ended up opposing the police until late that night. By the end of the confrontation, five hundred police and demonstrators had been injured and six hundred students arrested.

Among them, in the first batch bundled into the police vans at the beginning, was a then little-known Nanterre student called Daniel Cohn-Bendit. A red-haired, fresh-faced, gifted orator, he would soon become one of the emblematic figures of the events. An image of his grinning face looking up to a helmeted CRS towering over him exemplified the spirit of joyful defiance that would characterise much of May 68. Along with many others, he found his voice in that period.

One of the most significant of the posters that were created at the time symbolises starkly what French young people had been up against. It shows a young boy with the silhouette of a larger figure standing behind him, putting a hand over the young boy's mouth. The larger figure is easily recognisable as General de Gaulle, and the caption reads, "*Sois jeune et tais toi!*" – "Be young and shut up!"

Spiral

The whole 3rd May episode set a pattern that would be repeated time and again during the coming weeks: relatively modest demands from students, first refused point blank by university authorities, then met with over-reaction, and finally countered by violent repression from the state – thereby starting the whole cycle again on a larger scale. It is revealing to recall that the Movement of 22nd March in Nanterre, whose small meeting was the trigger for the enormous conflict that followed, had been campaigning for rights and freedoms that would have been taken for granted in British universities. Their grievances went from the appalling learning conditions (overcrowded lectures, no chance for student participation) to the ludicrous rules of their halls of residence: no right to move furniture in bedrooms, no right to put up posters, very limited rights of visits across male and female halls, no right to hold meetings (not even to discuss philosophy!), just a few TV rooms where you were expected to engage in worthy pursuits, playing chess or cards. Nanterre was not exceptional. Thousands of students throughout France faced the same situation.

In the aftermath of the Friday afternoon's spontaneous confrontation, the Sorbonne remained closed, a first in its history, and the whole Quartier Latin was occupied by police. During the weekend, many of the arrested students were charged and six of them were jailed in emergency procedures. Meanwhile, student activists were busy trying to organise a response: action committees sprang up in all universities and halls of residence, thousands of leaflets were printed (the main way of mobilising people in those clunky pre-social-media days), and a demonstration was called for the Monday. A new student paper called *Action* was launched and widely distributed, its bold headline declaring, *Demain, la parole est <u>à nous!</u>* (Tomorrow, it's our turn to speak out!) Many of the student activists were used to organising demonstrations against the Vietnam war and, based on that experience, they expected at best a couple of thousand to attend the Monday march. Instead, from their vantage point on the plinth of the statue at the centre of the very large Place Denfert-Rochereau, they could see a sea of faces. Over sixteen thousand had turned up, and not just students but young lecturers too and trade unionists. There were of course several revolutionary groups active among the students, Maoists and Trotskyists especially, but they were relatively small compared to the numbers involved. None of them could have claimed to have been at the source of the movement and certainly not to lead it. In that sense one could say this was a real mass movement, almost entirely spontaneous. A few leading figures emerged, mostly as negotiators with the authorities, but none of them were really leaders who could wholly control and give direction to the movement.

On that Monday, the crowd's impetus was behind calling for the liberation of the arrested students and the reopening of the Sorbonne. Buoyed up by the success of the mobilisation, people cheerfully marched right up to the police ranks blocking access to the university, thinking their sheer numbers would make the police give way. Instead, they were met with a response that far exceeded in its violence what had happened the previous Friday. In repeated charges, batons were drawn and demonstrators and passers-by indiscriminately beaten up. Tear gas cannisters were fired liberally at the crowd as students fought back with cobblestones. The battle raged in all the streets around the Sorbonne for several hours, well into the evening.

Needless to say, the Sorbonne did not get 'liberated' that day. Nor in the next few days as the authorities refused to budge.

Every day saw larger demonstrations, from sixteen thousand on the Monday to forty thousand by Friday, which was to be a turning point. The three student representatives who had finally been allowed to have talks with the authorities were making no progress and called on the demonstrators to occupy the Quartier Latin all night long, if necessary, until the government gave in. With hindsight, perhaps again a rather naive, rather foolish tactic, but these were rather foolish times. So, by that evening there were forty thousand demonstrators encircling the ranks of gendarmes and CRS, who were themselves encircling the Sorbonne. Talks were still taking place and people gathered around little transistor radios to listen to constant news reports on independent stations – the official ones, strictly controlled by the government in those days, were not reporting fully what was going on. By nightfall, because they were bored and they feared an attack by the police at any moment, people started building barricades. Within a couple of hours there were dozens of them throughout the *quartier*.

During that strange interlude, we noticed something quite unexpected. Many well-to-do middle-class residents watching from their balconies started throwing down bottles of water and food to the students – a first sign of what was to come, the start of public opinion turning against the government's intransigence and repressive over-reaction.

At 2am that morning, the news came that all talks had been abandoned and, a few minutes later, the gendarmes and CRS, all six thousand of them, charged. The clashes were extremely violent and lasted for four hours. Several hundreds were injured in the ranks of both students and police. In fact, it was a miracle that no one was killed. Parisians woke up to scenes of urban devastation that had not been seen since the end of the war. With all media now reporting and showing images of the fighting and its aftermath, the shock was enormous throughout the country.

It soon became clear that, by and large, public opinion was blaming the government rather than the students. All the main trade unions seized the opportunity to call a general strike for the coming Monday, 13th May. De Gaulle still thought it was the work of agitators and wanted to send in the army, treat it as an insurrection, but his prime minister, Pompidou, more adept in the art of compromise, prevailed and, finally, late in the day, he was allowed to defuse the situation. On Saturday evening he gave way on all of the three student demands: the Sorbonne would reopen on Monday, the police would evacuate the Quartier Latin, and the arrested students would be freed. The students had won.

'Imagination has seized power'

Monday 13th May saw by far the largest demonstration: nearly a million people, the majority of whom were not students but trade unionists and people of the left – anyone opposed to de Gaulle and his right-wing government took to the streets in what felt like a victory parade. It could also easily have been the final episode, with the main organisers, the official trade unions, satisfied to have done their bit and happy to leave it at that. But by the afternoon, the students, elated at their success and determined to press for a radical reform of the education system, occupied the Sorbonne and an amazing period opened up. *France-Soir*, the Paris evening newspaper, with unusual insight, was already calling it in its huge front-page headline 'a cultural revolution'.

This it was certainly going to be, but by the very next day it had become much more than that. On that Tuesday morning, I was in the courtyard of the Sorbonne where groups of students were again gathered around transistor radios to keep up with the string of surprising news items. From all over France, every few minutes brought reports of workers not resuming work after Monday's one-day strike but instead going out on unofficial open-ended strike and, even more significantly, occupying their factories and places of work. Just as with the student movement, this was a spontaneous action from the rank and file, not one called for by the union hierarchies. Young workers in particular – and there were many of them, a third of the population was under twenty-one – were by and large the ones initiating the actions. They had seen the government give in to the students' demands and thought, "We can do the same!" They too wanted change.

From the post-war period of the late 1940s, France had been experiencing an economic boom, but not one that benefited all equitably – in the ten years prior to 1968, manufacturing production had gone up by 51 per cent but wages and conditions had lagged far behind. A majority of people worked over forty-eight hours per week, sometimes as many as fifty-six hours. One of the first banners over an occupied Renault factory demanded, *Du temps pour vivre!* (We want time to live!) And, crucially, productivity in factories was being driven by constantly increasing work rates on assembly lines and by strict rules all too often enforced by petty supervisors and foremen. Just as young students found French society repressive, young workers found life in factories demeaning and oppressive. It was no wonder that the atmosphere in many of the occupied factories was one of joyful liberation, almost carnival-like with banners and flags abounding.

The same exuberance and sense of newly discovered freedom was also present in the occupied Sorbonne. "Be young and shut up" was no longer the leitmotif of the times; instead, as one poster proclaimed, *La parole est libérée*, the freedom to speak was asserted. And that freedom was enthusiastically exercised by thousands – and not just students – who came to fill the universities' amphitheatres, no longer to listen to old professors but to talk to one another. There were endless debates, day and night, arguing about how to change the education system – and, beyond that, the entire political and economic system. The virus of questioning and speaking out had spread far and wide. These debates also happened beyond universities, in an impromptu manner on many street corners. It was remarkable how often one came across small groups of ordinary people gathering on pavements, having all kinds of lively political discussions. I witnessed amazing scenes during that period, if not of people undergoing instant conversions, but certainly profound changes of attitudes – attitudes to young people, to politics, to the government, to the way society was organised. There was something in the atmosphere that made people question themselves and society in a way they probably had never done before, and sometimes visibly changing their outlook there and then. It was a time when radical change really seemed achievable.

The other key feature of the period was a great flourishing of free expression, characterised by an inspiring cocktail of humour, poetry and politics. It was the era of the silk-screen poster, with clear line designs, simple images with pithy slogans. These posters were to become a distinctive graphic expression of the events. The movement also gave rise to a proliferation of graffiti which creatively captured the spirit of the times. The utopian idealism: *Soyez réalistes, demandez l'impossible* (Be realistic, demand the impossible). Sometimes with a touch of surrealistic poetry: *Sous les pavés, la plage...* (Under the paving stones, the beach...). And often with a libertarian, anarchistic streak: *Il est interdit d'interdire* (It is forbidden to forbid). And a great deal of idealistic wishful thinking too: *Prenez vos désirs pour des réalités* (Take your desires for realities), and sheer hope: *L'imagination prend le pouvoir* (Imagination has seized power).

The contagious wave of '*contestation*' (as it was termed) of the established order touched almost every sector of society.

It was not just the industrial heartlands that were affected but also the normally tame employees of prestigious department stores, the taxi drivers, the professional football players, and even the employees of the *Folies Bergères* in Montmartre. At the other end of that spectrum, the Catholic Church was challenged by its more progressive members, and perhaps most significantly of all the journalists of the state-owned (and strictly controlled) broadcaster, ORTF, also rebelled for the first time ever. In that sense *France-Soir* had been right to call it a cultural revolution – in a matter of days it seemed that France was being transformed from a sclerotic society ('*coincée*', stuck, as the French would say) into one where every aspect of it could be, and was being, challenged by the rank and file.

By the third week of May, there were ten million people on strike. France was at a standstill and the government no longer in full control. On 24th May, de Gaulle made a televised speech in which he tried to reassert the government's authority but he sounded weak and disheartened, and his words had no impact. In fact, that evening there was one of the largest demonstrations of the period in Paris. Unfortunately, it ended up also being one of the most destructive and counterproductive, with the crowd invading the Paris Stock Exchange and setting fire to it. This marked the beginning of a change in public opinion, as concern mounted about the country descending into chaos – this change happened just as quickly as the initial sympathy for the students had done, but this time in the opposite direction.

De Gaulle was still keen to send in the army but Pompidou once again prevailed. De Gaulle wanted to repress, Pompidou wanted to manoeuvre and try to split the movement. He called a meeting of unions and employers and by 27th May he had made huge concessions to the unions: the minimum wage went up by 35 per cent, all salaries went up by 10 per cent, a fourth week of paid holiday was offered, the forty-hour week was reasserted, union rights in places of work were enhanced – all of which actually showing how far behind wages and conditions had fallen. These were significant gains, and yet when the union bosses put them to the rank and file the next day, a return to work was rejected and strikes and occupations continued.

The crisis was now deeply political. Opposition parties were on the verge of setting up an alternative provisional government. Another mass demonstration was called for the evening of 29th May, and was planned to go past the Elysée Palace. This is the nearest point to what could have been an enforced regime change as there was a real risk that the crowd might have tried storming the President's residence. In the event, nothing of the sort happened but, extraordinarily, it was at this point that de Gaulle disappeared for forty-eight hours. He was flown secretly with his close family to Baden-Baden in Germany to meet General Massu, the head of the French military forces still based there since the war. Massu later described de Gaulle as despondent, ready to give up and talking of retiring (oddly, to Ireland). After the two of them had been ensconced in his office for one-and-a-half hours, he claimed to have talked him out of it, telling him: "You are de Gaulle, you have to be the saviour of the nation once again!" Some say that he promised the army would back him and intervene if necessary.

Meanwhile back in France, once they knew that de Gaulle was returning, his supporters got busy rallying all right-wing forces throughout the country to organise a pro de Gaulle show of strength on 30th May. That same day, de Gaulle, in an echo of his historic London call to resistance, chose to make his next intervention in a dramatic radio broadcast. This lasted only four-and-a-half minutes but unlike in his previous TV appearance, he sounded strong and determined, even combative. Starting with a defiant "*Je ne me retirerai pas*" ("I will not resign"), he condemned the chaos and, crucially, announced he was dissolving Parliament and ordering a general election by the end of June, thereby shifting the ground from the streets to the ballot box. The Gaullist party had managed to bring hundreds of coaches from all over France and that afternoon about one million people marched on the Champs Élysées, confirming that not *all* of France had been radicalised by the events.

The tide had turned. The protests, strikes and occupations continued for another four weeks or so but, in view of the approaching elections, dwindled gradually and by the end of June most people had resumed work. A peaceful evacuation of the Sorbonne signalled the end of the events. The parliamentary election returned a clear majority for de Gaulle's party, though at 47 per cent versus 41 per cent for the left, it was not a landslide.

A poster marked the moment with rueful irony: it depicted a flock of sheep under the heading, *Retour à la normale*. But was it really a return to normality? Politically, in the short term not much changed, the political system remained the same, the same people stayed in power. But although de Gaulle won that electoral battle, in a way he lost the war, his authority was fatally damaged and by the following April he had resigned, having been defeated in a referendum. In the longer term it led to the unification of parties of the left, which eventually enabled the election of François Mitterrand.

'IMAGINATION HAS SEIZED POWER'

But it is socially and culturally that the change was most profound. In many ways the May 68 events gave voice to the voiceless, and that voice has resonated down the generations to become an integral part of the cultural fabric of French society. The events brought in a great liberalisation of social mores. In short, it was, for France, similar to the social changes that had happened in Britain earlier (typically with far less conflict), the arrival of youth culture, the so-called 'end of deference' and all that went with it in the 1960s. It marked the end of submission to rigid social and moral norms of behaviour. The women's liberation, gay liberation and ecological movements of the 1970s were direct heirs of May 68. In the shorter term, the education system was indeed reformed: students were given new rights and were allowed to participate in the running of universities; seminars and continuous assessment were introduced; schools allowed pupils' unions; and, to give a couple of examples of smaller changes, schools allowed girls to wear trousers for the first time, and primary school teachers were encouraged to organise class outings – an activity previously unheard of. And there were many other changes, all things that would have been taken for granted in the UK, showing how far behind France was before May 68. It was a defining moment in modern French history, a moment when France became a far less rigid, far freer society.

I have probably not escaped romanticising these events, at least to an extent. In many ways they were difficult times, often violent times, certainly not to be wholly glorified or revelled in, but I would like to conclude with one of my most abiding memories of the period because it is an upbeat one. On 24th May 1968, I was in the midst of a huge demonstration when we heard that Daniel Cohn-Bendit had been banished from France and, appallingly, had been referred to as a 'German Jew' by a government minister. I will never forget the thrill of hearing tens of thousands of voices spontaneously responding by chanting, "We are all German Jews!" Surrounded by like-minded fellow human beings, taking part in that inspired instantaneous outburst of collective solidarity was an ecstatic feeling, still with me today. To paraphrase Wordsworth, in the words actually written about the outset of the real French Revolution, there were mornings during that time when it was bliss to be alive, and of course to be young was indeed very heaven!

In the Gray zone

Even though we are now in Scotland there is no escaping the tribulations of the Westminster government, however much one would want to. Apart from the accumulation of bad news over the consequences of the absurdity of Brexit, there is a current ongoing kerfuffle about a report that everyone has been waiting for by a civil servant called Sue Gray. Journalists have been having a field day coming up with play on words on her name and, not to be left behind, I have made my own feeble attempt in the heading above. We are indeed in a grey zone of uncertainty, but as I have just been writing about May 68, it made me think that whereas political life in France tends to be black and white in Britain it tends to be more like a grey zone (or 'grayscale', as our printers will have it, conveying better a sense of gradation...).

Let me say up front that this does not imply a particular preference on my part. Even as a former *soixante-huitard* I have to confess to sometimes having feelings of 'not again' when I read of yet another street-based mass protest in France. Part of me can't help wondering if it's become an addiction since the May events, a sort of collective knee-jerk reaction. Maybe it's just the part of me getting old – wary of conflict. In many ways, the lack of extreme reaction in Britain is easier to live with on some level, more comfortable. But part of me is also, still after all these years here, astounded at the degree of acceptance and placidity of the

British people – or is it just the English people? A lying prime minister, a cabinet of incompetent non-entities, the BBC being threatened by a ludicrously ignorant minister, the health service being undermined to open it even more to private enterprise, the narrowing down of the purpose of education, civil liberties being trampled on, the justice system being allowed to wither on the vine, the blatant corruption of giving contracts to friends and associates – and more, much more. And still no outburst on the streets. Not that this absence of violent opposition has always been the case. The trope that while the French go for a cycle of extreme containment followed by sudden violent change, the British go for compromise and gradual evolution is broadly true. But there are at least some historical exceptions to that, and some relatively recent ones, especially when looking at street protests – you only have to think back to the anti-poll tax campaign of the early 1990s. Protest can, at times, be counterproductive – it could well be that in May 68, more political change could have been achieved if some of the protests had not descended into anarchistic mob excesses (the setting fire to the Bourse, the desecration of the Tomb of the Unknown Soldier under the Arc de Triomphe).

So, not going down that route may be a good thing, I suppose, if one can trust the way the polls are currently going: that one can hope that all the bad stuff will result in the good outcome of a deeper rejection of the sort of nationalist populism we have been plagued with for several years now, and that this will be expressed, as it should be in a democracy, through the ballot box. Not that this is not subject to manipulation, as shown by moves to make it more difficult for some people to vote – not to speak of a UK-level voting system that is intrinsically unfair when there are more than two parties in contention. A degree of progress has been made on that front with at least a form of proportional representation being used for elections to the Scottish Parliament. Like so many things here, this is of some comfort when compared to England. On a more banal, day-to-day level, I can easily entertain the thought that any stranger sitting next to me on the bus or the train is highly unlikely to have ever been taken in by the Buffoon-in-chief, and that in itself is heartening.

Anyway, back in London, political outrages are committed daily but for now, calm prevails. It looks like you can't have the advantages of a temperate country without paying the price in passivity. We live in a grey zone.

In praise of pubs

I had been living in Brighton for a couple of years when Gérard, an old friend from my *lycée* days in Niort, visited, so I was already familiar with that most British of activities, going to the pub. But as it was his first ever trip to England, he was not. It must have been in 1971. Admittedly he came at a most opportune time – it was during that week between Christmas and New Year, a time of unfettered celebration and general goodwill. But I was still surprised at the extent of his amazement and delight at our repeated pub evenings. Each night I had to drag him out at closing time in a euphoric state which was only partly explained by slight inebriation (I don't think he could manage more than three pints of bitter). He'd just reached that state of being not quite drunk but sufficiently relaxed and free of social inhibition. In a word, jolly. It was not just the drinking that caused his reaction. He just loved being in a pub. He loved the atmosphere. When he returned to France, his thank-you note waxed lyrical about it. It brought out again for me part of why I had fallen in love with life in England. I know it will sound reductive and trivial but pub life was definitely a part of it. (This is from someone who now rarely goes to a pub, except to eat rather than spend a social evening.)

The pub I took Gérard to was a typical, very ordinary Kemptown local, packed with regulars of all ages and backgrounds, quite a few students but also working people who lived in nearby council houses, and a smattering of bohemian eccentrics (real or alleged artists and writers – this was Brighton, after all). The place was heaving because of the time of year, and good humour reigned. Everyone seemed to mix happily, or simply in some cases at least to coexist happily. There was banter between the older customers and the students but it rarely got ill-tempered as everyone knew you were bound to come back the following night and see the same people again. Gérard was wowed by the atmosphere and, seeing things through his eyes, I was able again to see what had attracted me too when I arrived. The whole *modus operandi* was so different from cafés in France. The going to the bar to order and pick up your drinks – meaning you were not subject to the moods of a waiter, and the press while waiting being another chance to talk to people and fraternise. The pub games that facilitate mixing – people playing darts with strangers. The buying of rounds encouraging the joining in in a group – a rare practice in French cafés. The size of the glasses also helped – there is abundance in a pint glass being poured by a loquacious mine host as opposed to a mean-looking *demi* served by a surly waiter. Cafés are places where you sit and drink at separate tables – pubs are places where you meet people, mix and socialise. More like clubs where you settle in and spend several hours rather than somewhere useful to stop by at for a single coffee or beer. You spend an hour in a café, you spend an evening in the pub – and the next evening, and the next... At least, that's what we did when we were students living in Kemptown. You could go in on your own any evening and be certain there'd be someone there you knew.

And as Gérard's visit was during a period of festivities, there was even more communal singing and slapping of backs than usual. He was surprised to be hugged by strangers and receive many offers of drink – which he laughingly accepted, the language barrier dissolving as the beer flowed. He discovered that conviviality was on tap as much as the beer, and freely available. One of his greatest sources of amazement was the contrast between this experience and his previous perception of British people as having a reputation for being cold and distant, offhand with strangers. (This is not an uncommon impression among the French and is one of the myths and legends that exist on each side regarding the other...) His pub experience could not be more at odds with the stereotype.

His enthusiasm reminded me of my own delight at having such easy access to warmth and conviviality. Beyond pubs I had also found informality, friendliness and much easier day-to-day living when I first arrived in Brighton in the autumn of 1969. All of it was a welcome, soothing contrast to being an impoverished student in Paris (a condition, I discovered, which somehow made you blind to the beauty of the city, left you unable to enjoy its charms). After the turmoil of May 68, I found it impossible to return to the hard work and straight and narrow career path of *Sciences Po*. I did not sign the paperwork needed to register for the delayed end-of-year exams in a futile gesture against pledging to abide by rules, and therefore was not admitted into the second year. Behind that gesture was a realisation that I would not stand a chance anyway, having spent very little time studying in the previous six months. I had qualified for a state scholarship because my parents' income was, most of the time, only my mother's modest schoolteacher salary – my father ducking and weaving, involving himself in various small jobs and schemes that never seemed to bring in much money beyond keeping him in second-hand sports cars and nice clothes. Leaving *Sciences Po* meant that source of funding was gone. I was keen not to make demands on my mother's income, so tried to find odd jobs, but it was incredibly difficult to get temporary work. Students were looked upon as 'agitators' and were not particularly welcome. I spent many hours pacing the boulevards of the Quartier Latin selling *Le Monde* – my earnings not only paltry but also having the practical disadvantage of being bags of coins. (I remember well the awkwardness of buying food in supermarkets in fifty-*centime* coins...)

At least I was still a student, and in my second year of a *licence* (BA degree). *Sciences Po* encouraged its students to do a foreign language degree course in parallel with their main studies and I had registered for a degree in English at the Sorbonne. That end-of-year exam I had taken and passed. At the end of my second year, fed up with scratching a living on the streets of Paris, I realised I could apply to do my third year as a French Assistant in Britain. This is how I ended up in Brighton and it was a life-changing move for me. I don't know if this scheme still exists, it has probably been killed by Brexit like so many other things. It had the advantage of being paid, poorly but enough to rent a studio flat and be able to afford going to the pub every night. By my Parisian student standards, this was both secure and plentiful. True, I had to submit to giving several hours of torturous 'French conversation' classes with groups of reluctant, sullen teenagers in a couple of local schools but that was worth it. And I had enough time to do a bit of academic work, had access to Sussex University library, which also ensured I felt I was still leading a proper student life.

I was already a little bit in love with Britain before I came to Brighton. I had an English girlfriend in Paris and after she returned to the UK I visited frequently. I liked the free and easy life compared to France – even after the transformation of May 68, Britain still felt like a much more relaxed society. I did a tour of a few northern English universities, Lancaster, York, Sheffield and Leeds, to speak at meetings about the French events, and was received with warm hospitality everywhere. I have no memory of anti-French sentiment in all my travels and everyday interactions during those days. I am sure it existed then as it does now among some, but it took me years to pick up on it. In those university visits, I was astonished by what were, by French standards, lavish surroundings and facilities – and especially by the incredible fact, again compared to France, that universities provided the Students' Union with premises, including a bar! Even after that induction, I was still awed by what struck me as the magnificence of the Sussex University campus – architecturally designed, low-rise, brick and glass modern buildings nestling in the South Downs, just outside town. I watched lecturers in their own offices giving their time to individual students, groups having animated discussions in seminar rooms, uncrowded lecture theatres and a comfortable library, and thought this is academic heaven. It was worlds away from *Censier*, the grungy modern annexe of the Sorbonne where I had to do my first year.

May 68 for many of its participants had been a *cassure*, a rupture with conventional life that many never recovered from – they did not return to traditional paths. Many in the early 1970s opted out and set up communes in some of the rural semi-deserts of France, where they tried to lead alternative lifestyles in abandoned farmhouses, raising animals and growing crops. Most of these did not survive for long. I was never tempted by dropping out, to use the terminology of the time. I did not want to be out of society, I wanted to help change it. A minority foolishly fell into a vanguardist idea of revolutionary change which took some of them to the extreme of violent action. I was never in danger of losing myself in that false avenue. But like many around me, I continued to believe that political action could lead to a radical change in society and I told myself it did not matter whether I worked towards that in France or in Britain. I had no strong emotional attachment to France – at least not the kind you can feel for the place you were born in. And I could not wholly feel that for Algeria, so there was a void to be filled. I am often asked, "What made you stay in Britain?" The simplest answer is perhaps that I drifted into staying because I felt so much more at ease here than in France. Of such happenstance are life-changing choices sometimes made. And at the time, a bit for the pubs too...

A sense of community

Thinking of pubs, I have just read a headline that said, "Britain's oldest pub forced to close after 1,229 years". Whether or not Ye Olde Fighting Cocks in St Albans can claim that title (there are probably other contenders around the country), it appears that the pandemic has finally killed it. Even before the lockdowns and restrictions, the previous ten or even twenty years have seen thousands of pubs disappear. Closure is the most extreme fate. The evolution of pubs in the time I've lived here has followed two opposite trends. Many of the surviving ones have been transformed away from their essential nature as 'locals' by the invasion of games machines and huge TV screens always turned up to maximum volume for some sporting event, aping the sports bars of the United States. A long way from the demotic club-like atmosphere of a traditional local. The other trend, and admittedly more to my taste, has been the gastropub phenomenon, the arrival of good food in many pubs, starting in cities but having now spread throughout the country. In passing, I would say that this has had the consequence that you are more likely to get high-quality food, creatively cooked with fresh ingredients, in a British gastropub than in many an ordinary café-restaurant in France, where you will often be served industrially pre-prepared limp dishes. An historic paradox.

There are of course some residual locals surviving in many areas, playing their traditional role in the community. I enjoy

A SENSE OF COMMUNITY

their existence in a vicarious sort of way, mostly through my stalwart friend who lives in a small Sussex town and still makes regular use of his couple of favourite ones, not so much for extensive drinking but for the social connections they provide. And for me it is always heart-warming to hear stories about his cast of regular characters and tales of new encounters, quirky conversations and odd anecdotes – comforting to know that this sort of social interaction is still thriving in places like his home town. In an even more strongly affecting way, I always find myself deeply touched when I read of pubs saved from closure by their local communities. This is not an infrequent occurrence, people clubbing together to own the place collectively, often combining the reopened pub with a local shop or post office, helping to maintain, often in very small communities, a place where people can both get services and socialise. A communal effort for a common good.

Perhaps it touches me because it brings back what struck me when I first got to know Britain, when I first realised how this sense of community was so widespread and deeply rooted. That, and the feeling of being at ease with surrounding society that I've already mentioned, are what caused me to fall in love with Britain. I found myself in a country awash with initiatives involving cooperation with, and goodwill towards others. There seemed to be an unquenchable thirst for forming groups, clubs and societies around all interests and causes. Each one an affirmation that it is better to do things together for a common purpose than alone for individual gain. I think it is probably easier for an outsider to notice the exceptional extent of this.

Coming from France, the most visible part of this phenomenon was the plethora of charity shops and fundraising activities for good causes. My surprise was mixed with a degree of critical scepticism, imbued as I was – and still am – with the belief that funding cancer research and 'saving the children' should primarily be the task of a democratic state through a fair system of taxation. But one could not fail to be impressed by those thousands of people across the country volunteering to give their time and the millions contributing their hard-earned cash. Their good intentions could not be faulted.

It is sometimes said that the British are the most clubbable of people but I think this trivialises the importance of that characteristic as it implies that it is to do with entertainment only, which is far too reductive. Historically, it encompasses the formation of trade unions and cooperatives, the whole self-improvement movement of the Workers' Educational Association and more recently the credit unions, and now touches every aspect of everyday life, education, health, environment, as well as politics and economics. I found that this readiness to come together to do good permeates the country. There is nowhere where you can't find groups of volunteers running food banks, cafés for those who find themselves homeless or jobless, garden projects promoting mental health, engaged in urban wild planting transforming rundown areas, campaigns to save green spaces or still-useful old buildings from developers – a myriad of activities and causes in which people experience the joys of communal endeavour for the good of their community. Every time I see a report of such efforts in a local paper or on television news, I am deeply moved – and I would say this is where pride in a country and, if you want to claim it, real patriotism is to be found.

I once had a fantasy of a series of documentaries, a sort of weekly Best of Britain slot, that would feature a short fly-on-the-wall piece on groups doing good around the country – showing the highs and lows, the joys and challenges of working together towards a common goal, the range of characters involved, and above all the satisfaction of making a difference, however small. I thought this could have an enormous feel-good and inspiring impact, as well as honouring the people involved – and make good television. I spoke about it to a good friend, a TV producer, who liked the idea but felt he could not pitch it without a competitive element to fit in with prevalent successful formats – pitting groups against one another and asking the public to eliminate one each week, which to my mind went against the whole concept. But I am sure he was correct about how it would be received by TV executives.

It is true that this yearning to experience a sense of community has been weakened by de-industrialisation, made more difficult to fulfil by the dereliction of traditional working-class areas, vilified by the 'there-is-no-such-thing-as-society' ideology of Thatcherism, caricatured and misused by Cameron's Big Society attempt at distortion, and further undermined by the economic devastation of austerity policies. Yet in spite of it all, it has survived and, in some cases, even grown. One only has to look at the enormous, spontaneous upsurge in voluntary community support groups during the pandemic period to see that it survives in the fabric of society, to thrive when needed. I experienced it in my gut when I first came to Britain and it has stayed with me. It is still there, indomitable, persisting through it all, including the awfulness of Brexit, and certainly even more present, because more deeply anchored, both politically and societally, here in Scotland.

I don't mind sounding sentimental about it – sentiment is justified in this case and there is damn little to be sentimental about in our dispiriting times. I admit unashamedly that I am deeply moved by good intentions, by people meaning well, wanting to reach out and help others. But perhaps when evil intentions and nastiness often seem to have the upper hand (right up to the top of our very institutions), it should be no surprise that finding good is so affecting.

A Brighton honeymoon

Not that I had to join any group or organisation to find good fellowship when I first lived in Brighton – I was twenty and it was easy to meet people. The usual self-centredness of youth meant I was more concerned with making friends and enjoying myself. I think of those times as halcyon days. I realise the passage of years may have given them a rosy tint, but it still feels like a period when by and large fate smiled upon me.

I had not forgotten that first visit to England which had been a high point of my teenage years, that thrilling discovery of a very different society, of a freedom I had not imagined possible. Since then, there had been a few crazy journeys from Paris to visit a girlfriend, and the infatuation with the country had grown, but these brief visits were too hurried and I was too preoccupied with personal gratification to notice very much of the society around me.

Living and working here brought new sensations, and a deeper love, as I found in England an all-pervading and soothing benevolence that contrasted so starkly with the gruff harshness of life in Paris. I was discovering English life with new eyes and finding much to like. Both people and places.

There was the immediate upside of being in unfamiliar surroundings. A myriad of unexpected, disconcerting, fascinating details, however trivial, gave everyday life the shine and glamour of the extraordinary. Everything was noticeable and interesting. Double-decker buses, three-wheeler cars, red telephone boxes, advertising posters using surreal humour, parks where you could walk on the grass, traffic signals with amber lights that enabled you to get ready for green, multiple football pitches right next to one another, public tennis courts, bowling greens, jumble sales, milk bottles on doorsteps, fish-and-chip shops... Strangely, there was something both faintly exotic and reassuringly cosy about all of this. There was also an endearing quirkiness about the place. The first time I saw the Brighton Pavilion, having never heard of it before, it nearly made me laugh. It seemed almost unreal – such an incongruous building in the middle of an English city, it could have been a plywood set for a Hollywood movie.

Also, for the first time in my life, I had a little money. And with money came a bedsit (another English speciality), a stereo system, and the ability to buy *more* music – the day I got my first pay cheque, I went out to complete my collections of Dylan and Beatles LPs, and many others. After a while, I even had enough spare cash to acquire a battered old Volkswagen Combi minibus from some young Australians at the end of their European travels. By the standards of my Parisian student days, this was true abundance.

Even the staffrooms of the two schools I worked in turned out to be surprisingly welcoming environments. I was struck by the informality of the relationships between teachers irrespective of hierarchy. Everyone was on first-name terms, unheard of in a French *lycée* where you would have been expected to make frequent use of *Monsieur* and *Madame*, and where you might easily have gone several years without knowing the first names of your colleagues. It may appear a small thing to remark on but it coloured everything. In a way I took the use of first names as the British equivalent of moving from the polite and formal *vous* to the familiar *tu* in French. It has become more common in France now but was not so then. This informality was prevalent throughout society – from the bus conductor's banter to the market stallholder's greeting of 'all right mate?' Even shopkeepers were generally helpful. There was no longer any need to steel oneself for a possibly unpleasant encounter with a condescending or irascible two-bit counter tyrant every time you went into a shop. And it was not the sickly how-are-you-today fake cordiality of commercial America either. It was simply that most people chose to be pleasant first, as opposed to being aggressive first and pleasant only as a last resort, as was so often the case in Paris. What is more, it did not matter what you were wearing, at least it did not *seem* to matter. Long hair and casual, even outrageous clothes appeared to be accepted with equanimity everywhere. I encountered far more *bonhomie* (linguistic irony...) in Brighton than I had in all my years in Niort and Paris. Strangely, in that respect at least, it felt closer to the atmosphere of *pied-noir* Bab-el-Oued than France.

It was soon after having started that I met in one of these staffrooms someone who had himself only recently qualified as a teacher and he made a point of getting to know me and offer support. I was struggling with my reluctant learners of French, even though the groups were small. (Occasionally I was asked to look after full classes when a teacher was absent and that was even worse.) He almost immediately invited me to his local pub in Kemptown, which soon opened up friendships with a whole gang of people. The easiness with which this happened was a joy – an example of easy conviviality which I had not experienced in Paris. And it is one of the most gratifying features of my current stage of life that I can look back and know that through all changes of life and locations, two people I met then have remained the closest of friends for over fifty years now.

Next door to the high school in Portslade was a primary school and the head asked me over for a sandwich lunch there once a week and hold a 'French conversation' class with some of his staff. This was in the days of a long-forgotten educational initiative, the Nuffield French course in primary schools, an experiment in teaching some basic French to young children – soon to be abandoned, incidentally. This was excruciatingly painful, partly because I had no technique whatsoever to draw people out, partly because the teachers clammed up, not keen to expose their deficiencies in front of their headteacher. But what struck me most was again the extent of British tolerance. Here was a long-haired young Frenchman, a student fresh from the quasi-revolutionary events of May 68, not exactly proselytising his views but not hiding them either, being treated with kindness, generosity and good humour by a most traditional headmaster, an archetypal middle-aged man, steeped in 1950s manners, and a bunch of very conventional middle-class women, most of whom probably voted Tory. When we did have a conversation in English and I expressed, in answer to their questions, what must have been by their standards pretty radical political viewpoints, they would naturally mostly disagree, and even challenge me, but always with great politeness, moderation and apparent respect. I could not help thinking that in that same situation in France, the likelihood is that I would hardly have been heard for loudly expressed interruptions, acerbic remarks and expressions of dismissive contempt. This is another example of this feeling at ease in British society – an early concrete personal experience of the vaunted tolerance.

I revelled in this cornucopia of informality, conviviality and acceptance. Naturally, with the passage of time, I would later find hidden aspects behind these characteristics. As with all phenomena they contained elements of their opposite, everything is only what it is primarily, always with a bit of its opposite inside. But for now, I relished all of it.

Looking back on that period, years later, when magazine articles began to refer to the 'exciting days of the sixties', I realised that I experienced what was supposed to be the best of the sixties (relative affluence, music, freer sexual mores), right at the end of that decade and into the early seventies, in those last few years of optimism before the oil crisis of 1973. Luckily for me, they coincided with the initial flurry of my love affair with Britain, and gave me a kind of extended honeymoon in Brighton.

The power of parsley

Just as infallible as the joy-inducing effect of watching dogs running on a sandy beach is the power of parsley. There is no savoury dish that cannot be cheered up with a generous sprinkling of bright green, chopped parsley. And the cheering-up starts with the effects on the cook – or at least on me. Never mind comfort food, for me it is the comforts of food that do the trick and, to be precise, the handling and preparation of food, which every time are the source of sustained, sensuous pleasure.

There is plenty of self-help advice telling people to live in the moment, that life can only be good when you are present exclusively in what you are doing. The only problem is that in most circumstances this is easier said than put into practice, but I find that preparing food is something that forces you to do just that. When you are at risk of cutting yourself, you have to cut out everything else. It's a sublime form of escapism, shutting out all troubles and worries and concentrating on the joys of minuscule moments. The attention required to chop the parsley into tiny enough pieces to rain down properly on the ready dish guarantees this. Not missing the burst of aroma released by the first cut of the first leaves. Hearing the crunch of the stems as you cut them into small lengths to be added to the simmering stew. It's a rapturous invasion of all the senses, self-delivered and endlessly repeatable – with all kinds of foods.

Can there be any iteration of dark purple more beautiful than on a shiny aubergine? It provides visual delectation every time I pick one up. And its pristine look, slightly resistant to the first incision of the blade, harbours a soft abundance of flesh that you know will melt into a delicious mushy consistency on being cooked. Its immediate slight discolouration as you cut, a sign of how protected from the elements it was under the smooth, shiny skin and how vulnerable it now is to alteration when exposed. Then, there is the promise of later delights of taste as its pieces lie there for a while, under a light showering of sea salt. Here again you have had to concentrate, not to overdo it, lest you enjoyed too much the feel of the grains between thumb and forefinger.

I love the powerful and pleasurable olfactory assault one sustains when taking vine tomatoes off the stem – an immediate nose sensation whose only equal, not in pleasure but in strength, is when brushing against a geranium leaf. But in this case, if you are lucky enough to have chosen well (or even luckier, to have grown your own), there is the promise of an equal burst of that stirring mix of sweet and sharp when the little small wonders reach your mouth.

I am always in danger of overusing the word sensuous but it has to serve here, and not in a subtle way, when thinking of the peeling and preparing of a mango. It starts with the necessary testing of ripeness, providing a satisfyingly yielding fullness in one's pressing hand, which releases a faint aroma of the fruit. Then the peeling-off, to reveal the full lushness of the yellow flesh, accompanied by the strongest of exotic scents. It can't be other than a moist and messy act, best engaged in privately, to fully switch on all the senses, especially when sucking the last layers of flesh from the inside of the peeled skin, your mouth dripping with fragrant juices.

All food preparation requires such depth of concentration and therefore is true escapism indeed, but at the same time I find it floods me with evocation, diffuse evocation of feelings from other times and places which I can never identify completely when doing it – too busy watching the knife.

Why does cutting parsley give me the same feeling as that pleasurable sense of being wanted? I later hesitantly reconstruct it as a memory of a long-ago gesture, when in a strange kitchen, that promised intimacy (even though that promise was never fulfilled). Why does cutting cloves of garlic fill me with a perception of being in a different place, in Saint-Georges-de-Didonne, taking the children on a beach holiday so they could spend time with their grandmother? Was it simply because said grandmother always put too much garlic in the vinaigrette? But a long way from that trivial trigger, what it now leaves me with is a feeling of well-being, a sense of bathing in happy family normality.

To someone like me, not a great practitioner or fan of DIY, often cack-handed with tools (how was I to know you had to adjust the thingamajig *before* using the thingamabob?), there is an easily attainable satisfaction in successfully wielding that miracle of simple kitchen technology, a good peeler. The most joyful experience is using it on carrots, when the utensil effortlessly unpeels thin layers of skin to reveal the beauty of a bright and dewy bare carrot – I know foodie purists might suggest to only brush and wash to keep the goodness of the skin, and I sometimes do that, but often the temptation of that visual revelation is too much. Carrot pleasure does not stop there – there is the crunchy satisfaction of slicing, the firm resistance, and the repetition of the pleasing plonking noise of the knife hitting the chopping board. And carrots are always a visual gift, their bright orange jollying up other duller-looking vegetables. I can't help at least partly conceiving my dishes with colour very much in mind. Pre-cooking, in the assortment of ingredients, there is great initial delight in composing an assemblage of colours. Cooking tends to dull that initial vision but then the sensual pleasure will have shifted to smell. And if you've planned the ensemble well, there can be another go at being creative with a colourful display on the serving plate.

The cook wholly escapes into their own world not only during the preparation: the cooking itself demands complete attention to timing, stirring, smelling, adding, adjusting heat, synchronising various elements, and yes, even the serving out requires it too. To my partner's occasional impatience, I claim that I can't possibly engage in conversation at the same time as dishing up.

The whole thing is a feast for eyes, hands, nose and tongue – and of course head and heart too. The beauty of this is that it does not require a fancy kitchen or elaborate gadgets – just a small number of utensils and pans, and a functioning cooker. And it is easy to add an essential final touch to ensure a conducive environment, a large bowl filled with multi-hued fresh fruit, oranges, bananas, red and green apples, a vibrant promise of the raptures to come.

Which is lucky for me as we are still living in what we think of as temporary accommodation. For someone so keen on the importance of a nest, it is not a comfortable situation, this feeling of living on the cusp. It can indeed mean being on the edge of something better. But there is the risk of falling over before this has had a chance to happen. Morbidly, I sometimes fear, because of age and conditions, that the falling over could be terminal (given already one heart attack and diabetes, this is not an entirely incongruous consideration). So, in the endless febrile thinking of long nights of sleeplessness, I sometimes have a vision of this makeshift nest being the last one. That it could be this nest, too inadequately made, too provisional, too full of boxed possessions in transit to be loved, that I could fall out of. An inadequate ending for sure. Such are the fears of reaching the sort of age when obituaries don't bother giving the cause of death.

A view of the 70s from my seventies

I was sitting in a comfortable armchair, but feeling uncomfortable, outside the bank manager's office, dreading the moment when the door with the fish-eye spyhole would open to let me in. Was I being observed, secretly assessed by Mr Wagstaff? I thought at the time that it was an odd name for a bank manager, or for anyone for that matter. Then I remembered I had had a pupil called Stephen Wagstaff a couple of years before. Could be a relation of Mr Wagstaff the bank manager... Perhaps I could mention it, as a way of breaking the ice. But then I thought, how stupid, there was nothing odd about the name except to a foreigner, there were probably hundreds of Wagstaffs in Brighton. I went back to rehearsing what I would say. It sounded quite good, in my head anyway. Well argued and plausible, a sound enough case for a loan, even if for an unusual purpose. I had thought about it for several days before filling in the application form and arranging for an appointment. Those were the days when every branch had a manager, and when most customers, at one point or another, had to go through the ordeal of sitting across his desk (it was almost always a man) and wait nervously for his response. I was aware that asking for a five-hundred-pound loan to pay for a holiday in the US when one's account was barely in the black was not going to be easy. And I couldn't just tell the full truth, "Look, Mr Wagstaff, I've just had a painful breakup with my girlfriend and I need to get away for a while...". I imagined the answer.

"What's wrong with Cornwall, Mr Barbannew, or the bracing air of the Lake District?" I had come up with what I thought would be a credible rationale. After a few years' teaching, I had started writing for educational publishers and I was going to tell Mr Wagstaff that I had good reason to believe they would pay me for photographs I would take on my proposed five-week trip around the States. It sounded credible enough. But I knew it would not come out as convincingly as rehearsed. I knew that I was likely to be nervous and that my French accent would become more noticeable. That I would become aware of it myself and that in turn would cause me to make more mistakes, and possibly lose the thread of my argument.

But when I was ushered in, I actually managed to make my case reasonably well, albeit in a rather curtailed way. I still got the response I had expected from Mr Wagstaff. "You do realise that our personal loans these days are usually given to help people make a major purchase, like a car or carpets, or furniture, not to just go on holiday." I tried to come up with back-up arguments, my accent becoming stronger and my reasoning weaker, until Mr Wagstaff, perhaps to change the subject and end the meeting with pleasantries, said, "You are French, aren't you, Mr Barbarno?" "Well, yes, but I took on British nationality about a couple of years ago," I replied. I could see the expression of surprise on Mr Wagstaff's face – "Really?" – and after a short pause, perhaps recalling the gloom and doom of that period, the many strikes, the three-day-week, the constant talk of crisis, the general running down of the old country, the newspaper articles about the queues of people wanting to emigrate to Australia, New Zealand or Canada, he said, "You mean to say you actually decided to..., you *wanted* to become British?" "Well, yes."

"Excuse me for prying but what made you want to do such a thing?" It was not the first time I was asked that question and as by this point I had lost all hope of a loan, I had relaxed enough to expound smoothly on the matter with a catalogue of good reasons, with fluency and feeling, in fact slightly overdoing it when I realised it appeared to be sweet music to Mr Wagstaff's ears. Waxing lyrical about "the most tolerant and the most civilised country", I went on a flight of slightly clichéd but sincerely felt encomiums for Britain, interspersed with "jolly goods" from Mr Wagstaff who, when he could eventually put a word in, said with a broad smile, "Well, that is very interesting, Mr Barbernean. You wouldn't care to come and say all this at our next Rotary Club dinner, would you? Now about this loan, are you sure five hundred is enough?"

The Rotary Club dinner never materialised. Maybe it was one of those invitations that are often offered by middle-class English people out of politeness but are not meant to be taken seriously. I was still getting used to that. Anyway, it may have been a good thing as an extended conversation and further questioning would surely have revealed that I was not exactly on the same *Daily Telegraph* page as Mr Wagstaff and his Rotary Club friends regarding what was going on in the country at the time, economically and politically. While I was supposed to be working on a doctorate thesis for my French university, I had in fact been well settled in Brighton since 1969, becoming a British citizen in 1975. I had drifted into a teaching job in a way that would be impossible today, with just a degree and no teacher training qualification. Fresh from my political activism in Paris, I soon got involved in the National Union of Teachers and the local and national labour movement.

It has become a trope to talk of the seventies as a period when unions had too much power. The right-wing press to this day brings up the spectre of the so-called 'winter of discontent' at the end of the decade as a culmination of this, as a symbol of the alleged anarchy that results from power overreach by organised labour. This ignores a simple fundamental point, that strikes and other union activities are almost always defensive, not offensive – aimed at safeguarding and, if possible, improving the position of workers in the fragile balance that exists between the interests of capital and those of wage earners. It also ignores the wider cultural and societal role of the unions. In many ways, they were mainstays of working-class communities, helping to promote values such as solidarity, mutual aid and self-improvement. The absence of which since then has clearly shown its deleterious effects on society.

But by the late seventies, after a long and relentless campaign of press vilification of the unions, a majority of public opinion accepted the *Daily Mail* version of events, and this was to usher in the Thatcher era. The British car industry, often put forward as a typical victim of that period, was destroyed not by union militancy but mainly by the well-documented financial short-termism of its owners and the unsuitability and incompetence of its managers – too many only there because of their belonging to City-approved circles or because of the right school and university background. And when the latter failed, they were replaced by supposed hard men, professional trouble-shooters, often recruited from abroad to sort out the unions, but instead never failing to make matters worse. I am sure there were plenty of potential Red Robbos in German car factories too, but they also had sound, long-term policies of investment in research and innovation, and well-formed technocratic managers who understood the value of involving their workforce and showing respect for unions.

I am not fond of playing the games of 'branching history', but it is patently obvious to me that we would not be where we are today – the deep disparity between rich and poor, the worsening social inequality – if the trade union movement had not been so weakened. That the extreme imbalance in terms of value accumulating between capital and wage earners would not have been achieved in the last fifty years if unions had been strong enough to resist that particular overreach.

I balk at the usual descriptions of the seventies as basically a drab decade. One with terrible fashion, yes – I recoil in shame and horror at a photo of me taken at an outside party wearing a white suit and a stripy red and white shirt with enormous collars – but a period of lively social and political events and I often found myself in the midst of crowds shaping them, and this time not crowds of revolting students, but ordinary, working people taking collective action in defence of their interests.

I was recently reminded of one of the most significant events of that period by the death of a Labour MP, Jack Dromey, who had become known as a union leader during one particular dispute. Grunwick was a film-processing laboratory in Willesden. Its owner employed almost exclusively female workers from minority ethnic communities and imposed drastic working conditions: low pay, long hours, compulsory unplanned overtime, and petty restrictions enforced by bullying supervisors (women workers were asked why they needed to go to the toilet). Dismissals were frequent and the boss absolutely refused to recognise unions. In August 1976 several workers were dismissed for refusing to comply with a late demand to work overtime. Others came out on strike and the conflict escalated in the following months, including protracted and complex legal proceedings. Two things became significant: the resilience and courage of Mrs Desai, a middle-aged woman of Indian origin, and her fellow strikers; and beyond Grunwick itself, the fact that support for them extended widely across the still predominantly white and male labour movement throughout the country. I recall travelling with a coach load of supporters to attend the mass picket that took place on 22nd June 1977. This was a near riotous affair with thousands of trade unionists and a large police presence, including for the first time the anti-riot Special Patrol Group (SPG) destined to become notorious. In the middle of that crowd, I was reminded of previous times in both Algiers and Paris, and there was a degree of cognitive dissonance that this was now happening in a London suburb. The dispute went on for so long that the Labour prime minister, James Callaghan, appointed a judge to report on it. Lord Justice Scarman recommended that the union should be recognised and the sacked workers reinstated, but the Grunwick owner refused and the union finally gave up in July 1978, having held out for two years. Echoing the words of Jayaben Desai at the time, that strike had been not so much about pay as about human dignity. Its defeat was a portent of things to come in the following decade.

In the time of fear – part two

Right now, the invasion of Ukraine by Putin's troops is in full flow. Like many, I found it difficult to believe he would actually be mad enough to start such a conflict. Yesterday Russian troops shelled a Ukrainian nuclear power plant and a newspaper headline today spoke of a 'catastrophe narrowly avoided'. This came after several statements by Putin implying that he was prepared to use nuclear weapons – with many experienced analysts confirming that he was quite capable of taking this ultimate step. At first, it seemed so incongruous as to be difficult to believe. But gradually a perception built up from Putin's repeated hints that this was no empty threat. Thus, the real possibility of nuclear Armageddon became a reality for the third time in my life.

I have clear memories of the Cuban missile crisis in October 1962 because, unlike most of my contemporaries at the *lycée* in Niort, I followed the news daily, a habit from my Algerian war days that I had not broken. This was in the recent aftermath of our exodus in June 1962 when, irrationally, I still held on to a tiny, unrevealed and totally unrealistic hope that the newly installed Algerian government would issue an invitation to the *pieds-noirs* to return and help build a new multi-community Algeria. (I knew this was a foolish hope, too much blood had been spilt.) I was still in shock at losing the country of my birth and now all around me was the fear of world destruction. It seemed to appear suddenly and then to be gone in a matter of days.

Right now, it does not look like the current crisis will disappear in similar fashion.

It feels like a much more tangible and immediate threat than the other time it was present, but more in the background – in the heightened tension of the Cold War in the 1980s. As it happens, this also followed a Russian invasion, that of Afghanistan, after which Reagan launched a renewed and wider development of nuclear weapons, and notably the deployment of Cruise missiles in Europe. British women at Greenham Common led the opposition to Thatcher's support for US policy. I recall taking part in a CND march that was meant to go past various 'secret' nuclear shelters in south London. Since that time, I have read accounts by contemporaries that speak of living in constant fear, of being haunted by images of the nuclear cloud in their dreams, but I can't say I experienced any of that. Maybe I was too preoccupied with a complicated and often troubled personal life. The here and now was too demanding to worry about what I judged to be an unlikely eventuality. The nuclear threat never seemed more than abstract. Reflecting on it now, I don't remember any time in that period when I felt it was as concrete as it is today.

In all the death and destruction that we are witnessing – mostly helplessly – I find a degree of succour in two features of this war as evidence of the good side of humanity, surviving in a time of conflict. We see in real time a people's tenacity in resisting barbarity. Beyond feeling admiration for the daily acts of bravery, it has made me reflect on the importance of resilience. We live in a culture that elevates instant enjoyment as a desirable permanent condition, which goes with the belief that everything can be fixed, preferably rapidly, whether by drugs or money or other means. But of course, not everything can be fixed and I believe the test of our human mettle is whether we are capable of enduring, not just enjoying. Especially given that in most of our lives we endure more than we enjoy. A realisation that comes from growing older is that every life well lived in the end is a story of resilience. And there is plenty of that on display in Ukraine today.

The other inspiring aspect, in sharp contrast to the deficiencies of our own, is the quality of the leadership shown by Volodymyr Zelenskiy. While we are stuck with an unserious, incompetent buffoon performing a meaningless pseudo-Churchillian act, it is heartening to see a man given to humour live up to the moment, in seriousness, courage and determination, and with such humility. Maybe seeing the funny side of life is good preparation for resistance to inhumanity. It also seems to bring wisdom. In March 2022, in answer to a journalist asking how he was coping, Zelenskiy, casually hitting upon a fundamental truth about the human condition, said:

My life today is wonderful, I believe that I am needed... That's the most important sense of life, that you are needed, that you are not just an emptiness that breathes and walks and eats something.

Feeling needed as a source of happiness. I know this might sound dissonant, this segueing from the life and death issues of war to a general point about society in more ordinary times, but my thoughts on this are meant as a humble homage to Zelenskiy for having highlighted a concept that could be applied so widely. In particular, I believe it's a concept we should put into practice much more in how we organise our workplaces. If, as it appears, we are stuck with an economic system largely based on ownership and hierarchies, we could at least address in a more deliberate way one of the main causes of alienation, the feeling of being just a cog in the machine with no agency. However menial the jobs are deemed to be in any organisation, it should not be beyond the ken of humanity to find ways of making the people doing them feel needed: by listening to their views, by involving them in decision making, by giving them the maximum practical autonomy over their tasks. It is a simple concept that would yield huge benefits. To do everything possible so that everyone could feel able to say, in the words of the valiant Ukrainian leader, "I believe that I am needed..."

Lost in the labyrinth of language

This little story also starts with me waiting nervously in an anteroom, this time of a Magistrates Court in Brighton in 1975, not because of any crime, I hasten to make clear – though I was about to commit a minor offence of lèse-majesté... I was there for the final step in my acquiring British nationality, swearing allegiance to the Crown. I was nervous because I had just been given a small card with the words that I was to solemnly utter in front of the august panel I was about to face. And I could immediately see the problem. It was this bit that jumped at me "...her Majesty the Queen and all her heirs..." The difficulty might not seem obvious, unless you are French.

One of the banes of a native French speaker trying to pronounce English correctly is that troublesome letter 'h'. It is mostly aspirated as in 'house' but then to complicate matters there are words in which it is silent such as 'hour' or 'honest' (bear with me, I'm still learning after fifty years...). And the greatest difficulty for a French speaker is that there *is no* such thing as exhaling to pronounce any letter in French. It is a totally unknown concept. All right, you can point to the frequent French habit of exaggerated blowing of air that usually accompanies the clichéd '*Oh, la, la*' but that is a free-wheeling demonstration of emotion (in the French genes), not precise pronunciation of a word. The aspirated 'h' remains forever bizarre, as does putting the tip of one's tongue between one's teeth to produce the other sound that repeatedly defeats French learners of English, the 'th' sound. You can produce it in French but only if you want to talk in a silly way, imitating a toddler. Anyway, I am glad to say I have mostly mastered the 'th', but the 'h', silent or not, still regularly trips me up, so that I often incongruously morph into a faux cockney. Which can be amusing, to others. But this solemn declaration in front of their honourable (there it goes again...) justices was a serious matter. So, I practised discreetly as I waited to be called in: "...I swear allegiance to **h**er Majesty the Queen and all **h**er (h)eirs...", attracting strange looks from the police officer in the room. I went in anxiously and had to find inner assertiveness to turn down the Bible and to state that I wished to affirm, which caused a few raised eyebrows. Inevitably, when the moment came, I proceeded, in as firm a voice as I could muster, to swear allegiance to "...'er Majesty the Queen and all 'er **h**airs...". The justices were not amused.

By that time, I was speaking a fluent and only subtly accented English but I remained dissatisfied with my command of the language. When friends and acquaintances insisted that I was as good as a native speaker, it reminded me of people pretending not to notice a physical disability, well meaning but not to be wholly believed. In my relatively brief teaching years, no such sensitivity was shown by the pupils – in their cruel innocence, they knew how to be implacably truthful, never missing a chance to mock when I mispronounced a word. I was last in a classroom over forty years ago but those in my English family have never allowed me to forget that I once revealed I had caused students hilarity by pronouncing 'awry' as '**aw**-ry'.

After all these years I have become good enough to pass as a native speaker among strangers as long as conversations do not last very long – that is, until I am tripped up by the vagaries of stress. Being unsure where the stress is meant to fall is the curse of a foreign speaker of English, particularly anyone whose first language is French. I am not talking about the few words that are subject to a **con**troversy/con**tro**versy, but about the vast majority where rules (never fully integrated by my brain) or established practice (not naturally acquired) should apply. I can't always stop and think before I speak to decide if it's dependa**bili**ty or de**pend**ability. Stress is a real minefield, especially because French is an unstressed language. The French might be easily given to emotional verbal displays but their language is flat – or at least there is no ordained stress on a certain syllable as in multi-syllable English words. On that particular score at least, French is more straightforward than English – French *démocratie* is easier to deal with than English de**mo**cracy (if perhaps not in real life...). Even trickier is the handling of stress in compound constructions – the ones that can change meaning from a suit that is wet to a wetsuit you wear in cold water. It is all very stressful.

With an artificially learnt tongue, you are always an immigrant in the language landscape. You can never become as fully able as a native speaker, just more adept at concealing your impairment. Far from being fully bilingual, you end up being disabled in both languages. Stranded between the two. Awkward in both to different degrees.

And the more you immerse yourself in the new language, the more you become a less than perfect performer in your original language, gradually losing fluency through lack of practice. At first, it's a case of still being able to call up the right words but finding that they come into your brain in the syntax and constructions of the new language, and you soon get stuck. Frustratingly, the first thing that is curtailed in your original tongue is the language of emotions and feelings. (This is linked to my failure to bring up bilingual children, but that is another story.) If you feel emotions in English, it becomes really difficult to express them in French. There are too many hurdles and you quickly reach dead ends and blockages, falling prey to hesitancy and false starts. Not so much lost in translation as fumbling in translation.

Eventually after some years, you start having to make an effort to recall certain words (how do you say 'predicament' in French again?) Not to speak of the muddy waters of common words with different meanings in each language, the notorious *faux amis*. As an aside to this, I can't help feeling irritated by the currency that the phrase 'economical with the *actualité*' has acquired in Britain. It was originally created by a colourful English politician and is now widely used by journalists, even though it is nonsensical, a classic case illustrating the perils of *faux amis*, enticing because of using a word instantly recognisable in one's own language but in fact inappropriate. The word that should be used there is *réalité*. *Actualité* is mostly used in French to denote something happening contemporaneously or, in the plural, to mean 'the news'. But there is no going back.

For the sake of balance, I should say that the French are just as likely to get things wrong, and not just with *faux amis*. For example, not only have they adopted *faire du footing* for jogging, but they have now gone way beyond this to invent *le fooding* to describe everything that the people we call 'foodies' get up to – discovering new restaurants, going to farmers' markets, being interested in cooking, in ingredients and recipes. Then, to go back to *le footing*, they have a chain of shoe shops specialising in trainers called *Athlete Foot* – a monstrous creation if ever there was one. And there is the whole realm of mispronunciations that, in a meme sort of way, can create new words – or at least new *franglais* words – to the chagrin of the language purists. (Full disclosure is perhaps required here, as I may well be one myself.) I once could not help doing a slight mental double take when one of my brothers said to me, *"Passe-moi mon* sweet, *s'il te plaît"*, asking me to hand over his sweatshirt. You can easily see the genesis, a shortened version and a mispronunciation and you end up wearing a *bonbon*. Sweet, really. Another puzzling one was being told that this particular restaurant was very *hype*, mispronounced '[h]ip'. I then realised in coming across it in magazine reviews that this was being used to mean what we would indeed term 'hip' in English – fashionable, trendy. Maybe it had occurred because the places it was applied to had been the subject of 'hype', and the two concepts got mixed up, with meaning and pronunciation ending up meshed in a nonsensical way. You can easily get lost in the labyrinth of language…

Beyond issues of translation, you become aware of the conceptual distance between the two languages, some examples of which are mystifying and occasionally entertaining (the latter being an example of this itself as I don't think *amusant* conveys the same meaning). French people, it appears, don't 'look forward to' anything, or at least they have to use a lot more words to express something akin to it but even that to my mind is a long way from what is meant in English and how often it is used. Nor can you tell them to 'enjoy it' – there is no way that *profitez-en bien* (the closest I can think of) has the same connotations. It's more to do with 'making the most of it', which has less implication of delight to be had. Going in the other direction, why is there no English word for *frileux/frileuse*? English, usually pithier than French, has to use more words and say 'sensitive to the cold'.

This is in danger of turning into a nerdy disquisition on the intricacies of coping with two languages but it would have been difficult to avoid, as I have spent a lot of my life wrestling with words (sometimes desperately...), first as a learner of a second language, briefly as a teacher, and for a long time working as an editor in publishing. Come to think of it, I did also, at least for a few years in my 'alternative side activity' as a psychotherapy counsellor, spend quite a bit of time listening to others wrestling with words too.

Before leaving this theme, I will allow myself the indulgence of venting a little about two personal bugbears (maybe the mention of counselling has triggered this off). I will do this in an equal-opportunities way by castigating both sides – and inevitably there will be some generalisation.

First, I have never understood why so many French people when speaking English don't even try to at least approximate the sound and intonation of English. I recently heard a renowned French academic, based in the States, speaking fluently and at length about her subject (immigration and wages) in grammatically perfect English – but an English that for a few seconds sounded to my ears like French. It did not have the rhythm and sound of English; it was just a flat flow but made up of often mispronounced English words. Weird, especially as what she was saying was very interesting. It was not just the use of 'ze' or the missing non-silent aitches but many basic (which, by the way, she insisted on pronouncing 'b*aah*sic') mistakes in words she must have heard correctly spoken hundreds of times by students and colleagues. How come she did not take any notice? I once had to brief a French woman who came in as a supply teacher. She spoke in a similar fashion to the academic. To make polite conversation, I asked her how long she had been in England, expecting a relatively recent arrival. Her response was, "Oh, I 'ave bin 'ere sirty yirss." And I wondered, was it thirty years of deliberate resistance (but to what purpose?) or simply a kind of linguistic tone deafness? Whatever the reason for this deficiency, it has at least been a gift to comedy writers.

My other bugbear is the native English speaker's wanton use of idiomatic expressions that are bound to be opaque to their foreign interlocutors. This is particularly prevalent on the part of highly educated people and it has made me cringe on many occasions in my professional life in international publishing. I am making up these examples as I do not recall the details of actual long-past incidents, but they are not far-fetched. It is embarrassing to hear someone answering a stumbling, "How are you?" from, say, a Spanish collaborator with, "Fit as a fiddle!" And then to tell them that you can't make a delivery "at the drop of a hat" and that they should "cut you some slack". Or even that they should just "bite the bullet", otherwise it could be the "last straw" and you'd have to "call it a day". Taking a leaf (ha!) from the famous Manuel in Fawlty Towers, my poor hypothetical Spaniard would be fully justified in reacting with a bewildered and possibly irascible "Qué?" And one last petty point – please don't talk to foreigners of 'bank holidays' ("Oh, you have special days when banks are closed?"), call them what they are in every other country, *public* holidays.

Having got all this off my chest (yes, it's difficult to avoid...), it is time to close on a more positive note. In spite of all the hurdles, some of them insurmountable, learning another language is of huge benefit. A second language is not just for communication, it opens mental doors, gives access to new vistas of existence, develops a new state of mind. You think differently, you feel differently, you add a new layer to your whole being.

For me, learning English was also a form of emotional exile. It allowed me an escape from my post-Algerian traumas, from the profound ambivalence I was suffering from about living in France and being French. It had been symbolic of travelling in my teenage years, of escaping the narrow confines of a provincial town. It had saved my skin as a student after leaving *Sciences Po* by enabling me to slide easily into a language degree. And now, with permanently moving to Britain, it was a way of turning a page, of starting afresh – of immersing myself in another universe, shedding at least some of the burden of my childhood. As with many other aspects of my move to Britain, it was a kind of liberation. I did not fall in love just with the country, I loved the language too.

From school to books

Every French school pupil, by the time they reached their fourth year of high school, had to buy a big French–English dictionary, and in my days it was one produced by an old British publishing firm called Harrap. Given that English was a compulsory subject, there are millions of French people who will be familiar with what they undoubtedly know as *'le 'arraps'*. They will remember it as the bulkiest and heaviest object in their collection of textbooks with either fondness or profound dislike, depending on how successfully they grappled with their English homework. In many cases, their well-thumbed copy may still be gathering dust on a shelf somewhere. I did keep mine. Given all this, it seemed to me a strange twist of fate when, after five years of a teaching job that I was getting fed up with, I spotted an advert for a position at that very publishing company – and got the job.

This is hardly in the league of stories from famous thespians who proudly tell of realising their own success when getting work with actors they had admired in their childhood. But it is my own modest version, a still surprising and totally fortuitous coincidence in my professional life, my lucky break into publishing. Of course, to the people around me it was of little significance, as the *Harrap's French–English Dictionary* never had the iconic status in Britain that it had in France, and in any case I was not being employed to work on dictionaries (no lexicographer, I) but on their educational books. The kudos I got from French family and friends was gratifying but hugely disproportionate to the actual achievement. I was taking a significant pay cut – entry jobs in publishing were poorly paid then as they are now. From being a head of department in my last school, I was going to sit in a shared office with three other editors and would have to report to a mid-ranking manager. But it was publishing and the choice felt obvious at the time. Looking back, it was a turning point in my life, and one that more or less came out of the blue, found by chance in the job adverts pages of the *Times Educational Supplement* – pages that in those days every teacher in every staffroom in the land always at least glanced at, or in some cases pored over in a desperate search for a better post or a sideways escape. As I was to find on other occasions, it seemed right to go along with the haphazard unfolding of life rather than agonising over pros and cons and trying to think too far ahead. "Where do you see yourself in five years' time?" is a question I've always found quite pointless.

It meant I could stop fearing the prospect of getting stuck in teaching. My life-lasting admiration for Audier, my *lycée* mentor, had not turned his profession into a vocation for me. After finishing my degree, I had harboured a slim hope of getting into journalism or publishing – I knew it would not be easy for a non-native speaker but it proved even more difficult than I had imagined. The only bite I got was an interview for the French department of the BBC World Service and I failed to get that – paradoxically, my creative juices were already not flowing freely enough in French by that stage. So, like quite a few of my contemporaries, I ended up by default in a teaching job.

Not that I disliked teaching. It kept me in Brighton, where I had friends and a relationship and where I eventually bought a flat – a teacher in his mid-twenties could still do that without parental help in those days. Once I got over the initial tribulations of facing a class of troublesome third years and more or less managed the mysteries of basic classroom control, I enjoyed the cheeky rapport with the youngsters. You had to work constantly on your classroom presence, displaying confidence and selective firmness, drawing boundaries while showing you were interested in the students, and especially giving them the same respect you rightly expected from them – preferably adding an occasional dash of humour. A piece of cake, as you can see... Then if you were lucky you might overhear one of them say, "That Mr B, he's all right" – and be forever grateful for that faint praise. It was exhausting but strangely stimulating too. And there were moments of satisfaction whenever there were signs of real learning taking place, or rather when you could feel that some learning was occurring at least partly thanks to you. You had to cling to that, a miniscule contribution to the sum of human enlightenment. And it was gratifying, even though it had to be set against the hours of preparation, the dreariness of lunchtime supervision, the endless marking of piles of exercise books, the laborious writing of reports and the tricky parents' evenings – a tiny nugget of gold out of a long seam of tedium and pain.

Occasionally I could not help contrasting the working conditions and status of British teachers with those of their French colleagues. There was no doubt that the latter were better paid, had longer holidays, taught fewer hours per week, were not required to do any of the ancillary jobs such as playground and lunchtime supervision, or generally looking after discipline outside their own lessons, and, on top of that, were more highly respected by society at large. And not just because they are known as '*professeurs*', although there may be something in that. On the other hand, it was obvious that there was much more of a sense of community in British secondary schools than in French *lycées*, and relationships between students and teachers were much closer. The other difference that gradually became more evident was the full significance of British education being a two-tier system. This was not the case in France where private education was really limited to a very small number of cramming establishments in Paris and schools run by the Catholic Church. I had of course known, theoretically, of the existence of private schools in the UK but had not fully grasped how deep the divide was between a minority of schools lavished with private funds and the rest often being left to make do with inadequate resources and generally poorly funded by the state. The social and economic implications of this became even more obvious once I moved into the world of publishing.

Harrap had been one of the last few family-owned, medium-sized publishing firms in Britain. But when I joined it in the late 1970s it had just been acquired by the Eton-educated scion of a newspaper-owning family, with a view to stripping at least some of its assets, as it turned out – we were after all entering the money-grabbing 1980s. The new owner had very little knowledge of book publishing – and it transpired not very much more of ordinary everyday life. The firm had long been based in a large building it owned in Holborn in central London. Having much enjoyed its proximity to the restaurants of Covent Garden, I was sorry when the premises were sold only a couple of years after my arrival. Up to that point the chairman of the company, now fairly powerless having sold his stake, was a Harrap family member, quaintly known to all as Mr Paull, in old-style dynastic fashion. He was an old-fashioned avuncular gentleman who for some reason – possibly to do with my French background – took a liking to me. As I was promoted to a managerial role, he started inviting me to the regular lunches he had with some of the directors, which I suppose he imagined was a way of buttressing his position versus that of the new owner and managing director. I can't say that I fully understood the manoeuvring but nonetheless these occasions were hugely enjoyable. I was discovering that publishing's extended lunches were not just a cliché. There was plenty of rumour and gossip peppered with wit and humour as well as wider, intelligent and entertaining conversation – all of it agreeably helped along with abundant supplies of good food and especially good wine. It was no surprise, given the balance of power in the firm, that Paull Harrap soon decided to retire to his country house and beloved garden in a salubrious town in the Thames valley, and Eton boy (yes, he did look boyish) made himself chairman, sold the Holborn building and moved us all from fun Covent Garden to the edge of the city on boring Ludgate Hill.

Part of the fun of the early years was the camaraderie of four people working in the same room, a situation that I had wrongly dreaded. We bonded in part over our all being subjected to what we felt was fastidious scrutiny of our work from a rather stern and pernickety manager. The atmosphere was often quiet and studious as we bent over the preparation of manuscripts or the checking of proofs (unlike today, everything was done in-house). Not used to long hours doing the same thing, I did occasionally miss the hustle and bustle of school and the cheekiness of the pupils. Occasionally, though, there were moments of shared humour when we felt a little bit like naughty children as the manager left our office after one of his 'giving notes' and we broke the tension and embarrassment by sharing anecdotes.

Soon after I joined, the editor in charge of German textbooks sent the galley proofs of an annotated compendium of German poetry to its aged and eminent German academic author for checking. There were already some corrections marked on the proofs by the typesetter, including, alongside a passage of explanatory text which had been wrongly set with a ragged right edge, a vertical line and a note saying 'Justify' – in typesetting parlance, this means 'make lines all the same length'. We were greatly entertained by the three-page letter that came back with the proofs. Herr Professor was not amused. "How dare you ask me to justify my commentary? For the last thirty years, I have been considered the leading expert in this field...", and much more, couched in dark blue ink, no doubt from an old and expensive fountain pen. I think, because of his eminence, he'd never before been asked to check proofs and was obviously not familiar with the term in this context. This particular project yielded further repressed merriment in our office, when we had to listen to our fellow editor trying to convey euphemistically to our manager that having one of the chapters called The Poet's Tool may not be ideal for an audience of sixth-formers. The editor's series of gradually less euphemistic attempts were still met with a frown and a puzzled, "I don't see the problem."

Eventually, in the late 1980s, I found myself in charge of the French dictionaries of my youth. This came about when the Publishing Director, who I had been harmoniously working with (and frequently lunching with), left to found his own publishing imprint. Soon after that, Eton boy decided it was time to further cash in on his cost-cutting, and put the whole business up for sale. To avoid it being swallowed up by a large American firm, four of the directors (including me) organised a management buyout, an operation fairly common in those days. Unfortunately, shortly afterwards, we suffered badly from the effects of high and rising interest rates – at one point they hit 15 per cent, which for a highly-leveraged company was not sustainable. The recession of the early 1990s added to the firm's financial woes and in 1992 it was taken over by a French publishing conglomerate, which merged it with the Scottish dictionary publisher Chambers they had already acquired. This was part of a trend which over twenty years saw British publishing being concentrated into a handful of mega-firms. Sadly, the company that started in 1901 as George G. Harrap & Co, and in its heyday published some of Winston Churchill's history works and children's books illustrated by Arthur Rackham, is today reduced to a dictionaries-only imprint of Hachette, being run from the offices of the Larousse dictionaries in Paris.

Having said that, I should stress that it was the international aspect of publishing that was one of its attractions for me. Towards the end of my time at Harrap, we had set up a subsidiary in Paris and being a frequent visitor to it allowed me to reconnect with the city in more auspicious circumstances than in my student days. There were also the ritual pilgrimages to the annual Frankfurt Book Fair each October. For my first attendance, when I had just been made a director, Mr Paull had insisted that not only should we travel by car but we should also allow for *two* stopovers on the way, the first being in scenic Bruges – which did not take us much of the way but was justified on gastronomic grounds! A lot of real business was indeed carried out during the week of the fair but I have to confess my memory of that first occasion is that much of the time I was witnessing publishers at play rather than work. There was, of course, a complete meshing of the deal-making and the socialising – the latter involving large amounts of cross-cultural drinking... I recall not coping very well with the multi-toast protocol of drinking sake with Japanese dictionary publishers, who certainly were not as abstemious as the lexicographers I knew. Evenings usually started with post-fair cocktail parties hosted by the main firms, followed by long liquid suppers and ending up at a packed hotel bar. No wonder the story doing the rounds on the second day of that particular fair was of a Dutch publisher who, having fallen out of a bar after a long night, plucked from the top pocket his jacket what he took to be his hotel card, handed it to the taxi driver, promptly collapsed in a heap on the back seat, and woke up five hours later outside his offices in Amsterdam.

I was not used to this degree of consistent drinking, especially as something separate from meals, and I had my own more modest baptism of drunken embarrassment. As I was a late entry, I had to share a hotel room with my erstwhile manager who I had recently been promoted over – which was awkward enough in itself. He was a serious man, working at the time on a German dictionary, and he'd decided to retire at a sensible 10pm, while the rest of the gang went on carousing in the hotel bar, much to his silent but obvious disapproval. By the time I staggered up to the bedroom it must have been 2am. I soon became aware that I had only a hazy idea of our room number. Standing unsteadily in the corridor, and wondering was it 200 or 202, I saw that a key had been left in the outside lock of 200 – ah, I thought in my befuddled state, this must be so I can get in quietly and not disturb my roommate. (I know, it does not make sense...) So, in I go, into a darkened room. Leaning against the left wall, I divest myself of my clothes, and with a great effort of concentration I fumble my way to where I just about remember my own single bed being, past the door to the bathroom, in a recess on the right. Yes, there is the end of it, just coming around to the side, feel the bed cover and – oh, my goodness, there is a body in my bed! I never knew that a high degree of sobriety could return so instantly. By now, it is suddenly absolutely clear to me that our room is 202 and definitely not this one. Fortunately for me, my fumbling must have been hesitant and gentle enough not to have woken anyone. So now, more consciously quietly though in hastier fashion, I gather my clothes from the floor, move out into the corridor, holding some of my garments close to my lower body, turn to the door of 202, which thankfully is unlocked, and open it onto a fully lit room – where I am shocked to see my roommate propped up against pillows with an array of German dictionary proofs and an assortment of red and blue biros laid out in front of him. What he sees, no doubt just as shocked as me, is a naked man, still somewhat drunk, looking utterly befuddled. What he must also see at some level is the younger man who he used to supervise and to whom he now has to report. To this day, I am grateful that he passed no comment nor asked any question – nor indeed ever spoke of this shameful display of dissipation.

After the dissipation of that first Frankfurt Book Fair, I enjoyed many years of working in publishing in generally rather more sober fashion. It could often be demanding and stressful, given the deadlines and tight budgets, but I found most people in the industry convivial company. The vast majority were cultured and interesting people, almost all liberal-minded, many of them *bon vivant*. A few could also be terribly pretentious and status conscious, and addicted to name-dropping.

Not that there is necessarily a direct link with the above but I became aware quite quickly of the prevalence of Oxbridge people in publishing and beyond that of private school backgrounds. Given the subtleties involved, it does take years to fully realise all aspects of the stratification of British society and the extent to which people are categorised by accent and education, and interact accordingly.

Being an immigrant means you are always an outsider allowed – or perhaps more accurately, tolerated – inside. In a way I got a free pass, as people could not use their standard yardsticks to place me. It's difficult for me to judge but it may have served me well in my working relationships as I did not come with a label that could be instantly read. On the other hand, it often meant that people did not know how to engage with me, unsure of safe terms of reference, of what would be common territory. In social conversations, they often fell back on sport. Having readily assumed I could not know anything about cricket (not wrong there), they usually thought they were on firmer ground with rugby. I have long lost count of how many commiserations and congratulations on the performance of France in international matches I have been the perplexed recipient of. Perplexed, because unfortunately for my interlocutors I am profoundly uninterested in *following* any sport. A mild interest in major occasions as part of current events, but that is the extent of it. (Maybe I never got over being mocked in the *lycée* in Niort on my arrival from Algiers for not knowing the names of football teams or champion cyclists.) What is more, even if I had been interested, their assumption that I would support France would have been wrong as I would have easily passed the Tebbit test (I use the term as a shortcut not as a sign of approval of that reactionary politician's intentions in setting it): I would not root for France, but for England, or now Scotland, in other words for the country I live in, simply because a sporting win always seems to be good for the communal mood. Of course, I could not have expected anyone to know that my nationalist fibres had been cauterised to death in my misguidedly patriotic childhood. But there was always the weather we could talk about...

When I went for one of my anti-Covid vaccinations not long ago, the nurse asked me what I did before retiring and when I said that I worked in publishing, she went on to say, after a brief pause, "You know, I can't think what people working in publishing actually do when they arrive at the office at 9am."

There was no time to answer, but it made me reflect that most of what I did in my publishing career was in fact managing people and money. But it also caused me to remember that there was a time when, in addition to my main job, I engaged, hands-on and in my own time, in all aspects of publishing. This was because I had set up my own imprint as a side line, a small operation that published about eighty titles over a period of fifteen years. Most of publishing is very specialised, but having my own imprint allowed me to publish across various genres, from travel writing to self-help to children's books, and eventually even fiction. The main criteria for selection were that I liked the book (and the author) and that I believed it would appeal to a sufficiently sized audience. Publishing wisdom, in this case echoing reality, will tell you this is no way to make money. But for me it was gratifying because it meant I was personally involved in every step of the publishing process: reading proposals, assessing manuscripts, working with authors, copyediting, commissioning cover designs, choosing typefaces and page designs, proofreading, getting estimates from printers, writing blurbs and press releases – not even an exhaustive list and already far too long to recite to my curious nurse but it would have given her an idea of what people in publishing actually do. I could have also spoken of the anxiety and joy of receiving the advance copies of a new title from the printers – the apprehension that there will inevitably be missed typos but, oh, the pleasure of holding a finished book in one's hands after all those months. The sheen of the cover, the inky smell of the pages. Even though you haven't physically made it yourself, there is something of a craftsman's satisfaction – at least you know you have made it happen.

After that, there were the all-too-rare reviews to look forward to or, with a bit of luck, some authors' media interviews. These were cause for celebration but I treasure even more the memory of a less public occurrence that gave me greater personal satisfaction. Once, as I sat down in a London Tube carriage opposite someone reading a paperback, I realised, as their sudden laughter made me look up, that it was one of 'mine'. Not written by me, of course, but a leading title in my Travellers' Tales series, Frank Kusy's *Kevin and I in India*. On what was until then a dreary Northern Line journey, that stranger's laughter gave me a warm glow. It also made all the late-night work to produce it more than worthwhile.

I have now left the realm of books – but still miss its pleasures. Like most people I encounter them in browsing bookshop shelves and acquiring some of them (can it ever be too many?) And having now been involved in digital content rather than the printed word for nearly twenty years, I know there is no question of ever weaning myself off books. They will remain lasting objects of desire.

Throwaway thoughts

Every morning at 8am when I step out from the front door of our flat and into the centre of town, one of the first signs of activity I see is a couple of council employees picking up litter and emptying the communal bins. On my way down to the beach I come across another council worker driving a narrow, motorised vacuum cleaner doing the gutters and pavements. Where others might see this as a profligate use of their taxes, I see it as a laudable sign of civic pride and reassurance of still surviving public service. And, of course, the town is very clean. Not that there is much of a problem anyway, and it's certainly not as bad as in many places 'down south'.

Here I will take the risk of sounding like Disgusted of Tunbridge Wells, because for me litter has been such a visible signifier of something much bigger. When I first came to live in this country it was noticeable how much cleaner city streets were than in France, how much more socially unacceptable it was to drop litter. Since then, I have seen the litter problem get worse – a change which I think became manifest in the 1980s, part of what was happening in the culture during that decade.

Every love affair has to experience a period of disillusionment or at least of adjustment to reality. After the bewitching discovery of all the wonderful attributes comes the slow revelation of flaws and downsides, and having to face the fact that loved ones don't always change for the better. Thus, it was with me and England in the 1980s. As with personal life, it is possible to pull through and develop a more authentic, often profounder relationship and I am glad to say this did happen – at least until the catastrophe of Brexit and the coming to power of the Buffoon. There was not even as much dark humour to be had in the eighties, as there is now. The toxic plan was more competently carried out – a serious and systematic dismantling of all the pillars of the post-war consensus. Or, to put it in more personal terms, of so much that underpinned what I felt made this country so admirable. None of this was done surreptitiously, with Thatcher proudly declaring that there was no such thing as society. Everything she stood for was an endorsement of unfettered individualism. Unions were bad, nationalised industry was bad, local authorities were bad and, even more importantly, taxes were very bad.

Consequences of the policies of that period can clearly be seen today. The attack on workers' rights and protections has led to the spreading of zero-hour contracts, the worst aspects of the so-called gig economy, the use of fire and re-hire. The latter ironically was even condemned recently by self-proclaimed Thatcherite MPs, having realised, a bit late, that "things have gone too far". The negative outcomes of the privatisation of vast swathes of industry and utilities are clear for everyone to see: the mess of the worst and most expensive railway system in Europe; the scandal of water companies releasing sewage into rivers and seas; the quasi-destruction of council housing being a significant contributor to the current dire housing crisis; the big bang liberalisation of the financial sector, including the disappearance of most building societies, being part-causes of the 2008 financial crisis; the general degradation of public services, health, education, social services, meaning there are now mountains to climb to get them back up to anything like a decent level. (There was, admittedly, the beginning of a correction to this in the thirteen-year Labour period, but then austerity struck.)

All of this was based on a fundamental category error, linking the issue of efficiency with ownership. But maybe it was a deliberate act of dressing-up: with a fragment of reality, and a lot of exaggeration and distortion, a case could be made in the popular press that the private sector would do better – with the added bonus, in the case of council services, of reducing local taxes. But in reality it is now obvious that, if anything, privatisation has in many cases meant more inefficiency (see repeated failures of outsourcing firms). The only thing the privatised companies have been more efficient at is extracting more private profit through worse working conditions for their employees, higher prices and poorer service for the consumers, and lack of reinvestment.

The problem of any inefficiencies could have been addressed differently. Unfortunately, not by using the blunt tool of targets (self-defeating in the long run), as Labour did in the 1990s. A much more substantial transformation was required, based on the principle of giving people a sense of autonomy and a sense of mission. By autonomy, I mean recognising that the more a person doing a job is empowered to decide *how* to do the job, the more efficiently that job is done. So, give the widest possible responsibility to the lowest possible level. This promotes self-respect, and helps combat feelings of alienation, feelings of being reduced to a mere cog in the machine. The importance of the cog to the whole also needs to be made clear and explicitly appreciated. And by mission, I mean what is often referred to as a sense of ownership with an added vision of clear purpose, so that people are encouraged to develop a sense of guardianship, of being responsible for looking after a common good. The more you help imbue public sector employees with the feeling that they own or are trusted with a collectively owned public good, the more they will take care of it and want to eliminate waste. To achieve this, you could do worse than emulate the ethics and practices of organisations like clubs or voluntary set-ups, where it's a given that everyone feels responsible for protecting the assets and finding the most efficient way of doing things. There is peer pressure not to do otherwise and by and large it works. There is not much slacking in voluntary work. And, indeed, there would also be plenty to learn and emulate from the more progressive end of private enterprise – from the teamwork, flat hierarchies and ability to be nimble and learn from mistakes of the technology companies, to the kind of employee participation and incentives of leading companies such as the John Lewis Partnership, based on forms of employee ownership.

Along with the denigration of public services, another noxious notion was widely propagated in that decade – that a priority of government should always be to reduce taxes, irrespective of consequences. Over and over again stories in the right-wing press (especially by one newspaper shamelessly owned by a tax exile) helped to create and nurture the perception that tax money is wasted, that inefficiencies in public services are the result of too much tax revenue being allocated to them. A nonsense that does not bear examination but sadly has continued to have a hold on a significant portion of public opinion.

This ideology of tax as a bad thing led to the absurd situation of local councils being proud of divesting themselves from responsibilities. I remember living in London in the 1980s and Wandsworth council boasting of having the lowest council tax in the country – but on the ground, what you faced, as we did, for example, having a disabled child, was that it also had terrible provision of social services. We need politicians with the courage to defend the whole rationale of taxes – to ask people to imagine setting up a society as in a create-your-own-country computer game; they would very soon realise that it makes perfect sense to build roads, schools and hospitals with resources pooled together, fairly, from the whole community. When you take away the obfuscation and the misrepresentation, progressive taxation is really a simple and most sensible idea.

Instead, some now promote the insane concept that you should only pay for what you use, that you should be able to opt out of paying for services you don't personally need, which completely defeats the fundamental principle of mutuality, the very foundation of public services. Unfortunately, a version of this has already crept in and established itself in the realm of higher education – a public good that as a nation we all benefit from and we should all pay for through taxes (as in most other European countries). The whole idea of individual students paying fees for higher education is egregious. The answer to the point that they might derive personal gain in the form of higher salaries, is that a proper progressive tax regime can ensure they contribute a fair share to the system.

Moderation is admirable, it has a lot to be said for it – it makes for a more harmonious, less disputatious society, and was at the heart of what I first appreciated about this country. But sometimes there is too much restraint, in particular in affirming liberal values. We should never be apologetic about them, or afraid to defend them explicitly. Yet, in a kind of misplaced attempt not to confront a difficult subject, progressive people are often too hesitant to insist that yes, there is such a thing as society, yes, altruism has a place in it, and yes, it is morally right to pay taxes to fund what the state needs to do because it is fairer and more efficient to do it collectively.

The answer to inefficiencies in public services is not private provision, but better public services. The answer to concerns about taxation is not a smaller state but a better, more effective state. Subverting the words of a certain notorious film character of the 1980s, we should proclaim that Tax is Good!

Here endeth the Lesson.

I have meandered a long way from litter but it is all linked. The sanctification of private material success, and the desecration of the public good, underpin the attitude of not caring about the public space and thoughtlessly throwing stuff on the ground. It is no coincidence that the incivility of urban life and the general coarsening of life in England increased in the 1980s. When I think of this period, I have a recurring image of thin, pale, mean-looking, feral boys in baseball caps, wearing sports clothes with ostentatious labels, roaming the litter-strewn streets lined with boarded-up derelict shops. And I recall some of my pupils from a local Brighton council estate, who prefigured them in the mid-seventies, being 'parked' in a poorly resourced state school – already suffering from education budget cuts shamefully introduced by a Labour government – being taught in classrooms with broken desks and buckets catching rain from leaks in the roof, and thinking how could they possibly learn the concept of respect (and self-respect) when the state was treating them with such lack of respect. Unfortunately, some of them would never find a way out of that predicament and would turn into the shaven-headed, beer-bellied, foreigner-hating, angry men wrapped up in St George's flags, often seen in pro-Brexit or now anti-vaccination events, trying to mend their broken sense of pride in that usual last-resort, jingoistic nationalism. The mentality of everyone for themselves and the belief in being a nation above all others started to prevail then, celebrated daily by that red-top rag I will not deign to name.

I was once told by a colleague after I had voiced criticism of the government's policies, "If you don't like it here, why don't you go back to where you come from?" – an experience familiar to many other immigrants. (I could not begin to tell him why I could not 'go back' to Algeria...) So, I am going to allow myself to be a little defensive here. There are two reasons why I feel entitled to be so critical, even to sound a little bitter. The first is that having fully contributed to the country's fate, in work, votes and taxes, for the past fifty years, I do feel entitled to defend the values that first attracted me here, which by the way are surely values that a lot of British people still hold on to. It is also possible that, like many other long-term immigrants, I am better placed than autochthonous people, because of the initial appreciation of the good sides as new and different, to notice the shortcomings and the worsening of them. The second is that having gone through the disillusion phase of the love affair, I still profoundly love this country and its culture – and, indeed, now more realistically, its flaws and all.

Discovering the New World

My first encounter with the Microsoft universe in the autumn of 1994 was full of surprises – admittedly because I had by then absorbed much of the stereotyped view of the company. Sometimes referred to as an evil empire, it was meant to be driven by ruthless businesspeople intent on world domination for their products and remorseless crushing of their competitors. Some aspects of this were rooted in reality but what we found did not exactly fit. The environment for a start: a vast purpose-built modern complex of attractive buildings set in a landscaped area dotted with greenery, populated by casually dressed people, most of them in their twenties and thirties, looking quite relaxed and not at all evil. No wonder the place was known as the Redmond Campus. It did feel just like a well-funded, newly built university. And that feeling was confirmed in our first working meeting with people responsible for *Encarta Encyclopaedia*, which Microsoft had launched in CD-ROM format in the US the year before. We were there to discuss plans to help them create international versions of this work.

Leading our party of three was the founder of Websters International Publishers, a London-based independent company (which, by the way, has nothing to do with the American *Webster's Dictionary*). A contact at Microsoft had approached him because of his past involvement in the multi-language success of *The Joy of Knowledge*. I had just been recruited to Websters as a consultant to bring my experience of managing international reference projects. As a French version of *Encarta* was planned to be one of the first to be launched after a UK version, we had brought with us a leading French encyclopaedist as another consultant. We were expecting a difficult meeting as we felt we might have to convince the Microsoft team to go much further than they had anticipated in committing to the work necessary to make foreign versions. The existing US content had already been adapted and expanded from an American print encyclopaedia, *Funk and Wagnalls*, and they knew that it could not just be a translation, but we still had to make a persuasive case for having local teams in each country to ensure the content was culturally relevant – and this would mean the creation of some new content.

Our interlocutors were Ivy-League educated people, sophisticated and cultured, and we had reasonable hope that we stood a good chance of convincing them. Our discussions around the topic of how much localisation was needed were conducted in softly-spoken, but rapid, extremely polite and restrained exchanges. And some progress was being made. However, as time went on, I could sense a French storm gathering to my right. The French encyclopaedist, who understood English well but was rather tongue-tied when it came to speaking it, was simmering away, increasingly fidgety, sighing, grumbling and at one point even hissing at what was being suggested. Which was met with a gracious offer for him to make his contribution. And he was certainly going to put them right, in French... Speaking loudly, with much gesticulation for emphasis, and sounding, by the standards of our hosts, not just irritated but outright angry, he launched into a tirade of criticisms of their approach, peppered with far too many comprehensible

French words such as *impossible, ridicule, arrogance intellectuelle, domination culturelle*, which rather alarmed me as I knew what was coming. Running out of breath, he turned to me and said, "You tell them in English." So I found myself, not for the first time nor the last, with the interesting task of deliberately losing quite a lot in translation. Starting with, "[He] has a few reservations...", and then toning down every statement he had made to a more digestible version – a repeated search for a sort of Socratic golden mean on every point, shedding the barbs and the outrage. Our Microsoft colleagues looked slightly askance at my benign reconstruction, torn between doubt and relief. Anyway, the eventual outcome was positive. A decision would soon be made to set up substantial editorial teams in each country to ensure sufficient adaptation and creation of new specific content. Our US friends, conscious of European ways and contrary to their usual work habits, decided to take us to a restaurant for a proper lunch. Our French colleague calmed down and returned to his more usual avuncular persona, helped along by frequent outside cigarette breaks.

Part of all this was a clash of approach, with our American colleagues, displaying typically positive, optimistic, can-do attitudes, focusing on what they thought of as solutions, whereas our encyclopaedist would have liked a thorough examination of the problems, with much dwelling on some of their insurmountable aspects, a chance for some satisfying tutting and sighing, and plenty of heaving of shoulders, all much practised in French intellectual circles. And it is indeed the reality of life that worthwhile tasks are almost always fraught with obstacles and apparently insoluble issues that need to be thoroughly considered. But it was clear that this very French, analytical way would hold things back too much for our results-driven American colleagues – who wanted to progress and achieve.

As a fan of *bandes dessinées* (French-style comic books, known in English as graphic novels), I sometimes like to think back on that *Encarta* period as *Adventures in the Land of Technology*, Tintin-like. Intense, full of plot twists and turns, but mostly positive and enjoyable. It spanned fifteen years and would involve working across six countries, as Websters was eventually to manage the editorial work of *Encarta* not just for the UK but also in France, Germany, Italy, Spain and, in the latter period, in the US too. At that time many people had negative views of Microsoft as one of the first technology behemoths to have a worldwide impact, which, as we have seen since, has not always been beneficial. But we did not experience our relationship with the company as a commercial rival to be beaten or bought into submission. We encountered the human face, as it were. Not quite a pro bono side but certainly a benevolent side, a side that wanted to make a good impression on the world, producing content with an educational purpose. Part of the motivation, beyond the fact that there was a sound commercial rationale for it, was that it might help to improve Microsoft's public image.

The first new thing for me was dealing with an enterprise that had the means to do what it set out to do – as long as a compelling case was made for the need for resources, they were usually provided. This was an utterly new experience. I had never known this either in my few years of teaching or in my many more years of book publishing. I had always had to work within quite narrow constraints, even in publishing – there was always a feeling that things were not going well enough in terms of sales, or even if they were that we were about to enter another recession, or that what was needed in terms of resources was beyond what was sensible to allocate. So, you always worked in conditions of 'making do', sometimes more, sometimes less, but always hamstrung. Working on *Encarta* felt like a release from this, and in itself was professionally satisfying. And for Microsoft, the gamble paid off as for fifteen years or so *Encarta* was successful commercially, selling hundreds of thousands of copies throughout the world. Then, as is the nature of technology, change caught up with it, the world moved online and free Wikipedia and the growing ubiquity of Google combined to kill it.

The other new aspect that struck me was how much there was to learn from the ways of working of a new technology company, an environment that proved more enlightened and progressive than traditional publishing. In describing a few of these ways, I don't think I can avoid falling into management jargon, so be warned. What struck me most was the autonomy given to people – I am trying to avoid the cliché of 'empowerment' because I think it's misleading. What I observed was clear definitions of goals (a sense of mission) and a very high degree of latitude in the means by which to achieve these. This was helped by a marked absence of strict linear hierarchies and siloed departments. Instead, there was a prevalence of project-based, cross-function teams: developers, designers and editors working closely together under the leadership of a project manager, rather than each reporting to their distinct department's manager. The main benefit of all this was that it unleashed enormous creativity. This was also fostered by encouraging experimentation and the acceptance of mistakes, and of things not working out first time. There was a systematic use of post-mortems and time spent drawing lessons from shortcomings after every project cycle. All of these characteristics originated from working on developing software, where it would have been necessary to adopt them, but they were equally beneficial to our work on content. And I often thought how an injection of a good dose of these into the world of work in Britain would do wonders for morale and efficiency.

The software capabilities challenged our ways as traditional editors and encyclopaedists. For example, hyperlinks played havoc with established ideas of taxonomy. They enabled users to go on serendipitous voyages of exploration from one topic to another, without any reference to the logic of a standard categorisation. Not having the categories visible was a departure for many of our editorial teams, rooted in a 'tree of knowledge' approach. But the intuitive and random navigation suited the mostly young users well. As for our editors, being able to include a great variety of multimedia elements – videos, animations, interactive features – was an exciting change from the world of print, adding a whole lively dimension to the presentation of knowledge.

More of a challenge was handling the usual contentious cultural issues arising from working on the basis of a common corpus. Was the Scottish-born Alexander Graham Bell really the inventor of the telephone or could the Italian Antonio Meucci claim that title, having effectively developed a more basic version beforehand? In a similar way, could the British Sir Joseph Swan be said to be the inventor of the lightbulb because he developed it first, or was it right for the American Thomas Edison to have that honour because he not only developed the concept but commercialised it too? And then there were the many, sometimes amusing, idiosyncratic points of view of different cultures – exemplified once again by the French editor, who at a meeting allowed himself another outburst to complain that he could not simply use a translation of the UK entry on goats because it stated that people sometimes kept these animals as pets, a custom that was unthinkable in France. On a more serious note, we also had the usual difficulties associated with disputed territories, where the thickness of a line on a map could potentially lead to a ban on sales of the encyclopaedia in at least two countries.

Overall, our teams worked in a cohesive and collaborative way, which was no mean achievement across six nations. I was lucky to bring to Websters a colleague from my Harrap days, who I have now worked with for over thirty years. Our common approach, along with that of the chairman of Websters, was aimed at creating a working atmosphere that fostered both autonomy and respectful collaboration. Part of this was emulating the new ways of working, outlined above, that we were learning from our Microsoft colleagues.

I suppose the *Encarta* project was one of capitalism's few sweet spots: a worthy innovative product needed by vast numbers, from a company which, on this project at least, treated all the participants fairly and provided adequate investment. I was conscious at the time of making the most of that uncommon set of circumstances.

I have compared my time on *Encarta* to an adventure and indeed it was a mix of triumphs and tribulations but, unlike in a Hollywood movie, the jeopardy part of the plot came not halfway through but right at the finish. When the project came to an end, we had to close down our editorial teams. We had the means to do this properly and with generous termination packages. Almost everyone understood, having known from the outset that it was not likely to last for more than a few years, and we had by then been going for nearly fifteen years. The exceptions were half the French team, who used the arcane complexities of French employment law to pursue a claim in an industrial tribunal to try to get more than the package they had been offered, even though it already exceeded legal requirements. But it was common practice in France to do this systematically and tie employers down in procedural knots in the hope that companies would pay out additional compensation just to get out of a lengthy dispute. This led to five years of legal wranglings. But on a personal level, even worse was the sense of betrayal from people I felt we had always treated with respect and employed on the best possible terms. I have to acknowledge that I found myself in a painfully awkward position, as someone fundamentally favourable to the role of unions in defending workers, being forced to act defensively on the other side of that fence. The fact that I knew it was a preposterous case based on lies and distortions did not make it any less stressful. Anyway, it was dismissed in the end, but by then our French subsidiary had been put out of business and potential future jobs lost. A perverse outcome, sadly not unusual in France at the time.

To displace the bitter taste this has left in my mouth after all these years, I will end with recalling a sweet moment – which I wish we could have captured on video – in a meeting of our Academic Advisory Board for the British version of *Encarta*. Thanks mostly to the excellent contacts of our lead editor (who had an Oxford background), we had been able to enrol the help of prominent academics to advise us on the development of the content of the encyclopaedia. The fact that they had accepted to do this was an important step, adding legitimacy and gravitas to the whole project. Our first meeting was held in a hotel in St James's Place, London, suitably grand enough for this little gathering of a few of the great and the good. We wanted to make a good impression on this first occasion.

A senior marketing person from Microsoft Redmond was in attendance and, after we welcomed him, he suggested that, as was customary in all Microsoft meetings, we should start by going round the table for each person to introduce themselves. At which point my Websters' colleagues and I cringed discreetly and looked askance at Lord Briggs, who was chairing the meeting. Naturally, he very politely agreed having, with the slightest raising of eyebrows, exchanged glances with Mary Warnock and Richard Dawkins... And so, these widely known public figures, some renowned well beyond the shores of the UK, for most of whom it would have been an entirely new experience, subjected themselves to this Microsoft routine with good grace. They played the game, but played it in their own way, very much a British way, by turning it into an amiable competition in modesty, even self-deprecation. I paraphrase but hope to do justice to the humility. Asa Briggs set the tone when he said that he had "taught a bit of history at various universities and been particularly interested in the Victorian period" – with no indication of having been vice-chancellor of Sussex University, a professor at Columbia, the provost of Worcester College, Oxford, or having been commissioned by the BBC to write its history. Mary Warnock, the foremost ethical philosopher of her generation, went on in the same vein, mentioning that she had "taught a bit of philosophy at Oxford" and had "a particular interest in ethics", but omitting any of her several roles on government inquiries that led to society-altering changes in public policy. Richard Dawkins, whose turn it was next, topped this by saying simply, "I am an evolutionary biologist", and nothing about his groundbreaking book *The Selfish Gene*, or any of his other internationally widely known science titles. He was followed by our Irish member, Garret FitzGerald, who gave as good a performance as his British colleagues, in fact one might say exceeding it in self-effacement as this former twice Taoiseach (prime minister) of Ireland described himself as "having been an economist and then having dabbled in politics". This was getting ridiculous but everyone kept a straight face. Our cringing embarrassment had by then turned to repressed amusement. All the other Board members, which included a pre-eminent Indian historian, a leading educationist and an influential expert in disability rights, were equally pithy and modest in their introductions.

I sat there wondering how all this would be received by our American friend, who did look a little baffled and was consulting his briefing notes. Maybe realising who these people really were and then not quite getting their reticence, still puzzled by it. I also thought this could not have happened in any other country. Anywhere else, there would have been a greater display of one's own importance. It would have been the case in the US for sure, where it may even have been perceived as incompetence not to sell yourself, but I could also imagine an uncomprehending reaction in France where an opportunity to show off a bit, especially about intellectual accomplishments, would be just too hard to miss.

In an oddly-timed way, it reminded me of one of the reasons I love Britain.

The romance of wine

I was glad to see that our distinguished panel did not display the same degree of reticence in our subsequent meetings, especially when it came to enjoying the good food and wine served at the dinners that ended our sessions. Oxford University's Somerville College, our usual host for these, did us proud on the food front but Websters' chairman, a wine connoisseur extraordinaire, made sure that we brought a generous selection of fine bottles to go with it. All this seemed to go down a treat with our august advisers and it was lovely to see these usually rather serious people enjoying a relaxed and highly convivial time. Maybe it was no more than what they were used to at college high tables, but that would surprise me. There was something undemanding about the occasion and they could savour it simply as just reward for their earlier contributions. After a few of these repasts, when it began to feel like an annual reunion of old acquaintances or distant relatives, I could not help being reminded of ritual dinners with the French side of my family, of gatherings around a large table of aunts and uncles, and cousins and grandmother, where food and wine were the essential components of the ambience.

It brought to mind the fact that wine has been a presence throughout my life.

Admittedly only a small presence in my Algerian childhood – when I was first allowed to taste it with a bit of water added to the glass during meals on special occasions – but it did not feature much in family conversations as other preoccupations became more pressing. I do remember, though, that in my father's circle of friends was a vineyard owner from a well-known and prosperous *pied-noir* family, who possessed a large amount of agricultural land. Vine growing was brought to Algeria with colonisation and by the 1950s the country produced vast quantities of cheap and basic wine, which was then shamelessly blended to help boost the amount of *vin de table* from the Languedoc – the very bottles, probably, that British tourists were so surprised to find in French supermarkets priced at an incredible couple of Francs. It was these *pied-noir* landowners, by the way, the most ardent proponents and greatest beneficiaries of the colonial situation, who had been the first to transfer their fortunes to Switzerland when the war of independence started, later buying up wine properties in France, to which they moved before the disastrous debacle of the final two years of the war.

I became much more aware of wine when sent on summer holidays to my father's family in France, staying with my paternal grandmother or one of the great-aunts. That's where I began to discover the place of wine in relation to food – and, beyond that, in family life. It is during the many extended meals that I first got an inkling that different wines were being brought to the table for different courses and I gradually became aware of the attention being given to marrying dishes and wines. One or other of my great-uncles would often ask me to accompany them to their cellar – they all had well-stocked reserves – to help them bring up the chosen bottles, which I was given to understand was a privileged task, an honour. As the years passed, they would talk more about their choices and the wines' particular qualities and histories. I now regret that, not untypically for an adolescent, I became less rather than more interested. I could have learnt so much at that early stage, and there would have been the added satisfaction of knowledge being passed down within the family rather than acquired later from strangers. But it did set me up for a proper appreciation of wine, the idea that a wine cellar was something to treasure, that you sometimes had to wait several years to enjoy a wine at its best, that careful selection was needed to complement the food – that it was something to be handled with as much attention as was given to the cooking, and therefore worthy of equal respect.

Even though I was often desperate to leave the table to join friends, I still loved the ceremonial aspects of these meals. The beautifully set table, covered in a white cloth, the Limoges plates, the elaborately set-out cutlery, the several crystal glasses for each setting, the crisply folded napkins. All conforming to unwritten rules which for me, after Algeria, represented a longed-for normality. These occasions, after our loss of everything, also gave me a sense of achievable abundance, which was reassuring. I understand why people might be made to feel uncomfortable by the formality of gastronomic restaurants but when it is done with restraint and competence I find echoes of those family meals when eating in them, and a wave of *bien-être*, a sense of diffuse well-being, washes over me. This early exposure to what the French like to refer to as '*les arts de la table*', which encompasses everything to do with what appears on the table, both form and content, has left an indelible mark.

The respect for the conventions surrounding food and wine that every French child imbibes early at the family table may well have its source in the fact that French people of my generation are often no more than one or two generations away from people who worked on the land to produce that sustenance. This is perhaps now fast disappearing but, compared to Britain, there is still much resistance to the concept of individually just grabbing something to eat, to be wolfed down on one's lap in front of television or computer, or that of grazing, the strange, largely American habit of snacking at any time of day. The stubborn adherence of the French to regular and defined mealtimes probably also has its roots in the unfolding of the working day in rural communities. It becomes so ingrained – in my case reinforced by the needs of diabetes – that even after all these years I cannot abide the thought of having lunch in the middle of the afternoon.

What is also acquired by every child in France is an idea of the place and purpose of wine – that it is, primarily, to accompany and enhance the enjoyment of food. Sometimes I think this is a defining difference between a French and a British upbringing. A lot of wine drinking, on its own, is not common in France – if you exclude champagne. Yes, you might be offered a glass of rosé or a light white wine as a pre-prandial drink but you are far more likely to receive a suggestion of '*un whisky?*' as an *apéritif*, strange though that may sound. And yes, in contradiction to the above, you could bring up the stereotypical image of the lone man sitting at a café counter, drinking a series of *petits ballons de rouge*, but that's a minority occupation these days. In Britain, wine is more likely to be regarded as just another alcoholic drink to be had on any occasion, often on its own. In France, wine is mostly what appears at meals.

And what an appearance it makes, central (in the middle of the table) and ubiquitous (almost always present). In all its variety of colour, taste, origin and quality, it brings an added dimension to the feast. For day-to-day meals, its presence can be modest and almost as unnoticeable as the bread. In the Charente village of my now lost domain, not so long ago you could have lunch in the café on the little square and be served a no-choice, four-course *menu ouvrier*, literally aimed at workers, with a bottle of wine that had been filled from a *barrique* put on the table for you to help yourself from, which of course you would do with moderation as custom demanded, drinking only enough to add a layer of savour to the already tasty food. The whole thing cost eleven euros – nothing extra for the wine. The only reason the proprietress, who was also the cook, was able to make it work was that many of the ingredients were grown in the family *jardin potager* and that the wine was produced from small vineyards on her brothers' farm. No ownership of vineyards needed, though, for a bottle of *vin de table* to be placed on the dinner table in most French homes. On other, more special occasions, greater performers will appear, sparring with each dish in glorious two-part acts. And sometimes the wine will even be the star of the show, stepping to the front of the stage. In any case, I still find it difficult to conceive of food without wine or of wine without food.

Beyond its role in relation to food, and to push the metaphor further than maybe it should go, wine is as extraordinarily colourful and entertaining as the most exuberant thespian – in appearance, dress, personality, it shines in multifarious ways. Step into any decent wine shop, look at the shelves and be transported across the globe. The half-dozen usual suspects will dominate, but it is now common to find bottles from a score of other countries, some of which might surprise you – even China is now exporting some of its wines. Don't think in terms of only red or white, or even just adding the in-between rosé. It will not take you long to discover that red can be a gradation of that hue from light, translucent to deep, nearly opaque. Equally there are whites that are so pale that you could mistake them for water and at the other end ones that are the colour of liquid honey. Even rosé varies from pale reddish to almost white with the tiniest hint of pink.

Think beyond Merlot or Chardonnay and the shopkeeper should be able to amaze you with a multitude of grape varieties. There are some with wonderfully evocative names (not that you'll necessarily find some of the rarer of these in the average wine shop). I like the hint of friendship in a Tuscan grape called Bonamico. Then contrast it with a Ukrainian one – once they are able to grow it again in Ukraine – that goes by the more unsubtle Bastardo Magarachsky. In the Ariège region of France they have a grape called Canari Noir – I don't know if the wine made from it sings or if its presence in a blend presages a bit of a taste disaster. Petit Verdot, on the other hand, may be small but makes a qualitatively significant contribution to Bordeaux wines in both taste and colour. Varieties can sometimes change names as they travel. Charbono, as dark as coal, originates from the Savoie but is now more widely known in Argentina under the softer name of Douce Noire. The Italian Primitivo, often found in Puglia, is known as the more quirkily designated Zinfandel in California. Argentina in recent years has made Malbec famous but it originated near Cahors in France where it was known as Auxerrois or Côt Noir. Keeping to French custom, the name of the varietal never used to appear on the bottle, which featured instead the regional denomination, Cahors. Seeing the popularity of

Argentinian versions, French producers have increasingly relented and will now mention Malbec – rather than either of the local names. Marketing *oblige*. Some of the quirkiness of grape varieties also extends to the names of denominations, the specific areas from which the wines originate. Try remembering after just a glance, including the correct spelling, Pacherenc du Vic-Bihl. Or try thinking of the name Picpoul de Pinet without smiling. Yes, they are both real and rather surprisingly the latter has become quite a fad in British restaurants.

Don't leave my pretend wine shop without taking in the design richness and immense variety of the labels. They are a visual pleasure in themselves even though you need to guard against being enticed exclusively by a well-designed, original image. Some of the blandest wines hide behind the fanciest labels. With fine wines you normally don't have that risk as most of their producers eschew too much creativity and stick to traditional looks. But in recent years innovative small producers have increasingly brought originality to both labels and names. There is no need to search far to find examples of the weird and wonderful. Here are a few I gleaned from the online list of one of my favourite independent wine shops in La Rochelle: *A ma guise* (as I please), *Cause toujours* (keep talking), *A bouche que veux tu* (passionately, as in kissing), *L'âme sœur* (soulmate), *Truculence*(!). Just around the time of my beachcombing epiphany, the finding of interesting bits of sea glass and china fragments, that triggered the idea for the form that this attempt at a memoir could take, I bought a few bottles of a Côtes du Rhône, an unusual choice for me. An everyday sort of wine but one made by a seventh-generation wine-maker famous for his prestigious Côte-Rôtie, and perhaps not surprisingly given its provenance, it really sang. And its name was *Le temps est venu* – the time has come. Temporarily abandoning my rationality, I decided to take this as a sign, a bit like reading coffee grains, telling me to start putting together these pieces of a life. I am still unsure if it was a sign of *Sagesse* (wisdom, the name on another bottle) or *Un brin de folie* (a grain of folly, also a wine...).

Beyond this plethora of wine-related factoids, what I find even more fascinating are the stories of wine-making, the tales of human endeavour and character. The real romance of wine. It's a world where it is easy to come across deep attachment to the land and long-lasting family connections to particular vineyards, full of fascinating stories stretching across the years.

One of these stories, that sounds like a myth but is not, relates to the oldest champagne house, Ruinart. Founded in 1729 by Nicolas Ruinart, the nephew of Dom Thierry Ruinart, a Benedictine monk who, with a fellow monk called Dom Perignon (now a more famous name...), Ruinart was at the origin of the champagne method. Originally, the business was mainly the exporting of cloth to European royal courts for making uniforms. But when Louis XV authorised the transporting of wine in bottles, Nicolas was able to produce the first champagne that could travel beyond the local area, as previous transport in vats had not been suitable for a sparkling wine. The interesting thing is that what must have been a novelty was not at first offered *for sale* around the European courts but was given away *free* as an incentive to buy the cloth. The popularity of the wine soon outstripped the need for the material, and within six years Ruinart gave up the cloth trade to concentrate on making and selling champagne – which it still does to this day.

I recently told this to the chairman of Websters, who introduced me to Ruinart and who did not know the story behind it – a small token of my appreciation after all these years of enjoyment. Some wines remain forever associated with a person or an event – and in some cases, as here, with both. He was my boss at the time but after a few years of working together we had already become friends. At first, I had had some apprehension about working for yet another Old Etonian – having had to put up with the vagaries and oddities of the scion of the press-owning family who had swept through Harrap. Fortunately, I soon realised that the man I was working with now was a completely different sort of character. A big personality as well as a large imposing man, confident and assertive, he was by contrast with my previous OE very much of this world and, as I was to find out many times over the years, his heart was certainly in the right place. Despite our different backgrounds, personalities and even physiques, something clicked between us and our collaboration has now lasted over a quarter of a century and, even more importantly, has remained a friendship too. The latter being greatly helped by our common love of good food and fine wine. As the original publisher of Oz Clark's books and other wine titles, his expertise on the subject is extensive. I sometimes feel I have imbibed a little bit of this vast wine knowledge with the content of every bottle we have drunk over the years, perhaps by a sort of miraculous vinous osmosis...

There are times when fate, even business fate, smiles upon you and those times are certainly the ones for drinking something sparkling – and the very fine bubbles, the clean, subtle, elegant taste of Ruinart is perfect for that. Contrary to what the name might imply, there was, as I discovered, nothing ruinous about it; rather it left me with a lasting taste for its celebratory brio. We had just taken over responsibility for the content of French *Encarta* and the champagne was for a launch party to mark the opening of our Paris office. It was a late June evening in Paris, the slanting sun streaming through the windows, in a room full of bright young editors who all seemed so enthusiastic about working for us, and the champagne flowed – it was one of those times when it feels like everything is falling into place, when you feel, well, bubbly, and you allow yourself to look ahead with optimism. A rare moment, the taste of which I recapture in a fleeting and somewhat elegiac way every time I have a glass of Ruinart.

At the origin of another human story of wine-making is a wine that left a similarly profound impression on my senses when I first tasted it, also in Paris, probably around the same period. It was one of those occasions when the initial sip of a wine stops you in your tracks, makes you pause to take in fully the varied sensual pleasures being unleashed. It can start before the glass has even reached your lips, as aromas are released as soon as the wine is poured and even more so as you swirl it in your glass. In this case a scent of freshly picked raspberries assailed my nostrils and transported me back to my great-aunt Henriette's garden and my childhood holidays in France. Next was the joy of a wine that floated silkily across the palate, and then slowly revealed its substance and character as I swallowed, so that I became properly imbued with its flavour, adding a touch of violet and cherry, and a hint of liquorice to the confirmed raspberries. This is when you realise this is not just a well-made wine, when you know you have found that holy grail of wine, a harmonious balance between the different elements

– with the softness and concentration of fruit, the structure and texture of tannins, and the level of acidity in perfect consonance. The wine is singing to you. And I definitely felt all that when I had my first taste of a Morgon from Marcel Lapierre.

The setting was appropriate, a meal at Le Square Trousseau, a café-restaurant not far from Place de la Bastille in the 12th *arrondissement* – a rare establishment that has kept its turn-of-the-century (the previous one, that is...) art-nouveau décor intact. The two-tone marble tiles on the floor, large mirrors on the walls, a zinc-covered bar counter and varnished dark wood tables and chairs make you believe that Jean Gabin (who apparently was a regular) playing a 1930s' stylish gangster could at any time walk through the door. In fact, the interior has such atmosphere that it is often used as a set for period films or TV series. Anyway, its authentic feel was the perfect foil for tasting this wine for the first time.

But the lasting significance came not so much from the moment or the location but from getting to know the story behind the wine. Beyond enjoying it, I got to admire the man who made it. Although I never met him – he died far too early, in his sixties – he became a bit of a hero of mine for re-establishing traditional wine-making values and becoming a leading light of the renaissance of his Morgon *appellation*, and more widely of his wine region, the Beaujolais. With the advent, since the 1970s, of the Beaujolais Nouveau marketing operation, the region had become prone to the over-production of insipid wines. Marcel Lapierre's story is one of reaction against this, a story of redemption in a way. Resisting the prevailing commercial pressures, he railed against the fashion for beaujolais nouveau, which he castigated as tasting of "banana and boiled sweets" (ironically, *bonbons anglais* in French), and described it as a wine "*sitôt fait, sitôt bu et sitôt pissé*", quickly made, quickly drunk and quickly pissed away. In stark contrast, Marcel Lapierre's name itself, to me, has an earthy and peasanty (in a good way) authenticity to it. Lapierre evokes something of the stony ground where the roots of his old vines have to go deep to search for nutrients. In the 1980s Marcel jettisoned all use of chemical fertilisers, herbicides and pesticides, as well as the use of sulphites as much as possible, in order to make what he called "*un vin tout raisin*", a wine where the grape can express itself fully and exclusively – what is now known as a natural wine. He reduced the productivity of his vines to increase the quality of the retained bunches, and in the vinification process he allowed plenty of time for the Gamay grapes to do their best. Soon he was producing wines of great depth and purity, which also retained the supple, joyous nature of Gamay, so typical of Beaujolais wines. A few other producers adopted the same methods, and worldwide commercial success followed. Beyond that, there was a degree of emulation in the whole region and I think even Beaujolais Nouveau improved somewhat...

Marcel Lapierre died in 2010, but in the way that is both common and admirable in many wine regions his children have taken over the domain and continue his tradition of making "*tout raisin*", voluptuous Morgon wines. In reading up about Marcel, I discovered he had been friends with Guy Debord, philosopher, film-maker, critic of consumer society, and author of the Situationist tract *The Society of the Spectacle*, whose ideas had a strong influence on the student movement of May 68. I thought at first that this was an odd pairing, the intellectual *provocateur* and the third-generation *viticulteur*, but then realised that not only were they both rebels, what they also had in common was their search for authenticity. One could imagine their joint slogan might have been 'real, pure wine for a real, just society'.

Listening to the secrets of strangers

In a somewhat stretched link, I could say that I too spent some time in a search for authenticity, or rather helping others seeking to reconnect with their authentic self. This took the form of listening to the troubles and secrets of strangers when, in my fifties and sixties, I did some voluntary work as a counsellor. Voluntary but not amateurish because I had trained part-time over five years, and gained a university diploma in psychodynamic counselling. Aware of the precarity of my main job and the difficulties of finding a similar position in publishing in middle age, I wanted something to fall back on. I had always been interested in psychoanalysis and psychotherapy – ever since my times in the leather armchair in my teacher/mentor's study back in Niort. Those were counselling sessions in all but name and I knew how much I had benefited from them. So, for several years, I volunteered with an organisation offering free counselling in a deprived area of Oxford. Attendees were usually referred by their GPs for at least six months of weekly sessions.

Throughout the country, at any one time, there are hundreds, probably thousands, of similar scenes being played out – a quiet room, not too brightly lit, two people facing each other, at an angle, one looking tense, hesitant, sad, relieved or even angry, who seems to do most of the talking; the other, head inclined, keeping eye contact, an understanding expression on their face, looking concerned, but calm and reflective, and always, always interested. And in these many repeated scenes, the often hardly glowing embers of human empathy are being fanned into life again, for a few moments at least.

In the first of those sessions with each person I was struck by two contradictory things. One was how much courage it took for people, often in the midst of chaotic instability, to come to see a therapist. And immediately following that, how much people wanted to be heard. In many cases there was no one else to tell their stories to, whether because the partner at home had stopped listening, the children lived on another planet, the friends were too busy, or quite simply they were on their own. These realisations in themselves foster empathy for the patient – I prefer that term to the widely used 'client'. It takes patience to reflect on one's life, patience with oneself, patience with others and patience with the world at large. There is a lot of patience and attention required of the therapist too in creating a safe haven where the patient's past and present can collide in conducive circumstances so that often, out of that collision, feeling better can emerge.

In many ways, effective therapy is a joint exercise in emotional archaeology, peeling away layers of self-deception, or just confusion, to reach moments when something from the past can flood the present with a new light. For the patient, introspection is not usually easy. It can feel like probing a wound, like worrying the many scars of adult emotional survival. In listening to patients, an image used to come to my mind, that our childhood pains and traumas were like shards of broken glass dropped on a freshly concreted floor that we walk and cut ourselves on for the rest of our lives. Sometimes we can lay softwood flooring or carpets over them but the sharp edges still come through at unexpected moments. And at one time or another we need to get down on our knees and work hard on filing them down until they are smoothed over, and in some cases work even harder to chisel them out of the concrete – both long and arduous tasks, but ones that at least give you the prospect of walking through life more easily.

For the therapist, it can sometimes feel as if you are a mental sleuth, doing detective work, searching for meaning in the mysterious byways of someone else's psyche. Often it is like a slow exploration of little-explored emotional lives, through the clutter and confusion of memory, to help reclaim territory obscured by illusions and chimera that are more superficially seductive than the complexities of the life actually lived.

It is certainly helpful for the therapist to reach a state of *understanding*, to see clearly a narrative and where patients are in their stories. But there are also dangers in that. First, for the therapist to stray into self-gratification for being clever – and ending up treating all patients' problems as intellectual puzzles to be resolved. Also, this can lead to the therapist thinking that a clear vision is a solution to the patient's problems, and that apprising them of that vision will be sufficient to make them feel better. I found out that although this *can* help, if sensitively done and timely, it is rarely enough. Clearly, when people strive to make sense of their stories it is not just the mind at work but the heart needs to be engaged too.

So, for resolution or even just improvement in how they cope to happen, it has to be a felt experience. Time and again I was made to realise that, beyond understanding, what patients needed was an emotional apprehension of the roots of their problems. Which in many ways is much more difficult for the therapist to achieve as it needs to come out of the very dynamic of their relationship with the patient, a fluid circumstance not always easy to manage with that specific goal in mind. Occasionally, there is a moment of grace when it happens, and you are not always sure exactly how and why. This is not a scientific experiment. It is an encounter between informed empathy and emotional turmoil, not in the least subject to set formulas. It can happen almost by stealth, when what can seem like an innocuous question about a memory can give rise to a surge of feeling that unmistakably fills the room. Other times, it can arise from what has unwittingly become a tense exchange, suddenly causing a breaking wave of emotional relief. In my experience, the moment it happens, however it does, is always unexpected.

I once experienced such a moment of grace in somewhat odd circumstances – in a way, it was thrust upon me. I had been counselling a nineteen-year-old woman who had been raped the year before by someone she knew. She lived with her parents and since the rape she found it extremely difficult to relate to them. Although she had been able to talk about what had happened and they had at first been supportive, she increasingly felt that her mother was irritated with her and that her father was either openly rude or ignored her completely. Her relationship with the latter had become particularly difficult to bear. He had never been the most demonstrative or talkative of people but now she felt there was real antagonism in his attitude towards her. I had noticed the profound hurt this caused, which occasionally found its expression, in a typical case of transference, in angry outbursts directed at me. I sensed that she felt her father held her partly responsible for what had happened and disapproved of her. Over the weeks I did my best to be the recipient of her feelings of anger and to explore ways to help her cope better with them and assuage the hurt. A few months in to the sessions I felt I was making only little progress beyond having established a good level of trust. Something must have been working below the surface, however, based on that trust, because one day when she arrived for the session, I discovered she had brought her father along, saying she had spoken to him about her therapy. She had asked him to come and he had agreed.

This had never happened to me before and it posed a double dilemma – I was unprepared, had no experience nor any special training in family therapy and, strictly speaking, letting him in was breaking the rules of the counselling service. After a moment's hesitation I decided to go ahead – and what followed, fortunately, did not make me regret it. Not wanting to waste any of the time we had, the daughter immediately started to explain to her father how his attitude made her feel, which she managed to do with controlled emotion. Even more surprisingly, the father did not respond in anger or retreat into curtness or silence but opened up, a bit hesitantly at first, about how difficult he had found it to deal with what had happened, that he did not disapprove of her but just "did not know what to do". It was a clash of strong feelings, for the first time openly and honestly expressed, but a clash that defused rather than inflamed. You could call the rest of the session an intense time of reconciliation. My more or less silent role in this was simply to bear witness to a cathartic moment. It remains the most memorable of all my counselling sessions. She came back for a couple of sessions after that, during which she confirmed that things had been much easier at home. Of course, the trauma of what had happened to her had not vanished but it was good to see that she was facing life with renewed fortitude.

Fortitude in the face of adversity is something I came across so often during those times listening to strangers that it has become for me an abiding legacy of that period. It was not just the overcoming of fears needed to take the step to come for counselling. What I often came across too was a kind of everyday heroism, when in spite of everything that life threw at them, up against a variety of vicissitudes, often without the traditional support of family or community, people still managed to find forbearance and endurance and, in some cases, even a cheerful determination.

It is this resilience that I always looked for – to help bring it to the fore and nurture it for a while. And in many cases I found that it was within reach. Enabling people to articulate their sorrows, to share their distress, can lead them to develop a sort of autobiographical competence, a clearer apprehension of what makes them who they are. Which in the first instance can calm the turmoil they came with, and in the longer run help them cope with life's trials with greater equanimity.

As part of the increased attention justifiably being given to mental health, there is a risk of casting people too much as victims, as living in a permanent state of hopeless vulnerability, and under-estimating the ability of humans to handle emotional suffering. In a society that posits relentless cheerfulness as the ideal condition, it is difficult not to be made to feel that distress, or even just sadness, denotes failure. When in fact the reality of human life is that we have to carry aching voids and absences as well as positive experiences and happy times, that we endure as much as we enjoy. Hence, to my mind, the importance of duly valuing the human capacity for resilience.

Myths and legends

This is going to be a jump from individual psyches to collective ones, inevitably involving a liberal use of generalisations, including some that may be deemed outrageous. But generalisations, like clichés, do not come out of thin air – they are formed from an accumulation of small truths. Before laying into well-established myths, I will claim as credentials over half a century of close observation of the English and the French, and their perception of one another. And in this case, I mean the English rather than the British as I think what I am about to describe is primarily an English phenomenon that is not so prevalent in the other nations of the UK. (I will still use the term British when referring to attitudes coming from the French, as regretfully for our Scottish, Welsh or Northern Irish compatriots, the differentiation is rarely properly appreciated. Anyway, I will do my best to use English and British appropriately.)

I start with a revelation that came surprisingly late to me, couched in my acquired very English way: there is quite a bit of anti-French sentiment about in England. I know, I know, there is also no shortage of (mainly middle-class) Francophilia about but this does not invalidate the previous statement, especially as for many a Francophile I have often thought it is the French lifestyle, food, countryside, culture that they love – the French themselves, not so much... Maybe in my early years in this country I was so bathed in the initial love affair with it that I was seeing everything through a reality-distorting filter. Maybe because I was trying to get away from my own 'Frenchness', I might even have semi-consciously colluded with these negative views at times. And it would only rarely have been directed at me personally – and if so, in such a deflected way that I probably did not notice. Over the years, as I became better at seeing through covered-up meanings, it became more obvious. In fact, beyond the anti-French sentiment, I became increasingly aware that there was plenty of evidence of a widespread preoccupation with the French and their imagined attitudes to Britain. Ever since, this has remained for me, after a lifetime lived with a foot (a head and a heart too) in both cultures, one of the strangest, oddest features of English society. And it has niggled me quite a bit.

I now believe there are two aspects to it. On one level, it seems to be rooted in a fundamental misreading of French attitudes, thinking that the French, to put it bluntly, have systematically got it in for the English, which I believe can be described as a case of collective projection, and as with all projections is based on a misunderstood premise. I have occasionally addressed this rather facetiously in response to friends and acquaintances still smarting from having been at the receiving end of some unpleasantness from a French shopkeeper or official by telling them, "If you think the French have got it in for you as a Brit, the key thing to understand is that the French have got it in for everybody, including other French people" (particularly true in urban settings). Keeping to this not entirely serious register, I wish I could find a way of telling the whole nation, don't take it personally... The French are just very good at giving the impression they don't like anybody. It can be that simple.

On another level, if I slip my acquired English skin on – I have to say English here – I can see quite clearly how of lot of Frenchness can rub up the wrong way against English sensibilities. And that this can have quite a lot to do with creating and perpetuating the above misunderstanding. If I think too much about it, I sometimes feel it's a miracle that the two nationalities manage to get on at all.

Going back to the first aspect, what is noticeable is that there is a much greater awareness of the French in England than there is awareness of the British in France. Put quite simply, the French don't concern themselves with Britain and the British as much as the English concern themselves with France and the French – often in a mode of antagonism or mockery. The 'French and their anti-British ways', as a trope, never seems to be far from the minds of politicians, journalists, commentators, newscasters, stand-up comics, or pub pundits. And the strangest thing about this is that it is often done with reference to the historical concept of the 'old enemy' – a concept that you would be hard pushed to come across on the other side of the Channel, unless you were to consult historians who were specialising in the relevant periods…

This widely displayed belief that the contemporary French are still in the grip of an historically rooted, almost atavistic animus against the British is unfounded in reality – and is certainly not reciprocated. As mentioned, the French by and large don't pay that much attention to Britain and I am certain that awareness of the Hundred Years' Wars, the burning of Joan of Arc at the stake, or Napoleon's defeat at Waterloo does not surface in French popular thought when it comes to contemporary issues. To most French people it all belongs to the history books and certainly has not contributed to create, as in England, this pervasive and still actively perpetrated myth of an old enmity lasting to this day. The oft-repeated view that the French are always all too ready to oppose the British has no counterpart in France – in fact, again, the French mostly do not overconcern themselves with the UK and the British. French people just don't grow up with this view, and if and when they are made aware of it, it comes as a surprise. If the historical enmity is ever brought up, it is more likely to be as a subject of jokes than as in any way relevant to current problems. There is no equivalent in France of the British press's persistent shoring up of this view, the way it is periodically called upon, especially by the tabloids, to drum up largely imagined petty feuds or to inflame disputes and disagreements. Even at the height of the mad cow disease outbreak there was no vicious or even general turning against Britain in the French press, commentariat or public opinion.

The most critical view of Britain widely held by the French is that it is too prone to siding with the USA, rather than with Europe. (Iraq was a seminal moment in that respect.) Allied to that is a perception that there is a greater acceptance in Britain of unfettered capitalism, especially since the Reagan–Thatcher era. As a result of both this perceived fealty to Atlanticism and the embracing of neo-liberalism, it is, sadly, not uncommon for the French to lump the UK in with the USA in what they refer to (oddly to a British ear) as the 'Anglo-Saxon world'. Also, more recently it is true that there has been the occasional reappearance from the mists of history of the old concept of Perfidious Albion, but that is entirely due to the Buffoon's government trying to renege on an international treaty that now appears to have been signed in bad faith. Although it is worth noting that it is puzzlement and, for many, sadness that are the most common reactions to Brexit (which, by the way, are shared by most Europeans); it would be difficult to find feelings of anger generally directed at the British because of Brexit.

Notwithstanding the fact that the relationship with Britain does not occupy centre stage in France, there is no doubt in my mind that, contrary to the myth, there is a deep reservoir of goodwill towards the British. More recent history than that usually dredged up by the propagators of the 'old enemy' trope can explain this. For my parents' generation, the part that British troops (along with the Americans) played in the liberation of their country in 1945 is still very much in their consciousness. For my generation, when we were young, and as I have written earlier, Britain was a shining beacon of a freer, more congenial society within reach. We loved its music, its youth culture and street fashion. Fondness experienced in those formative years tends to last. And with the generations that have come after mine, even though post-1968 France became a more relaxed country, the fascination with Britain has not ceased. I can say with certainty that for young French people over the last sixty years London in particular has been, well, at times extremely cool, at times less than that, but always, always cool. See how many of them still want to spend time living there, even after Brexit.

Prior to my latest self-imposed exile to Scotland, I spent fifty years or so immersed in English society, and whenever I allowed the ambient temperament to fully permeate my own and to experience thinking of the French from the perspective of an English sensibility, I could clearly see how some of the French ways and attitudes can easily be triggers for misunderstanding. Relating these observations may come across not only as wild generalisations but also as brutally critical in some cases, so I should acknowledge that I do not give myself a free pass from their being applied to me. In spite of all my efforts to shed the more lurid parts of my 'Frenchness', some of the original colouring has remained stubbornly indelible... But at least this might give me a degree of legitimacy, and permission to be candidly rude about the French.

They may not be deliberate or specially targeted but it is true that some aspects of the French national character and ways of being do not mesh easily with English culture – in fact one could say they go against the grain. There's a kind of abrasiveness and over-assertiveness in mannerisms common in France which can come across as lack of restraint, unpleasantness, and even in-your-face rudeness. It is not meant with as much noxious intent as the English recipients of it imagine (they mis-measure it by using an English yardstick) and, to reiterate, they don't realise that this behaviour is not kept as a special offering to them alone but is available to everyone, including other French people. But nevertheless, the damage is done.

It is not unusual for the French to display a high dose of prickly self-regard, to react far too quickly with irritability and not hold back from showing it. There is often a thin-skinned predilection for taking offence and for that offence to be voiced and immediately made manifest. Silent, delayed retaliation using passive aggression is not, unlike in England, a sport much practised in France. Nor is deflection, another much used English defence aimed at containing any threat. For the French, this would puzzle or possibly cause anger. There will be a suspicion that reserve and false politeness are codpieces for hypocrisy and condescension, and will be received as hurtfully patronising. Neither is mordant irony, another English forte, likely to be well understood by the French. I can see how to an English sensibility there is plenty to be irreverent about, but the French default is to take themselves seriously and irreverence can often clash with that.

The French are not always good at weaning themselves off the sullen pomposity and grandiloquence typical of a clever adolescent. Admittedly they can be unwittingly trapped in that by the very nature of their language. Utterances that can sound reasonably well founded and articulate in French do not always 'travel' well into English, where they will often come across to an English ear as convoluted and, especially, pretentious. (If this is ever reviewed, a perspicacious critic will in all likelihood find examples of precisely this in my own writing – though, as I do my thinking in English, it will not entirely prove the point, just that one is forever tainted...) It is a mysterious phenomenon that would require an explanation worthy of quantum physics, involving how the same thing can be different depending on who is experiencing it, but it is nonetheless ubiquitous. I remember a clear demonstration of this during an interview on British TV news with a particularly media-friendly French public figure and philosopher. Longish mane of black hair much in evidence, white shirt open to the second button down, he was answering short questions in what would have been well-crafted paragraphs in French but which came across in his accented, though grammatically quite good, English as the verbose outpourings of an arrogant pseud. No doubt unwittingly, he had managed to make both his appearance and his words irritating to an English (and in this case probably British) audience.

In a way similar to the Italians' concern with *bella figura*, the French are prone to wanting to appear more profound than they are. (Funnily enough, it is not uncommon for well-educated English people to do just the opposite.) They can far too easily give the impression of wanting to show off intellectually all the time, which to an English sensibility with an often uncomfortable relationship with the very word 'intellectual', is not only unimpressive but off-putting and tiresome. In French adulthood, you never forget that as an adolescent you carried around obscure tomes which you would never read but would confidently pontificate about, *gauloise* in hand – and perhaps you want to recapture that moment... (You see how easy it is to mock.)

There are interactions between the French and the English that on many occasions make me cringe. There is a certain puppy-like, unbridled enthusiasm in the French that can be irksome. The exaggerated gestures, the overemphatic statements, the readily raised shoulders, and the all-too-readable (and all too easy to misread...) facial expressions cannot not be noticed. With 'English eyes', I can at times see it all in myself, and that can be even more vexing. I can see how easy it can be to make the French appear faintly ridiculous – how all the elements are there to make up the Inspector Clouseau stereotypes that regularly appear in popular culture. (Not forgetting the fact, written about in an earlier section, that, unfortunate though it may be, the French do sound silly and comical when speaking English with a bad accent.) Often included is a too overt interest in sex, food and wine and a perceived overindulgence in all three (by the way, apparently real in only two of the three; I'll let you guess which is more of a myth). Sometimes I can't help wondering whether the instantly triggered mocking from the English is not just yet another defence against an ingrained reticence to examine their own repressed sides, but maybe I am reading too much into it. (Or am I now indulging in a bit of passive aggression?)

As if all this was not enough, there is another fundamental difference that gives plenty of opportunity for misunderstanding. I know I am still treading in blanket generalisation territory but if it had to be described in a pithy headline, I would say the French are literal, the English allusive. The English excel at not telling it as it is; the French never let you forget that it is as it is. It is a clash between the rule of the opaque metaphor and the rule of unforgiving candour. The metaphor will involve imagination, occasionally stray into exaggeration and fantasy, and sometimes sacrifice precision and accuracy for the sake of a good story. It will dare to be loose with facts, chronology and logic to help foster an entertaining conversation. The candour will often take liberties with politeness and good manners, but will plough its furrow in a straight line, stolidly if often roughly, and will aspire to analysis and rational triumph rather than polite debate or banter. Using phrases typical of English middle-class circles in post-dinner-party debriefings, the metaphor, if personified as a guest, would likely be described with the words, "She's good value!", whilst I could well imagine the candour attracting the comment, "He can be a bit much!"

Speaking of laughs, humour is yet more dangerous ground. The French will not always get the wry repartee that comes readily to the English. They will be baffled, needing a mental pause to understand it, and then to decide whether it contained a sting in the tail. Falling on equally stony ground could be the French predilection for play on words or, even worse, for the kind of shaggy-dog, long-winded telling of jokes that requires much gesticulation and possibly crude, or these days outdated, references. All of this is not exactly conducive to shared jollity.

All in all, you might say it's a volatile mix. So, I should perhaps shift to a more benign way of illustrating the difference. And what better way than to ask you to think of gardens. Conjure up an image of an English garden, lush and pragmatically mixed in abundant, creative but controlled chaos, and contrast it with the straight lines and square parterres, ordered ranks of plants, pleasing symmetry of a classic French garden, and I suggest you have a schematic representation of how each nation's brains are primarily fashioned. I have a vision of an abundance of varied forms, creatively arranged, colours at their best against the all-too-frequent grey of the English weather, and by contrast, of angular shapes, strongly defined, shining starkly under a hot sun on the French side. Each has its particular beauty.

It is at least a gentle metaphor with which to conclude these observations – which some, on both sides, may dismiss, feeling that they come from someone stranded between two cultures rather than rooted in either. (Such is the fate of the expatriate. I suppose I was a citizen of nowhere long before the term was coined.) It is difficult to tackle these issues without shamelessly generalising. This has been a well-intentioned attempt at crystallising essential aspects of a reality that I have personally been affected by, for better or worse, for a long time now. I fully accept that a case can be made that this reality is more complex, more multifaceted, and that it contains opposite aspects of the main features I have chosen to highlight. I hope it can be read with this in mind.

Having said that, I will allow myself a last flourish of gross oversimplification with this not entirely serious but punchy summary:

Yes, the French can be abrasive, impolite, too direct, thin-skinned, overdemonstrative, bad tempered. Which often causes the English to feel the French don't like them. Which then causes the English to respond with evasiveness, deflection, irony, mocking and, for good measure, scapegoating the French.

Simples.

Standing rather shakily in this liminal space, on a flimsy bridge over the chasm between the two sides, I can only end optimistically with a modest plea for a clearer understanding from everyone, for a better *compréhension cordiale*.

My first vote

To all intents and purposes, I am now a citizen of Scotland and I recently first exercised my right to vote in local elections here. It was a new experience because a different electoral system applied from what I was used to in England. It felt good to get away from the dreadful first-past-the-post (FPTP) system, which only works fairly in a situation where there are just two parties in contention). I welcomed the chance to use a form of proportional representation. The single transferable vote (STV, where you vote for as many candidates as you like in order of preference) is fiendishly difficult to fully explain but suffice to say that it ensures the outcome represents fairly the diversity of views in a local area. Rather than go into detail, I will just quote as an illustration of this from the results of a vote in a Glasgow ward where four councillors were elected, one Scottish National Party (SNP), one Conservative, one Labour and one Green – had the vote been held under the FPTP system, all four elected councillors would have been SNP.

The inadequacies of FPTP seem to have ensured, particularly in recent years, that the worst of us are chosen to misrule over the rest of us. For years now, over 50 per cent of the voting population of the UK (if you add together the votes for Labour, Lib Dem and SNP, all pretty close in terms of ideology and policies) has consistently voted against the party that has clung to power over more than the last decade. The result of the 2019 general election can be considered a landslide only if you look at the elected MPs, not the popular vote. And that's without taking into account the issues around abstentions. In today's British political landscape, FPTP is an irrational and ludicrously unfair system. So, under this STV system, and with a bit of hesitancy because of having arrived here only a year ago, I was able to split my preferences. First, for the SNP because of its social-democratic, progressive stance on most issues, second Green because both locally and nationally they can help bend priorities the right way, and third Labour, partly out of loyalty (possibly not so justified here, but Scottish Labour has been getting better recently) and partly because some oppositional scrutiny (from at least a morally sound quarter) on a hugely dominant party is quite healthy. It was the first time in years that I was not forced to vote tactically just to prevent the candidate from the most awful party from being elected on a minority vote – and it felt gratifying.

I am not sure that it will be so easy to feel the same on the key poll that is likely to come at some point in the next few months or years – to make a decision on the fate of the nation. For a start it will be a binary choice and the decision about going for independence or not is not a straightforward one. It is not only that I am temperamentally uninclined to embrace nationalism – the concept has too many negative connotations to be comfortable with it. The misplaced patriotism of my childhood has left deep scars, meaning I am acutely averse to anything even vaguely resembling it. (I currently see it raising its ugly head again, in a parallel way to the *pieds-noirs*' historical blindness, among the Northern Ireland unionists, and being cynically used by a bungling UK government.) A narrow chauvinistic element can be at the heart of any nationalism. But not all nationalisms are the same or arise from the same context. To pick an odd illustration, Orban's Fidesz in Hungary and Sturgeon's SNP could not be more different.

But opposing the cause of Scottish independence primarily by using a standard critique of the nefarious aspects of *some* nationalisms does not stack up for me. I find Scottish nationalism understandable and acceptable only because it is progressive – aspiring to a fairer society and based on values of community that have been part of this land for ever. I was asked recently by former English colleagues how I liked living in Scotland and when I answered that one aspect I particularly appreciated was the more pervasive sense of community compared with England, I was surprised that they did not seem to know what I was referring to. And yet it is obvious to me that community is in the air and in the mood here. I would have thought the slightest acquaintance with Scottish society would make that clear. I see it in a myriad of small and not so small ways in my everyday life here.

One aspect of it is that, in spite of budget constraints that apply everywhere, local councils seem to pay more attention to community needs. It is not just that the bins are emptied every week, and every day in the case of the street ones. It is also that driving through towns around here you can't help noticing how good the provision of tennis courts, sports centres and swimming pools, and other sports facilities is – reminiscent of provincial France in that respect. Similarly, as we've discovered recently there is an abundance of free health activities for older people. As you walk around you can't fail to see municipal gardens being assiduously maintained. My window looks out onto a small area of grass in a public park – periodically I see this being mown by no fewer than three council employees (it is possibly more efficient being done that way). Whilst a stereotypical Tory-inclined voter in south-east England might immediately think 'waste of our council tax', the words that come to my mind are 'employment' and 'taking care of public space'. It's a difference of attitudes. It makes a change from the decades of deliberate dismantling of council services that I've known in England.

And this pro-community attitude goes way beyond the municipal and pervades many sides of daily life. I notice that many storm-porch outer doors are left open. There is a hardware shop near where we are staying that sees no need to take in new garden furniture for sale from the pavement overnight. An unknown woman in the queue to the baker insisted on paying for my bread when I realised I had forgotten to bring money. On the small walls near the ramps to the beaches there are makeshift wooden boxes with buckets, spades and water toys found on the sand – scrawled on their sides in marker pen are the words, "Please use, replace and add." And, indeed, as I pass by in the evening at the end of a sunny day, their content has been replenished. There is daily evidence in the streets of an enormous amount of volunteering for the good of the community, notably looking after the environment. Sometimes this level of engagement has a more activist character, in defence of local facilities. In this small town, I saw about a thousand people of all ages march to oppose the closing down of the local cottage hospital. More broadly, there is a readiness to take a stand on a community level against perceived iniquities. Twice recently, in Glasgow and in Edinburgh, local people have more or less spontaneously (and peacefully) gathered in large enough numbers to prevent the police from carrying out what they felt were unjust deportations of refugees who were their neighbours.

These actions are in a way symbolic of a nationalism that is not narrow and nativist but outward looking, open to the world. It is also one that wants to assume its place in the European community of nations, not set itself apart, contrary to England, as the results of the 2016 referendum clearly showed. It rejects the overdefensive, utterly unrealistic, quasi-neurotic version of sovereignty that has poisoned the polity of the UK in last few years. It is a pride in country and culture that does not need to be defined *against* other countries and turned into the ridiculous bravado of 'world-beating' boasting. It does not suffer from the insecurity of a post-imperial hangover that requires constant claims of exceptionalism.

Scotland is an old country but, as a result of its revived national ambition, it feels and behaves as a young country. There is an energy and sense of common purpose that is not present in England. By contrast with this feeling of newness, of potential ahead, England (and what the UK frame offers) appears old and tired, and confused – fraught with contradictions. Not knowing what it is. Whereas here, even the half of public opinion that is not fully convinced of the cause of independence is mostly in agreement that they want a *different* society from the current English model.

The prevalent attitudes to Europe here throw into relief the awfulness of what happened in 2016. A country that feared assuming its geographical fate chose, albeit by a narrow margin, to step back into uncertainty. A gigantic waste of what could have been a leading role in Europe – bringing its many strengths, pragmatism, creativity, scientific and technological innovation and more. (Sometimes it makes me want to weep.) Sadly, there seems to be a tendency for many English people to look backwards, to appear desperate for reasons to feel good about themselves and their country, which they seem to search for in the past (often a past that never existed) rather than in the real world of today. By contrast, many in Scotland find validation in wanting to shape a renewed, distinct national destiny. This helps create a sense of optimism and potential ahead – and especially opportunities for young people to feel part of that.

There is a young Scottish woman who puts out TikTok clips on Twitter, doing a 'Scots word of the day' feature. Addicted as I am to words, I find it both fascinating and entertaining. But beyond that, it's symbolic of this new energy turned towards the future. It is not coming, as it could easily have done, from an old male digging nostalgically into the Scots language as a relic, but from a highly educated, intelligent and extremely articulate young woman, who is also an accomplished poet, and who presents it as a lively aspect of her nation's culture for today and tomorrow. Every time, it makes me feel I want to sign up to all this enthusiasm. I sometimes feel I am not sure how entitled I am to do this but there are lots of encouraging noises here about new Scots being welcome. Here again, I can't help contrasting the anti-foreign sentiments stirred up in England since the referendum with the fact that Scotland seems to be confident enough in its national identity to open itself to immigration. Confident that national identification does not need to be exclusively based on genetic inheritance and that newcomers will enrich the country in all kinds of ways. (I can also tell myself that my partner's maternal grandfather and other family members are buried a few miles from where I am writing this so there is at least a degree of original legitimacy by association.)

I am probably too old to see much of the potential come to fruition but I occasionally find myself toying with an idealistic dream of a federation of the nations of the UK within the European Union... Though going in an utterly different, in fact opposite, direction, I see that a right-wing pundit has recently advocated the idea of England going it alone, dropping the antagonistic Scots, dumping the stirred-up Welsh, and presumably abandoning the rump of Unionists in Northern Ireland, to be free to be the England he dreams of, *global* to him, *little* to everyone else – a negative beacon of nativist nationalism, an object lesson in how not to handle a post-imperial role.

Scotland instead appears to me not only confident of what it is but very conscious of its position on the northern edge of the British Isles, aspiring in the first instance to closer relationships with the Scandinavian countries that it faces across the North Sea (other small countries doing well), and as soon as possible to take back its place in Europe. It's tempting to think, "We can be more like Denmark."

The random pursuit of happiness

An unconnected thought about Denmark... A moment of happiness. There is a certain kind of slanting light from a low winter sun here in Scotland that sometimes brings that moment, however fleetingly, out of the blurry area of old memories of youth. It cannot reignite fully the feelings of the time but it is enough at least for a clear vision of the scene to be brought back.

My seventeen-year-old self is sitting at a table with three other people. On my left is my Danish girlfriend or, more accurately, as the relationship is too distant and episodic for her to be called that, my first ever lover. At either end of the small table are the two elderly aunts we are visiting. Across the table I face the largest window I have ever seen: it has one of those enormous single glass panes common in northern countries. Beyond it in the bright haze is an expansive countryside view over the flatlands of Funen Island, not far from Odense. The afternoon sunshine is beaming through the window almost horizontally and fills the room with golden light and warmth. It must be cold outside but inside it is as if the whole scene, people and objects, are burnished with a warm sheen. Everyone is bathed in light and emanates gentle bonhomie. I feel suffused with love and sated longings. But this is not the paroxysm of physical pleasure but a diffuse, profound wave of contentment that rises inside me. A feeling that at this moment, here and now, everything is right with my world, that I am happy. I don't understand what they are saying but Hanne is answering her aunts' questions – about me, I guess – and is smiling, and then the old women look at me and smile too. It is, in the parlance of the times, a feeling of being high, except without the drugs, an undefinable, but oh so tangible atmosphere that seems to be made up of nothing other than meaning well and well-being. The unfamiliar sounds of the foreign language help me stay in this semi-trance state, in which I am aware this is real life but which also feels dreamlike. There is no trace of striving in that moment, just pure living.

The vision now suffers from the inescapable evanescence of happy moments – it is like a glimpse of a rarely seen painting, a scene in a forgotten film, an attempt to recall a much loved melody, a familiar taste of something you can't name, a wisp of the smell of soap that used to be in her bathroom. It all pulls in delicious pain at your senses. You want to grab it all, capture it, fix it for ever – but it soon flits away, leaving you only with a dwindling sense of something wonderful that happened once.

Happy moments almost always come upon us by stealth. At least with this one *I knew*, and lived it fully as such, though I did not realise at the time how it would remain so defined as symbolic and significant for the rest of my life. Often though we don't recognise those moments as happy, except in hindsight, only recognising them for what they were, precious and unrepeated, once they have become memories. Maybe at the time they were obfuscated by what had happened before or the fear of what would happen next, so the passage of years has to erase all the attendant clutter, and those moments have to be reconstructed in all their spare glory – a kind of retrofitted happiness. But this was different.

I sometimes come near to experiencing something approaching what I felt that day, this diffuse and permeating sense of all being well with the world – or my little world anyway – when I walk by the sea on sandy beaches. This is something I have rediscovered in the last year or so since we moved here. But it must go back a long way. Perhaps as far back as my early childhood, walking under a Mediterranean sun on the Algerian beaches in a 1950s world. A world that only consciously existed, trouble free, for a very few years, just for that very brief time of insouciance before the descent into war. Short enough for me to have only one lasting image of it, a memory that is probably not a real memory but one drawn from an image, that black and white photograph of my father showing me a locust he'd caught as we walked through the seaside dunes. A touch of a life that could have been, but now only exists in the realm of ethereal memories. A chimera that still haunts.

Time plays tricks on us. It makes us forget much more than it allows us to remember. It creates great gaps of darkness in our past, on which light is only sometimes thrown by the smallest of sparks – in this case, grains of sand. Not falling out of a hand as the symbolic gesture of time passing but simply as the feel of walking on soft, yielding sand. And so, I remember all the beaches I've known. It means that here, for whatever future is left, happy times of the past have a chance to emerge from the darkness and in turn at least give rise to happy thoughts. That surely is the point of consciously *living with* one's past. To enrich and enhance the present rather than to wallow in simple nostalgia. (Although I think nostalgia has an undeserved bad name anyway. We are what we've been.) This walking with both past and present, fully engaged in what's around here and now but also charged with feelings and memories of what once was, needs the right stage, and the beach is certainly that for me – where the potent trilogy of sand, sea and sun works so well.

Although it may not have been entirely conscious, it must have been at least a significant part of what persuaded me that this place was a good choice for this phase of life. Maybe there is a satisfying circularity to it, a neat way of moving towards the end somewhere that has similarities to where it all started. A seaside setting, the walking on sand and going into the sea – only a move from a southern beach to a northern beach. Yes, from warm to cold, but thankfully with still quite a bit of sunshine, if now often of the slanting variety. But even that is apposite. Could it augur a gentle, contented slant towards the end? (If that is not jinxing it, says the author who claims to be a fervent rationalist...)

Not that the choice of moving here was fully worked out. Like so many things in life it was mostly happenstance. It's become a cliché of the purveyors of self-help advice that you cannot pursue happiness, that you find it mostly as a side effect of whatever you are engaged in, and I think it is the case that chasing happiness, or even constantly treating it as a *goal*, can be a sure recipe for unhappiness – usually involving wrong turns and disappointments. Happiness is a derivative of other endeavours, the lucky fruit of other pursuits: jobs, travels, relationships, achievements. But even that is no guarantee. We just have to accept there is plenty that is haphazard in the pursuit of happiness.

It is one of the most difficult things to accept but we live in a landscape of contingency, constantly at the mercy of the random unfolding of life. We are surrounded by complexities, a myriad of factors, the vagaries of timings, the unpredictability of events, the traps of history, and increasingly in the future the effects of climate change. Faced with this befuddling mix, some may find refuge in the fanciful notion that "everything happens for a reason", a fallacious concept spewed out by every other schmaltzy, usually American, movie. Or, more widely, by the obsolete delusions of religious belief, that would have some orchestrator at work behind it all. The concept could be updated to be an almighty AI figure responsible for the algorithms determining all of our lives. (This could be the basis of yet another religion – or just a way of dressing up the debunked old beliefs in contemporary garb.)

I prefer to simply accept it as a given of human life. That the old conundrum of free will versus determinism is a false dichotomy. Free will can only operate in the context of shifting, complex circumstances, in a dynamic interaction that, once again as with nature or nurture, is impossible to disentangle objectively. I have come to accept that being able to put up with uncertainty is a prerequisite for finding at least some happiness. Complexities can also be seen as having a positive effect, as they foster human resourcefulness and, paradoxically, can lead us to look for pleasure in *simple* things.

Being often confronted by the fortuitous and the unforeseen can leave us dismayed by the capriciousness of fate, confused by the mysterious workings of providence, and often feeling that a full comprehension of the real eludes us. In the famous words of TS Eliot, humankind cannot bear very much reality. Fortunately, we have evolved a way to escape too much reality, or too much determinism in our lives, at least temporarily – we can always pull out of our human armoury that particularly effective weapon, imagination.

The lure of imagination

Perhaps it was the fragrance of a freshly cut piece of lime that sent me on this particular trail. Then something in the taste of a Scottish sort-of-gin, a botanical spirit by McNean, a small distillery on the west coast. It had been recommended by the local wine shop for being "interestingly aromatic" and that a slice of lime and tonic water worked well with it. And, indeed, there was an unusual layer of flavour that seemed familiar but which I could not place at first – something botanical which, even after realising what it reminded me of, I still to this day can't identify by name. But there was a definite connection, that strange underlying taste reminded me of something you get in cachaça, the Brazilian white sugarcane rum that is used to make caipirinha. It is a mysterious connection. I have checked the botanicals that go into the McNean spirit and, wonderful though they all sound (locally foraged plants such as juniper, coriander, chamomile, bog myrtle, thyme, sorrel or heather), none of them appears in cachaça. The only possible explanation for the similarity in taste is that it must come from the aromas and flavours given to cachaça from the wood barrels it is aged in – and these are usually made from local types of wood, the exotic names of which are just as evocative of a range of flavours as the Scottish botanicals: amburana, cabreúva, jequitibá, ipê and balsam. There must be some overlap somewhere, but it will remain an enigmatic bonus. In any case, the Scottish gin reached across the ocean to another continent to conjure the memory of my first caipirinha, the drink that for me never fails to induce a rush of happiness.

That first hit was in highly appropriate celebration of a long-hoped-for friends' reunion in Rio de Janeiro. It was August 1979 and the drink was prepared by Luiz with slow and deliberate ceremony in the small kitchen of his flat in Botafogo for J-M, my old friend from the *lycée* in Niort, and me. The three of us had been a trio of close accomplices in our student days in Paris, and J-M and I had not seen Luiz since his return to Brazil back in 1969. In my years in Paris prior to that, Brazil had been for me the subject of much fascination. I had met many of Luiz's and J-M's Brazilian friends (some of them political exiles as these were the days of the military dictatorship), and almost immediately felt an affinity with them. I had heard all J-M's stories from his own Zellidja trip to the Amazon, which had awakened my interest in the country. I already knew and loved Brazilian music. But mixing with actual young Brazilians took it to another level.

I discovered the beguiling power of the language – the melodic intonation of Brazilian Portuguese (so different from what I had experienced in Portugal). I could sit for hours listening to it, understanding little but enthralled. Gradually I absorbed more, to the sounds of Caetano Veloso, Chico Buarque, Maria Bethânia and others. But what I found I had the most natural, easy affinity with was the temperament of the people I spent time with – extrovert, open, warm, physically demonstrative, good-humoured and usually with a healthy dose of charming self-derision. I felt at home in their company. In the turmoil and uncertainty of my post-May 68 situation, it was not surprising that I often let my imagination run free, to come up with elaborate fantasies of a life there.

However, circumstances, the randomness of life (and a bit of choice) all meant my way to England was easier instead. It took another ten years from my Paris days before I made my first visit to Brazil, so that first caipirinha was loaded as much with poignancy as it was with cachaça, limes and sugar. For years I still imagined alternative Brazilian lives, mainly as an idle distraction. I did go back for trips there on several occasions – lately to see Luiz one last time just before cancer felled him and to visit J-M who had gone to the Amazon to settle there in retirement, a project which ended in a tragedy that forced him to return to France. This latter event has somewhat tarnished the feel of the place in my imagination, not to mention the awfulness of the political situation there in recent years. But in a corner of my imagination, Brazil remains a symbol of something that could have been.

I have to be careful not to give the wrong impression here, that worlds of make-believe overwhelmingly occupy my mind. It's never been a total evasion – more a case of feet still on the ground and head sometimes in other worlds. Looking back on my life I believe I have always engaged fully in the here and now, embraced unreservedly causes, loves, interests – if anything often with too much rash enthusiasm, with not enough pause and reflection. But this has not stopped me from indulging in imagined scenarios about roads not taken. I suppose it is a common activity, though I find it is not one that people often talk about, except when it has been used as a survival mechanism in dire circumstances, such as hostages recounting how it helped them to cope with their ordeal. Maybe, in ordinary life, it is considered childish or immature. Maybe most people are too embarrassed to reveal it, or that doing so could upset the fragile apple cart of their actual reality. I suppose if they are very good at it, they

The lure of imagination

become novelists. I have failed to do that, I am just a private dabbler, but I have always found these bouts of imagination a comfort when things get difficult, a welcome diversion when grappling with tight spots of the present, especially in the middle of the night, an effective form of succour.

I have to confess that it is not just about exploring the missing branches of my personal history, it can also involve free-range fantasies that span the world and different epochs. Some of these fictional alternative lives have followed my own for years – more detail being added as I rediscover them each time I revisit the scenario. Like revisiting an old friend and finding out more about them. The story builds up, becoming more complex, richer in jeopardy, in obstacles surmounted, and in achieving modest successes. Even in this make-believe world this consciously rational human cannot help giving in to the irrational superstition that you must not tempt fate and overreach. There is no imagined grandiose triumph, no ludicrous king-of-the-world ambition fulfilled, just enough success to trigger a dose of serotonin. It just has to be credible enough to be a gentle, easily accessible balm for the vicissitudes of real life.

Sometimes it is pure compensation for what is longed for but irretrievably absent. If I slip into the shoes of a concert pianist it is only because I rue the fact that I have no musical ability at all. If whilst listening to choral music I drift into an elaborate fantasy life where I can know the joy of singing with others, it is because one of the greatest regrets of my life is that I cannot reproduce a tune – and it hurts, since music has always touched me deeply and I ache from the frustration of not being able to be an active participant in it.

Other times, I shameless give free rein to banality and the indiscriminate absorption of sentimental tropes, to concoct happy scenarios that can act as emotional cushions. There is a long-standing storyline that sees me grow up in a stereotypical east coast small American town, wide streets, large houses, picket fences. It has seen me going to high school there, going away to college, coming back to it in adulthood to take over my dying father's business, encountering plenty of difficulties but naturally overcoming them all to make a success of it, and of my private life, reaching the ultimate prefabricated goal of the happy-ever-after marriage. A story where everything is quite simply as it should be in an ideal world. A full reality-denying trip, whilst willingly hooked on delusion. But what joy.

There are many others, in different geographical and historical contexts, often equally trite and sappy, but always with me in charge of the narrative – no contingencies there, no capriciousness of fate, no arbitrary twists and turns. I remain in control of crises and good times, of reverses and achievements – which is the therapeutic point of it all.

Imagination, our ability to create mental Shangri-las, seems to become more powerful with age, one of the few upsides of getting old (or is it, in a way, a return to the imagination of childhood?) In any case it is a blessing, a temporary salvation for the earthbound. As the territory of the real narrows down, as the boundaries of what can be accomplished in real life close in, all that will be left, apart from the pleasures derived from smaller and smaller things, will increasingly be memories and, above all, imagination. I aim to treasure that. To keep imagining, whatever circumstances throw in my path, private and enchanted worlds. But enough – I need to say something about what I will only offer a glimpse of.

A glimpse into the hinterland

In gathering these fragments of a life, I have found it odd that the most difficult of all was to write about who and what I have cared about most. The people I love, family and friends, the relationships that have marked my life. I don't know if it is the fear of not being up to the task, of saying too much or too little. It may also be motivated by a desire not to impinge on the lives of others. A memoir cannot but reveal a lot that is personal but I hesitate to go into this last redoubt of privacy. And yet a memoir would not be complete without mentioning at least something on this topic. So, this will be just a glimpse into my private hinterland. It has not always been a peaceful and decorous setting. Certainly not a classic French *jardin* offering beautiful symmetry. More of a fairly wild area, with lots of weeds, and at times, in some patches, a bit of a jungle – though in its late incarnation I hope it is more like a settled, mature English garden.

On the positive side of my hesitancy is a fear of falling into the mawkish, especially when mentioning my three sons. So, I will stick to an unadorned, sober appreciation – that in this part of the garden there has been nothing but fine growth, light and sunshine, and a bit of necessary rain too, enough to make everything flourish. In contrast to the bouts of turbulence of other relationships, this has remained a gratifyingly untroubled area of my life (so far...). I am not sure I can say with certainty that I have been a good enough father but I have tried. I hope I have remained engaged in their lives as much as circumstances allowed. I know I have been better than my own father but he set a low bar. Anyway, all I can say is that my relationship with each of my sons have together been the most untainted aspects of my life.

The same desire not to gush applies to friendships, and to my relationship with my two siblings too. I associate the latter with friendships, as strangely over the years I have felt that brothers have become like friends and close friends have become like brothers. The most comforting thing is that I can see familiar figures in this landscape that have been there for most of my adult life and, in one case at least, since my adolescence. This continuity matters a great deal, it gives heft to one's life. There is accumulated substance there, something thick and solid and not as given to crumbling as many relationships of love. There is plenty of ongoing mutual benevolence to draw on – a web of ropes to hold onto when buffeted. Of course, there is loss too. Friends lost to death, friends lost to drift – the latter sometimes my fault for failing to make more of an effort, for letting the everyday wholly displace the yesterdays. It's the stuff of regret, but it's an easy trap to fall into. You allow time to pass without contact and then it becomes a reason for not getting back in touch. I have let too many people slip out of my life in this way. Gérard, my French friend in our moped-riding days in Niort, is one. He was a conventional boy, serious, a little shy, who followed in the footsteps of his single mother to work as a regional civil servant in the French Treasury. I heard he got married and had a large family. I lost touch after that. I did Google him about twenty years ago and found out where he worked but I hesitated, fearing there would be too much time and distance between us. By the time I steeled myself to make contact, I looked again and his name no longer appeared where I had found it – he must have retired, and I could find no other online presence. A ghost, but still a friend.

Naturally, there is also a negative side to my letting much fall into a black hole – at least in these pages. I will spare this account the details of the shames and embarrassments that have at times been abundant in my personal life. In my twenties and thirties, there were several significant relationships that did not last. I believed in each of them but they were far from trouble-free. I did eventually achieve longevity but only after much turbulence. But I am not up to emptying out that particular ragbag of regrets. It is only mentioned here because, as a key, if painful, feature of my life, it has at least to be acknowledged. Also, in a way, to bear witness to a predicament that was not uncommon at the time. This is bound to find an echo in others of my generation, littered as it is with histories of broken relationships and divorces. We all grappled with the radically changing nature of relationships brought about by the social changes of the sixties. A shift that many of us were ill-prepared for, imbued as we were with the illusory expectations and inbred attitudes of another age.

This is by way of context, not to abrogate my own responsibility in my personal failings. I brought to it all a specific mix of my own insecurities and shortcomings. I was often incapable of making the necessary compromises with the foibles of others. I could not cope with mercurial behaviour, displays of unreason, and especially what I considered to be unfairness. My obsession with fairness (or at least my concept of it) often derailed things. As did my unrelenting approach to perceived wrongs, including a very un-British inability to always control my temper. Intent on wanting perceived wrongs to be put right, not being able to let go and forget about things. Let it drop, said my friends, but I could not. I was more terrier than Labrador... I have largely avoided dwelling on the scars of adult survival – mine and even more importantly the ones I have inflicted on others. I suppose it is the prerogative of the storyteller, a memoir is a self-constructed narrative. You become the editor of your own life – sadly too late to make changes to it but still in time to make some sense of it.

I am heartened by the fact that the generations that followed have fared better than my own in this respect at least. I can see this in the lives of my sons and all around me. There is still a great deal of continuing, significant change in the nature of personal relationships but younger people seem to take to that with much more equanimity than my generation ever did.

My generation

For a generation that is supposed to have had it easy, we don't half get a lot of flak these days – 'boomer' has even become a sort of insult. I think it is meant to denote privilege and the ignorance of being privileged, and a lack of appreciation of the subsequent generations' predicaments. We are also accused of being responsible for at least some of these. We are, for example, made to carry the can for all the ills of the housing crisis hitting the young. The very politicians whose policies have actually been responsible for this like to hide behind the myth of a generational culpability. As if it was a deliberate individual choice of every member of a particular age group to have decided to deprive their children of housing opportunities. This is arrant nonsense. Belonging to a generation does not mean an equal distribution of resources among its members. There are rich boomers, comfortably off boomers, poor boomers and many destitute boomers trying to survive on paltry state pensions. Where you are placed on the socio-economic scale does not depend on *when* you were born, but on your financial situation. There is no individual culpability for the housing crisis, just political culpability – notably the destruction of social housing that begun in the Thatcher era. Nor do I feel that people of my generation – who benefited from effectively free higher education through the grant system – have pulled up the ladder behind them. If there is collective responsibility for that, it is with people *of all ages* who voted for governments who got rid of the grant system and introduced tuition fees. Don't blame the cogs in the system for how the system has been designed. If there is failure on our collective part, it is not that we have despoiled any younger generation, but that some of us have failed to convince enough people to democratically change the political and economic system creating such iniquities.

Having said all that, I can now go back to more justifiable generalisations – and talk about some of the features people of my generation do have in common, in particular, music and, for many, a progressive political outlook.

Very specific circumstances have shaped my life: the Algerian war in childhood; my mixed relationship with France, including a popular uprising; the exile and adoption of England first, then of Scotland as a home – in so many ways so different from my contemporaries in this country. Yet, I am so obviously rooted in this generation and share its trajectory. From embracing the hopes that were common to many in the late 1960s that radical societal change was possible, through enduring the backlash against the post-war consensus of the 1980s, to coming to terms with the limited remedy that social-democratic compromise can offer. Looking at how I wound my way through all this, it would be impossible to completely isolate my individual fate from that of my cohort. We are to a large extent the product of our time, of our circumstances, of our climate even. There is nothing without context. We move in a common social and cultural landscape. And so I will accept with good grace the label 'boomer', along with '*soixante-huitard*', its French sort-of-equivalent.

We now live in a world where digital tentacles reach all corners and everyone is on the same page, as it were

– commonality of data is inescapable. It may seem strange to the young people of today, but we were a generation for which it was new to discover that other young people in different countries listened to the same music – rock and pop became our lingua franca across continents. Say the words 'Woodstock' or 'Isle of Wight' to anyone my age and not only will they know for sure what you are referring to, but this will evoke common images and sounds, whether or not they actually attended those events. This sense of experiences in common has bound this generation in much more benign ways than the previous. My father's generation had the war – and the risk of getting killed. We were lucky to have 'peace and love' – and a chance of getting high. For most of us, these latter themes have passed but music has stayed with us. It is as if our lives have been lived against a constant soundtrack.

There is a series of songs, tracks, artists that mark the milestones of my life, like aural monuments erected to last. They retain awesome powers over my emotions. After all these years, they still pop up periodically, causing delicious disruptions of the present. Randomly, I can think of the swell of evocation of the Beatles' 'Twist and Shout', first heard as a French schoolboy in that church hall dance in Newport, Shropshire in 1963, just before that first kiss – and the rich flow that came after that: the not-easy-to-enjoy at first *Freewheelin' Bob Dylan* album bought on a visit to my grandmother in Paris, with 'A Hard Rain's a-Gonna Fall' bursting open a window on the world beyond Niort – and Dylan lasting to this day as our bittersweet troubadour; in some cases, a rediscovery was even stronger than the initial encounter, the pathos of Van Morrison's voice in *Astral Weeks* and *Moondance* becoming the most poignant sound of a troubled phase of my life, listened to on long road trips to the Highlands; and then there is the one that never fails, time and again, to plunge me into a warm well of nostalgia, Procol Harum's 'A Whiter Shade of Pale', which to me has come to be the musical expression of that lovely Portuguese concept *saudade* (you have to hear it the way Brazilians pronounce it, slow and long, *sa-o-da-dge*, a word that conjures up a blend of remembrance and longing, a touch of regret, a mix of sadness and joy) – first heard in the summer of 1967, and which marked my turning away from a teenage love and a more ordinary fate in provincial France.

We all have our life's playlists, which can be so long and varied that we fail to put together a short selection for our imaginary *Desert Island Discs*. These days, we also catch ourselves compiling the soundtrack of our putative memorial function – this is unexpectedly not as morbid as it might be, but instead almost pleasurable, or at least satisfying. Interestingly, this features more and more classical music – I am surprised because I was a latecomer to a full appreciation of it. Hours of compulsory listening to Saint-Saëns' *Carnival of the Animals* in my first two years of secondary education were enough to put me off for quite a few decades. That and having to stand up in class and sing notes from a score and failing miserably in my attempts to do so, being mocked by the teacher, and being the cause of much hilarity all around. It is a strange but not uncommon phenomenon this embracing of classical music only in maturity, but it is in full bloom now, with going to live concerts especially pleasurable. Maybe you need to have experienced enough of the intricacies of life to be able to relate to the complexities of this music. But whatever the genre, music seems to have been a permanent presence in our lives.

More problematic, and with more shades of grey, is our relationship to political engagement. Not that I can really generalise to an all-encompassing 'our', but I do feel justified in observing that many, possibly the majority, of my contemporaries were touched in their twenties by a worldwide wave of wanting societal change. This desire started clearly enough but has become opaque and confused over the years. For many it began with seeking peace, with campaigning against the Vietnam war, but for some of us it went way beyond that, believing there was a chance for radical, even revolutionary change. We had seen the failures of the Soviet system, so that could not be our lodestar as an alternative to western capitalism, but for a while it was possible to be taken in by what was happening in China as an inspiration – an example of a revolution that would not go off course, but, as we now know, that proved a cruel delusion.

Our hopes for change were justified – and still are – and our intentions were good but it is clear now that our energy was largely wasted. I find it difficult, almost intractable to reflect on this, because our diagnosis of the problem was by and large correct, and has in fact become more evident as the years have passed, but we addressed it in a way that led nowhere. As a result, we carry confusion and embarrassment over our political activism. But this will have to stay in the hinterland for now. Nothing dreadful – no fateful acts, just ideological campaigning and defending of things that on reflection have turned out to be indefensible. In fact, we have long fallen back on good old social-democratic tinkering – going for its temporary, partial, but more achievable small fixes. And now we are in a new era, where the continued existence of our species is going to overtake all other issues.

Maybe I should have called this section 'My ge...ge...generation'. We started out listening to the deliberately stuttering words from one of our favourite pop songs and we are entering the last phases of our lives, still hesitantly stuttering in our answers to the main problem of our time.

Time for a last goodbye

It turns out that my childhood past is literally another country, or perhaps I should say a country that no longer exists – and only ever existed as an impostor country, an historical construct, one of the constructs of Europeans in their colonial phase, lasting in this case just one hundred and thirty-two years, a short span of time in the history of humanity. In the form in which I knew it, it has long vanished and soon, with the disappearance of my generation, all *pieds-noirs* will have vanished too. They will not be fondly remembered, except by their descendants maybe. History books will not be kind to them, their fate brushed aside – deservedly so. For they ignored history, were blind to where their objective interests lay, and lost their way. So this is in no way a paean to the *pieds-noirs*, just a last goodbye to my estranged tribe. Not 'only an *au revoir*' as in the words of the French version of Auld Lang Syne they sang on the ships that took them away from their beloved city, but a final adieu.

I am often asked if I ever returned to Algeria. For years I fantasised about a return by boat so that I could have a reverse version of the experience of leaving that is imprinted on all *pied-noir* minds, whether they actually lived it or left by other means, the whiteness of Algiers slowly fading in the distance. I dreamt of watching the recognisable bright vista emerge as we approached the bay to dock in the heart of the city. But unsurprisingly, when I finally faced up to a return, in 1979, aged thirty, I went by plane and landed prosaically in a renamed and rebuilt airport, an event devoid of the imagined poignancy. There was only one strong pang of emotion: when coming out of the plane onto the steps and onto the tarmac, I was assailed by a fragrance in the air which, though undefinable (hot dust, a hint of eucalyptus scent?), was immediately familiar.

After that, there was a degree of nervousness. How would a returning *pied-noir* be treated? A part of me wondered if I was venturing into enemy territory. But I did not seem to attract any attention, not even curious looks. During one of my long peregrinations, I was even asked the time in Arabic, so it seemed I could have passed for an Algerian. The whole place had the strangeness of a familiar stage set but with a whole lot of characters missing. Contrary to what my *pied-noir* relatives had predicted, it was not, in general, more dilapidated. In fact all the buildings on the seafront had been repainted white, with all the shutters painted the same blue – an inoffensive consequence of the power of an autocratic regime. The city looked good. But it was much more crowded, mostly with men, and mostly young men, evidence of the post-independence demographic explosion.

On my first full day, I walked up to El Biar where my parents had their last flat and from where, along with a group of friends and hundreds of other people, we had marched down to the centre on that fateful day in March 1962 to break the blockade of Bab-el-Oued – but had instead been fired on by a panicking platoon of French soldiers. I wanted to face head-on one of my worst memories of that period, so I retraced our steps all the way to the Grande Poste, the site of the shootings. Once there, amongst the busy, peaceful crowds, I stood in solitary remembrance of the misguided souls who were killed that day – and felt small tremors of retrospective fear. On the way down, seeing the many children playing in the streets, I found myself, instead of getting anxious, having recollections of some lighter, more normal aspects of my childhood. On those narrow sloping streets there had still been children hurtling down on makeshift wooden carts with little metal wheels filled with ball bearings. There were kids kicking a ball, and also younger ones playing with apricot stones – our more unusual alternative to marbles. You set up a small heap of three stones with one on top, and from a marked distance your opponent had to flick another stone to destroy your heap and pocket the lot. Innocent games in the midst of an urban war. Even at the height of the conflict – or perhaps especially then – we seemed to be always out on the streets.

For the three days I was there, I spent my whole time criss-crossing the city in a quasi-random fashion, recalling places I had known and walking to each in turn. A lot of walking but I did not get tired. Occasionally it was like being in a trance, hardly noticing the surroundings, for the real distance covered was inside me. And predictably I ended up spending the most time in Bab-el-Oued, the crucible of popular *pied-noir* culture. A real melting pot of immigrants from all corners of the Mediterranean basin – and further afield. I can recall names to show the mix of origins: Susini and Scotto, Pons and Padovani, Martinez and Muller, Cuesta and Casassus – these, picked at random, from Italy and Spain, Corsica and Sardinia, Malta and Alsace.

All of them immigrants responding to the calls of colonisation. A few, mostly from France, came with enough means and enterprise to take over land in true colonial fashion. Others were of more modest stock and stayed in

Bab-el-Oued and the other coastal cities. Among the first to arrive were poor Spaniards from Valencia and the Balearic Islands who came to work in the quarries, farmers from Alicante who became market gardeners. Then fishermen from Naples and dairy farmers from Malta. Because expanding Algiers needed fish, vegetables, milk – and stone. Masons, plasterers, painters, carpenters, shoemakers and locksmiths: I came across the descendants of all those in Bab-el-Oued. Between the wars, there was an influx of Sicilians, among them the father of my grandfather Adamo, who may well have been Jewish. Sephardic Jews came to Algeria from everywhere around the Mediterranean.

With such a mix, it is hardly surprising that the *pied-noir* dialect, *le pataouète*, had such a diverse lexicon and exuberant syntax. In addition to French, it took freely from Castilian Spanish but also from Valencian and Catalan, from Italian dialects from Naples and Sicily, from Maltese and the *langue d'oc*, and from Arabic too of course. You did not need to be fluent in it, but if you did not at least understand it you could be cast as a *francaoui*, or a *patos*, an assumedly pretentious incomer from metropolitan France. Unless, as my own father did, you could throw yourself into the *pied-noir* lifestyle – and later lost cause – with the fervour of the convert.

I walked to a central landmark of the *quartier*, the Place des Trois Horloges, appropriately named after its three-faced clock – the saying went "one that works, one that's stopped and one that gives the wrong time" – but this was always the right location for demonstrations to start from. I lingered around there a while as memories of dramatic events whirled in my mind. And then at last I made my long-anticipated pilgrimage to the most loaded location of my childhood days in Bab-el-Oued, my grandparents' flat at the corner of Rue Cadix and Rue Rochambeau. All the street names had been changed but I could have got there with my eyes shut. I had imagined knocking on the door of the second-floor flat, hoping to be asked inside, but I failed to summon up the courage. Too many children around, too strong a sentiment of being a stranger, an intruder. I just peered into the courtyard and walked up and down the street looking up at the balcony, wondering if my grandfather's armchair was still there in the corner, by the old wireless, and if it had become the acquired domain of another patriarch. I imagined the smell of simmering *tchoutchouka* coming from the tiny kitchen, just as grandmother Adamo would have prepared it. I saw that the Mozabite-owned grocery store to which I lowered the *cabas* with the shopping list and the purse was still there. But the café on the opposite corner had closed down and been turned into lodgings.

I recalled its livelier days. Open onto the streets on two sides, it was easy for me from the flat's balcony or the shared little terrace to spend time observing its constantly entertaining life. There were the classic wooden tables and chairs of a Parisian café spilling out onto the pavements and, inside, the walls were covered in mirrors and azulejos tiles like in a Lisbon bar. Peak time was early evening. The women would go out for a walk arm-in-arm, '*prendre la fraîche*' they used to say, the local form of the *paseo*, and the men would go to the café to meet friends and drink *anisette*. That colourless, transparent liquid that magically turned cloudy white on the addition of water and release a powerful fragrance of aniseed that could even reach my observation point. At *anisette* time, all cafés offered small plates of food to nibble, and there was great competition to offer the best *kemia*, as it was known. My uncle Christian, a regular attender, was an aficionado and on his tipsy return to the flat would delight in telling me what he had sampled, occasionally adding the gesture now known as 'chef's kiss' for cheerful emphasis. There was enormous variety: dried sardines (called Spanish cutlets), whole small peppers pickled in vinegar, green and black olives, diced cheese, anchovies, tiny merguez spicy sausages, pickled carrots and tomatoes, salted peanuts, roasted almonds, grilled chickpeas known as *biblis*, haricot beans cooked in a chilly and cumin sauce called *loubia* – and a lot more.

From my vantage point I could just about catch a glimpse of some of the inside tables where the older men sat playing dominoes or cards, with much demonstrative flapping down of either, and with as much noise as possible. But the real spectacle was provided by the gaggle of men either sitting or standing, half in the café, half on the pavements, when they engaged in one of the *pieds-noirs*' favourite pastimes, *la tchatche*, the loud, voluble, boastful, usually humorous telling of tall stories, full of embellishments and exaggeration. With a good *tchatcheur*, the hands spoke as much as the mouth, and all the features of the face were on the move as the story unfolded and meandered. When the right words failed to reach the lips, an outraged facial expression or a good strong gesture would do instead – a common one being the vigorous flicking up and down of a hand, so that loose fingers made a noise as you shouted, "*Poh, poh, poh!*" All stories at one point or another had to involve a defiant *bras d'honneur*, that ubiquitous Mediterranean gesture of putting your left arm in the crook of your right arm while raising your forearm, not forgetting to form a fist with your hand. Meaning the same as a raised middle finger but so much more expressive, and displaying (and exorcising) much more angry energy to good effect. The *tchatcheur* usually had a complicit audience – though not one that was wholly taken in. They just had to provide the right mix of appreciation, interruption, encouragement and challenge.

There was always the risk that someone would take some barb personally and feel aggrieved. This could lead a display of *rabia*, an escalation of raised voices and threats, an exchange of increasingly elaborate insults usually involving mothers and sisters. There could be a facing-off between two people that might include some shoving and grabbing of collars but it would rarely go further. Everyone was keen to avoid a real *baroufa*, the coming to actual blows, because then it would be so difficult for the protagonists to save face, and that was the main thing, for among *pied-noir* males honour was always at stake. So, one of the older men or the café owner would shout, "*Basta!*" and someone would buy another round of *anisette*, the opponents would clink glasses and do *tape-cinq*, the high-five slapping of palms (which I used to think had been invented in Bab-el-Oued…) to seal the peace. And everyone laughed. There was always a lot of laughter in Bab-el-Oued. The laughter of insouciance – that they would discover too late was also a laughter of ignorance of reality.

I then went up the hill above the *quartier* to Notre Dame d'Afrique, the basilica where I had often gone as a child to look down at the city – to enjoy a panoramic view. There, with the byzantine building (looking as incongruous as ever) at my back, I went to the edge of the steep hill and stood by the eucalyptus trees, suddenly understanding why the gaunt look of their peeling trunks, the droopiness of their thin foliage, had, wherever I encountered them in the world, never failed to move me, to fill me with melancholy. I looked down at the sprawling city as I had done so many times as a young boy, a neat model of peace, order and beauty. The white and pale ochre of the buildings, the dark green of cypress trees on the flank of the hill, the blue sea – the familiar triangle of Bab-el-Oued where it seemed from this viewpoint that nothing had changed, where everything, now as then, always *appeared* to be as it should be. Being moved, as always, by this mythical vision of an orderly world where human confusion and turmoil had no place. For a moment there, I did shed a tear for my repudiated childhood – and for the illusory images of security and continuity planted here in the mind of a child.

This was the real return, in real life, filled with exquisite sadness. It provided some relief but no new clarity for my troubled relationship to my childhood. It took years to work out how something that felt so right could in fact have been so wrong. But this is meant as a symbolic return, as a way of finally packing it all away. I have found over the years that there is no joy or comfort in nostalgia for that phase of my life.

It is also time to put away any leftover black and white condemnatory thoughts of my parents. Blind to the iniquities of colonialism, they were ill-equipped to be buffeted by historical events. It's in this gap between history's progress, society's evolution and our understanding of it and our role in it, whether as individuals or as groups, that tragedies and failures, both personal and collective, are born. At the root of many of our troubles is our inability to make our thinking alter quickly enough to understand and fit our circumstances. My parents, having failed to apprehend the reality of colonialism, were out of step with the pace of history. As a result, they lost everything, including what they thought of as their country. We often pay a heavy price for the tension between our emotional engagement and the lack of a rational approach. We get easily lost in between, in the quicksand of that dangerous, foggy territory. Our emotional side enables us to enjoy the present to the full without pausing to understand it, in many cases leaving us blind to aspects of reality. The rational side of us does give meaning to what we experience but usually only a posteriori. Indeed, if it was brought to bear on it concurrently, it would often hold us back and curtail our enjoyment of the present. The *pieds-noirs*' attachment to Algeria was certainly mostly emotional, with almost all of them failing to seek the reality behind the surface.

We all have contradictory pulls at the core of us. Part of what I have carried is an unstable mixture of emotionalism, at times extreme – excessive enthusiasm, excessive exuberance, excessive sensitivity and occasionally anger – my southern, Algerian, inheritance – and at the same time I have felt the need for extreme rationality, the need for explicit stating of reasons, the need for a constant analytical dissection of problems, which could be labelled the mental habits of the North – acquired during my French education – and which, by the way, have not been particularly congruent with the culture of avoidance that is dominant in the society where I have spent most of my life. The pursuit of rationality took hold so deeply precisely because of the awkwardness and confusion of my relationship to my Algerian childhood. I hesitate to call it guilt – more accurate to say that it became impossible to claim my childhood, to turn to it in simple, straightforward and pleasurable remembrance. It became tainted with shame, too complex to explain, a minefield of misunderstandings, and therefore largely ignored for quite a long time. Algeria, the place that had made me discover so young those rare heights of feelings, the place that had filled my childhood with extreme emotions, was also a place and a time that I was unable to turn to with an easy heart. It could not even have the allure of a lost domain because I had no right to lay claim to it. I have now come to accept that there is no escaping this conundrum. James Baldwin once wrote: "People are trapped in history, and history is trapped in them." Without knowing the words, I have felt this in my bones my whole life.

The thing with displaced people, whether their exiles were righteous or not, is that they forever feel that the life they lead is nothing but a substitute, forced upon them, for the life they could have had.

A thread of beads

Today is a red-letter day, an appropriate expression as it marks the day we have 'concluded the exchange of missives' on our new house – for non-Scots, that quaint wording is the equivalent of 'exchange of contracts' in England. Something more old-fashioned about it, less banally businesslike, akin to a deal sealed by a shaking of hands. It is a relief because we had been trying to buy a house for over a year and a half. We were caught up in the post-pandemic rush out of cities and in particular in the unfortunate phenomenon in seaside towns like ours of people searching for a home having to battle with rentiers buying properties for holiday lets. So, we faced another twist of historical events, if not of the magnitude of ones I have known before, but still involving strong enough societal currents to threaten to blow us off course. And as our search is now drawing to a conclusion, by an odd synchronicity my gathering of these fragments is coming to an end with this final section.

I have written about how this town is congruent with this phase of my life – to be blunt, old age. I don't want to misrepresent it in saying that. It is nothing like a senior enclave – it's a lively small town full of young families, for whom it is a very congenial environment too. But for me, with the presence of the open horizon over the sea and the long sandy beaches, it is a haven. I am entering a phase of life when the agitation of city life, whether in London or Edinburgh – or even Oxford where we last lived – can only be borne in small doses. Maybe as you become conscious of carrying the copiousness of seven decades of life, you need less clamour and clatter, less 'living' around you. Not that it is entirely straightforward. I find myself increasingly grappling with the contradictions of old age (although, come to think of it, hasn't the whole of life been taken up with endless contradictions, and often exhausting ones at that...).

I have reached the age when you occasionally feel you've had a bellyful of life, when you've accumulated so much past that it can seem like a burden. But at other times – more frequent, thankfully – you can be hugely comforted by the richness, colour and patina of your accrued life. Its very thickness, its weft and warp, its texture can make you feel more real than you have ever felt. The substance of the life behind you providing the virtual solidity that you need as you become frailer.

Although that too is contradictory. I am struck by how one's life can appear so full, so substantial, while at the same time being conscious of how insignificant it is in the greater scheme of things. A burst of light in the endless night of nothingness. How strange that a life can amount to both so little and yet so much too. That there is both solidity and evanescence.

The latter quality comes to the fore when a growing awareness of the shortage of time ahead comes upon you. You become old when you realise you are past the concept of 'later' in the frequently occurring thought, "I'll do this later" – I will travel to India, Australia, New Zealand later in life... When you realise 'later' has come and gone. And you recall that you spent too much time living with that sense at the back of your mind that you were sort-of-waiting for real life to begin. Then you start feeling that life has become a race against time. And not an always comfortable one, as the encroachments of ageing become more evident, the chances of being struck down by disease greater – and in my case the ever-present fear of another heart attack switching off the light at any moment. All this comes as a shock because for a long while you had been lulled into an illusory sense of durability by the slow pace of the erosion of youth. Now you have to walk on the cliff edge.

And you need to remain calm. But you don't want the price of calmness to be renunciation, as there is still plenty to embrace and live for. Everyone over the age of seventy should keep in mind the famous saying of Sophocles that "nobody loves life like an old man" (take that last word as being generic, meaning 'human being'...). This last period need not be a confused retreat – you can aim to make it a serene culmination. Or if not serene, at least interesting. The centre of gravity of pleasure is shifting from the body to the mind. But there is no shortage of old and new sources of joy, often small, to be appreciated with possibly greater intensity than ever. After a lifetime of sampling everything, our senses are at their discerning best. It can be the age of refinement and quality, instead of indiscriminate indulgence and quantity – and that can provide a new type of exquisite satisfaction.

Failing everything else, there is a bank of memories to draw on, and if these are too much of a mixed blessing, there is still the unfathomable realm of the imagination to explore. If your own falls short, or is stunted for any reason, you can always share those of others in books and films. The aim anyway is to manage getting old with aplomb, to walk straight for as long as possible, and not just to shuffle towards the end. As a generation, we don't exactly have an established path to follow. We have to make it up as we go along. We were the initial adopters of youth culture, and became rather addicted to it. As a result, we are now the fumbling pioneers of a new 'old age'. Occasionally blindly refusing to face reality – ironically, in an unconscious final embracing of one of the most utopian slogans from Paris 68, 'Take your desires for realities'. But it is not fanciful to see ageing as an accumulation of layers of experience that more often leaves you feeling enriched rather than burdened. And who knows, perhaps also endows you with more sagacity than you've ever known.

However, if no amount of newly acquired wisdom or stoicism can help you deal with the ghosts of the past, if pesky memories and too many regrets keep haunting you, then you can always try to metabolise the past by constructing your own narrative, as I have attempted to do here. I believe it is in any case the only meaning you will find in your life. The purpose is not just solace, but to achieve greater clarity – which can in itself be soothing. You need to get over the thought that it is presumptuous to assume that anyone will be interested, and just believe there are enough people who want to hear the stories of others. (In part at least because these often tell us something interesting about ourselves.) It helps to think that one of the consolations of advanced age is that you acquire a tone of experience which feels authentic enough to be shareable.

The cliché is that life is a rich tapestry and indeed it is, but what I have done here is a much more modest quilt. Or to go for a possibly more appropriate metaphor, in case the whole has not quite come together in a properly stitched way, a string of beads. For many years of my life, I have taken notes, as a repository of remembrances, ideas and reactions.

In some cases, they are just words or expressions that struck me as capturing well various moods and events. I thought of them as a collection of beads and, at long last, I have gathered them, tried to polish them up and then threaded them together as a way of telling my story – not entirely randomly, perhaps searching for, if not a pattern, at least a semblance of continuity. So, think of it as a string of beads, a secular *tesbih*, to accompany reflection on real life rather than illusory prayer.

Language is a refuge as well as an instrument of clarity, though a difficult one to wield effectively. It is not easy to order events into a narrative, especially disparate, disjointed events. Nor to find a simple way of saying complex things – and I may on occasion have fallen into the trap of doing the opposite. My tale had to be in English partly because of the dissolution of my native language (a loss), partly because I find it more natural to convey emotions and complexities in this medium. I have loved the English language for a long time. I have lapped it up – the sound of it, its idiomatic expressiveness, its lack of formality, its suppleness once you've mastered its colloquialisms, its sheer efficiency, and what it has represented in my life. The fact that it freed me up, liberated me, that it allowed me to be 'other'. I was both nurtured and given another chance by it.

I have threaded these few beads, retrieved from the attic of my memory and from my treasure box of inspiring words, to leave behind a small trace of this odd dash across four countries from south to north, from hot to cold, from war to peace. It is also a modest way of bearing witness to some of the events that have formed the backdrop to a life spanning the second half of the twentieth century and the beginning of the twenty-first. I have witnessed the bloody end of French colonialism, the last gasps of what were the well-meaning but vain revolutionary hopes of youth, the destructive triumph of neo-liberalism, the all-too-brief return to social democracy sabotaged by a pointless war, the crisis of financial capitalism and the ensuing devastation of austerity, the confusion of so-called 'post-history', soon exposed as wishful thinking, the return of war and the risk of nuclear conflict in Europe. And now, at the front of the stage, the climate emergency that threatens the very existence of humanity – and the repeated tragedy of our consciousness of it lagging behind reality.

I am in danger of ending on too mournful a note but any ending (of this writing, or the bigger ending…) cannot be other than melancholy – and the best you can hope for is that there is something elegiac about it. A bit like a twilight, which, especially here on long summer days, can be beautiful, turning from a glorious bright sunset into a lingering crimson afterglow, and then leaving a brief whoosh of colour disappearing behind the horizon, in a final flourish.

With that in mind, I would like to conjure up a small final, virtual bead, a beautiful shiny one, like a child's marble, a composite of swirls of colour that would evoke the joys, laughter and pleasures of all kinds of what has luckily already been a long life, a bead that would encompass both the fires of passion and the cool waters of reason. One that would have in it the sun-bleached whiteness of the buildings of Algiers, the red clamour of near-revolution in Paris, the ever-present soft greenness of England, and all the blues and whites of a Scottish horizon over the Firth of Forth. Everything from the urban bay of Algiers to this no less spectacular but wilder coastline of northern Europe.

Walking on beaches on this coast, I continue to collect the fragments that started me off writing this, sea glass and tiny pieces of broken china for putative collages. And just occasionally, I come across a piece of driftwood, bearing the marks of having been hurled around by incessant waves, hardened by the sun, reduced to its bleached core, but still there – resilient.

Acknowledgements

In relation to the writing and publication of this book, I have many and varied reasons to be grateful to the following people:

Adrian Briggs, Elfreda Crehan, Nick Darton, Roy Greenslade, Jean-Marie Royer, Peter Terrell, Philippa Tomlinson, Adrian Webster.

Reactions and appreciations from early readers

A number of people from the worlds of publishing, journalism, teaching and social work read sections of this memoir as it was being written. Here are some of their comments.

social, political and historical background

Both *"Where do you come from in France?"* and *"Auld Lang Syne"* have such a light touch. They combine a lot of info about the social, the political, the historical background. Unpicking such complexity could have added confusion or wordy weight – except it does the opposite while weaving in the threads of the writer's biography as well as those of his family.

The historical/political explanation of the complex situation [Algerian war] is straightforward enough to understand and it made pleasurable, interesting, informative reading. It's fluently written and I thoroughly enjoyed it.

"Imagination has seized power" caught me up in the excitement of those times [Paris 68]. This is history made compellingly readable.

a long journey

There's a feeling of contentment here – as if arriving home after a very long journey.

full of humour

The author's sense of humour shines through. *"What's in a name?"* made me laugh out loud on the train.

familiar memories

These recollections spark memories in the reader and will do so with more than just me, I'm sure. And so a sense of familiarity is created, of inclusivity perhaps. It's a strength to see such engagement with the reader in this way.

changing directions

I very much like the way that the successive sections take me by surprise, giving multi-sensory pleasure in the unexpected. They're like changes of direction on a walk. At the same time each has its themes that touch on others elsewhere. Meeting those again gives additional pleasure.

the grapes of joy

"The romance of wine" brings the subject to life in such an engaging way and with such knowledge.

the French and the Brits

I was variously intrigued, amused, taken aback, appalled... In *"Myths and legends"* I recognized familiar truths and found the witty observations and analysis stood up really solidly.

pleasure in simple things

The rich description of the afternoon with Hanne and her aunts in *"The random pursuit of happiness"* is enchanting. It makes time stand still.

it's Scotland for me

Incidentally and utterly unrelated, this is doing an excellent sales job on a move to Scotland.

no joy in nostalgia

"Time for a last goodbye". What a terrific piece of writing and almost a short story in its own right. It's inviting, reflective, insightful, informative, full of wisdom. It's a pleasure to read and perfectly placed.

roundedness

There's humour, understatement, delicacy, modesty, consideration of others' feelings (readers as well as participants).

tapestry

The way in which the various themes, characters, locations and concerns continue to weave their way through different sections is a delight.

If I read no further and was asked how I found the pieces so far, I'd say that in part it's like observing the weaving of a multi-coloured, multi-textured fabric. I'm watching illustrated strands emerge as in a tapestry. If they fall out of sight for a while it's not that they've disappeared. Rather, ways have been found to hold onto their structural strength beneath the surface until their visibility needs to re-emerge. Locations, characters, themes, history (personal, national, international) dilemmas, politics – all these, and many more, have begun to make up the developing weft and warp.

triumph

A very good ending, a great final paragraph and what a perfect word to finish on: RESILIENT.

I have just finished this brilliant memoir with its triumphant ending.

An excellent storyteller.